Exploring Science in the Elementary Schools

Exploring Science in the Elementary Schools

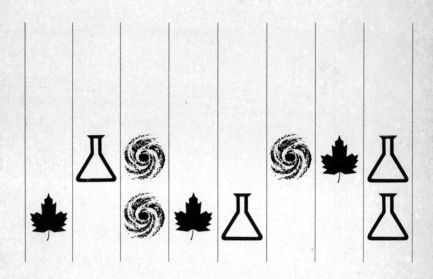

Donald Kauchak
University of Utah

Paul Eggen
University of
North Florida

Rand McNally
College Publishing Company
Chicago

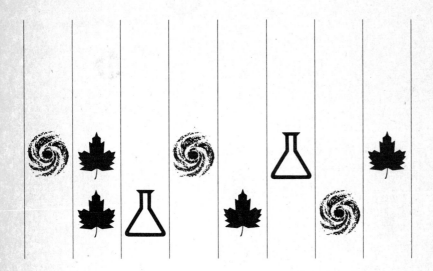

Rand McNally Education Series

B. Othanel Smith, Advisory Editor

Photo Credits

2 Edith Royce Schade from National Audubon Society/Photo Researchers, Inc.; 24 Michael Goss; 52 Bruce Roberts/Rapho-Photo Researchers, Inc.; 102 Vivienne della Grotta/Photo Researchers, Inc.; 144 Judy Hill/Hill Photography; 180 Charles Frizzell Photography; 216 Alvin E. Staffan from National Audubon Society/Photo Researchers, Inc.; 264 Leon R. Lewandowski; 296 Michael Goss

Sponsoring Editor	Louise Waller
Project Editor	Kevin Thornton
Designer	Harry Voigt
Photo Editor	Marcia D. Golightly

To our wives, Kathy and Judy—
Their love, help and encouragement are
always there.

Preface

This book discusses the meaning of science and how it should be taught to young children. The authors hope to accomplish both goals by using many tangible examples of science and of science instruction in elementary schools. The years we have spent instructing pre-service and in-service teachers in the methods of teaching science to elementary school children have made us realize that while teachers can learn about science and can understand it and the ways of teaching it, they should have illustrations, case studies, and examples to help them to conceptualize these sometimes abstract ideas.

Understanding science is a necessary prerequisite to teaching about science. We discovered quite early that elementary school science teachers rarely consider themselves to be experts in the subject. We also found that there were few teaching materials which did an intellectually honest job of describing science and science instruction in a manner easily understood by non-science majors.

This is not a "cookbook" of science activities; nor does it offer a definition of science that, once read, is then ignored or forgotten. Our purpose is to move from teaching about the nature of science to using that definition in order to develop a collection of conceptually based teaching methods related also to what we believe science instruction should be.

The book is organized into two major parts. Part 1 provides the conceptual background and themes for the remainder of the text. Chapter 1 describes our view of science and gives examples. Chapter

2 relates this view to the goals of an elementary science curriculum, and discusses the process and content aspects of elementary science learning activities. In selecting process goals for the elementary science curriculum, we have limited the discussion to observation and the various forms of inference. These are the generic processes from which most others derive. A thorough understanding of observation and inference provides the teacher with a base that is widely applicable to teaching all the process skills to children.

Chapter 3 discusses the development of the child, and how this parallels the development of science instruction.

Part 2 is based on the themes developed in the first three chapters. Three developmentally sequenced teaching models are described, and their use in teaching the nature of science, together with content and process, is then discussed. Each of these chapters is followed directly with a chapter of science activities designed to serve both as additional illustrations of the strategies described and as sources of ideas for teachers who want to plan a science lesson on their own. Chapter 4 describes the Experiential Model, a teaching strategy that provides learning experiences for young children. Chapter 6 discusses the Discovery Model, a strategy that teaches concepts and generalizations to children. The Inquiry Model is covered in Chapter 8. Related activities for each of these models are contained in Chapters 5, 7, and 9.

The teaching models in Part 2 are flexible, independent strategies that can be used alone or in conjunction with materials and activities from curriculum projects or elementary science text series. A thorough understanding of the models will allow a teacher to use effectively or adapt nearly any elementary science text in order to reach the goals discussed in this book. Although examples and illustrations come from a variety of elementary science sources, specific texts and project materials are not included.

In using these models and the related activities, teachers are encouraged to maintain an adaptive posture in their planning. Learning activities can thus be adjusted to the unique experiential backgrounds of their students. Because of this adaptive posture and the developmental factors that have been considered in designing the activities, grade level designations have not been assigned to the activities.

A planning matrix introducing Part 2 of the text should prove helpful to readers who want to incorporate separate activities into cohesive subject matter units. This matrix describes common conceptual threads found in all three activity chapters (5, 7, and 9). Other aids to unit planning are the *related activities* found at the end of each lesson.

To help the reader learn the material contained in the various chapters the authors have included objectives and exercises with feedback as an integral part of the text. Readers are encouraged to complete these exercises before turning to the answers given in the book or before continuing with the next section.

The anecdotes and case studies are written for the explicit purpose of reinforcing understanding of the material. They are written with clarity and brevity in mind, and as such are not actual classroom transcripts. They represent edited teaching activities which have retained the essential points, but peripheral dialogue has been removed. We hope the compromise in authenticity will be more than outweighed by the clarity of the examples.

No textbook is written and developed without help from many people. The authors wish to thank the following reviewers for their suggestions and criticisms: Lowell Bethel of the University of Texas at Austin, Willis Horak of the University of Arizona, Glenn Markle of the University of Cincinnati, Lennie Middleton of the University of Miami, and Sheila Wineman of Bowling Green State University.

D.K.

P.E.

Contents

Chapter 6

Chapter 7

Part 1 Science in the Elementary School

Part 1 of this text provides the background and conceptual framework for the remainder of the book. This part describes and illustrates the nature of science and discusses its implications for the elementary school science curriculum. The three chapters in this section are based on the theme that teachers must first understand the nature of science before they can teach it to elementary school students.

Science is described as a search for regularities in chapter 1. The description is supplemented by a number of anecdotes and exercises to provide first-hand experiences with science. Because they are an integral part of the book's makeup we encourage you to complete the exercises before continuing with later sections.

In chapter 2, the major goals of an elementary science program are outlined as consisting of content learning, process skill development, and an understanding of the nature of science. Content goals are divided into facts, concepts, and generalizations, with primary emphasis given to the latter two. The relationship between content and the processes of observation and inference is developed, and ways of integrating the three major goals are presented.

Chapter 3 describes the cognitive development of the child and relates these changes to the development of science. Emphasis is placed on Piagetian stages of development and their effect on elementary school science. A hands-on approach is used, which involves the reader in administering different developmental tasks. As with the chapter exercises, we encourage you to administer these tasks to elementary school students. Doing so will not only make you more familiar with developmental theory, but it should also better acquaint you with the students you will be teaching.

In a parallel treatment, science is described as occurring in three developmental stages. The first of these is the data-gathering or *experiential phase,* in which the primary emphasis is on gathering information in the form of facts. In the *conceptual phase,* the information that has been gathered is organized into concepts and generalizations, which guide investigatory efforts in the *inquiry phase.* This material builds on the content in chapter 1, where the nature of science is developed, and chapter 2, where science in the elementary school is discussed. The development of the child and the parallel phases of science then serve as the organizing themes for the teaching strategies described in part 2.

When you are through with this section of the text, you should understand what science is, what comprises science instruction, and how to adapt this instruction to the unique developmental needs of elementary school students. In sum, you will have the background to allow you to successfully implement the specific teaching strategies described in part 2.

You may have begun to read this book because you are enrolled in an undergraduate science methods course. Or perhaps you are a teacher interested in improving your science instruction. You have probably taken one or more courses in science such as biology, earth science, life science, or physical science; now you want to learn more about teaching science to young students. This is what this book is about. It has been written to help you learn to teach science to elementary students. However, before you can effectively teach science, you must have some understanding of science itself, and it is unlikely that you've had any formal training in this area. Your science courses taught you about the content of science, for example, "Vertebrates are animals with backbones," but probably did not teach you about the way science works and what its limitations are. This is the purpose of our first chapter. We want to introduce you to the world of science, perhaps in a way you have not previously en-

Chapter 1 Science: A Search for Regularities

countered. Typically, students are introduced to science through a definition such as the following:

> Science is an accumulated and systematized learning, in general usage restricted to the knowledge of natural phenomena. The progress of science is marked not only by an accumulation of fact, but by the emergence of scientific method and of the scientific attitude. (Bridgewater and Kurtz 1968, p. 1910)

> Science is the attempt to make the chaotic diversity of our sense experience correspond to a logically uniform system of thought. (Einstein 1940, p. 487)

> Science is systematized knowledge derived from observation, study and experimentation carried on in order to determine the nature or principles of what is being studied. (Guralnik 1972, p. 1275)

> Science is both a body of knowledge and a process. The body of knowledge is the product of solving problems scientifically. (Sund and Trowbridge 1973, p. 21)

If you can form a clear idea of science from these definitions, you are probably unique. Our experience with students suggests that people cannot acquire a complete understanding of science from definitions like these. This is true for two reasons. First, *science* is a *concept,* and research shows that concepts are learned most effectively when definitions are related to or combined with concrete experiences (Clark 1971). For example, if young children are to understand the concept *mammal,* they need to have sensory experiences with mammals. They need to see, hear, and touch mammals to make the concept meaningful to them. Second, science is an abstract and complex idea. Because of these characteristics, the idea is especially difficult to grasp from words alone. This is true of all abstract concepts. It means that concrete experiences are even more important in learning a concept such as science than they are in learning a more tangible concept like mammal.

All of this suggests that for people to understand science they need to have actual experience with science. This is precisely what we hope to do in this book. We plan, through the liberal use of anecdotes and examples, to illustrate rather than merely define science. Our goal is for you to have *experienced* science when you finish this book, not merely to have read about it. In addition, we hope to provide you with teaching strategies that will allow you to teach your students about science in the same way.

It may seem unusual that the writers of an elementary science methods text feel a need to teach the concept of science to people who have had several experiences with science in the elementary and secondary schools as well as in college. Because of the way they are taught, however, these courses don't usually reflect the true nature of science. They emphasize memorizing rather than doing. Taking a "traditional" science course does not necessarily give the learner an accurate idea of the way science works. With that in mind we want you to approach our discussion of science without the typical images of white-coated men and women in laboratories, discussing words that are hard to pronounce. Instead, consider science as a human activity that is natural for, and can be learned by, everyone.

Science as a Human Activity

To illustrate the natural human activity of science, we can look at an example involving a woman's attempt to raise house plants.

Ms. Williams was interested in decorating her home and wanted to bring some of the living outdoors inside. She decided plants would make a nice addition to her household, but she had little experience in caring for them. One day, when she was passing through a department store, a Swedish ivy caught her eye. She bought it and took it home. Ms. Williams had no books on the subject, and the plant itself came with no directions, so she started her botanical career by placing the plant on the windowsill and watering it every second day. She checked the plant every day to see how it was doing, inspecting it for bugs and dead leaves. The plant flourished.

Flushed with success, the woman bought another plant, this time a jade, with beautiful, thick waxy leaves. She put this plant on the windowsill by the ivy and cared for them both in the same way. After a while she noticed that both plants were doing poorly. She was surprised and disappointed, considering that one had flourished and both were given identical treatment. She wondered if somehow the jade might be hurting the ivy, since the ivy had previously done well. She inspected both plants for bugs and found none, but still she wondered if there wasn't something on the jade plant that was harming the ivy. To check this idea she moved the jade to a different windowsill to see if it would make a difference. Still the plants declined. She tried pesticides, fertilizer, and sprays, all with no luck.

Finally, she noticed a rather unpleasant smell coming from the jade plant. She gave the plants one more good dose of water and placed them in the garage, planning to throw them away later. The plants somehow slipped her mind until, while cleaning the garage, she happened to notice that the ivy was looking much better while the jade had died and smelled bad.

She thought carefully about all this and then considered the fact that the garage only received sunlight part of the day while the window from which the plants had been moved now received full summer sun. She wondered if perhaps too much sunlight is not good for some plants. Also, in digging in the pot that had held the jade plant, she found that the roots of the plant had rotted. This seemed strange since the ivy was all right, but then she thought maybe the jade was the type of plant that needed less water. Feeling much better for figuring all this out, she went back to the store and bought two new plants. She put the new jade in the window with small amounts of water. She placed the new ivy in indirect light in a corner of the living room. She watered it liberally and watched both plants. Both grew beautifully.

Another example of science in our everyday lives comes from the history of medicine. As you read through the following example try to think of some similarities between it and the first example.

Since the beginning of time, humankind has been concerned with health. Disease has always been a factor in existence, and because of curiosity, fear, or an innate need to understand, humankind has attempted to explain why some people get sick while others do not.

One of humankind's first explanations suggested that disease was caused by demons and spirits. This may sound primitive until you consider that people lacked a body of knowledge to guide them in their explanations and had no instruments such as microscopes to help identify disease-producing organisms. Actually, people were attempting to construct explanations for disease in the absence of data. Because they could not see the bacteria and germs responsible for disease, people constructed demons and spirits to explain their ills. Though the demons and spirits were not directly linked to observations, these spirits were attempts to order or explain a heretofore chaotic world.

Some interesting and amusing sidelights came out of this view that illness was caused by evil spirits. For example, one proposed cure for these spirit-caused diseases was to ". . . pare the patient's nails, put the parings in a little bag, hang the bag around the neck of a live eel, and place the eel in a tub of water. The eel will die, the patient will recover" (Winslow 1967, p. 22). A suggested cure for fevers was to fill an old shoe with salt, bread, and garlic, rise before dawn, and throw the shoe into a river, asking the fever to follow the shoe. In both of these practices, the way to cure an illness was to induce the spirits to leave the body. Interestingly, some people today still carry a garlic bag around the waist as a preventative against disease.

An alternative way of eliminating malignant spirits was trickery. The ancient Chinese believed sickness to be caused by demons who chased people about but who could be tricked into leaving. Even in modern times this view of disease exists in some eastern cultures, as can be seen by Winslow's account of travel in China. "The motorist in China is frequently enraged by the coolie who dashes across the road just in front of the car and grins happily because he believes that he has succeeded in having the familiar demon who has been dogging his footsteps run over and destroyed (Winslow 1967, p. 7). Though these remedies may now seem ineffectual, if not amusing, we can see that the method of treating disease was consistent with the explanation of its cause; demons caused disease and the way to cure disease was to eliminate demons.

As time passed, people noticed that certain diseases were contagious and that the spread of the disease could be prevented by isolation. Consistent with these observations, the process of quarantining was begun as a means of checking the spread of disease. People also noticed that certain diseases, such as malaria (which literally means *bad air*) were much more common at certain (rainy) times of the year, and that the disease could be avoided by closing the windows at night. Based on information such as this, it was suggested that disease was caused by humours, or gaseous substances that floated on air. The idea of humours as an explanation marked some progress for humanity, because now the explanation was at least partially based on information. (Closing windows at night did lessen the chances of contacting malaria, even though we now explain this observation by suggesting that closing windows prevents malaria-carrying mosquitoes from entering the room.) Explanations such as these, based partly on observable evidence, moved the science of epidemiology one step further away from superstition and closer to a reliance on observable information.

In a similar manner, people began to make other observations, and tied them to their explanations of disease. Galen, a third century scholar, observed the following connection between physical fitness and disease. He noted that in the unfit,

> . . . there is present already general obstruction of the pores, so-called plethora, an inactive life given over to drinking, high living and sexual indulgence; that in the others which are pure and free from corruption there is wholesome transpiration through pores that are neither obstructed nor constricted, that they take moderate exercise and lead a temperate life. . . .

He concluded by asking,

> . . . supposing all this, which of these two types will probably be affected by the breathing of air which is favorable to putrefaction? (Winslow 1967, p. 73)

Again, we see a view of disease based only in part on fact, (that is, physically fit people *are* more immune to disease than others), but yet another step away from pure superstition.

As time passed and people were able to gather more information in an attempt to explain disease, they discarded the view that sickness was caused by bad air. They focused on the concepts that disease was caused by organisms that were too small to be seen with the naked eye. This new view took into account all the facts that were known at the time: the relationship between exercise and illness (the fit person would be less susceptible to the organism) and the transmission of disease from person to person (the organism could be transferred from one to another). In addition, it explained why habits such as cleanliness were an aid in disease prevention, while humours, if they existed, would be present whether an individual practiced good hygiene or not. This new view is the germ theory of disease. It is accepted today as an explanation for many illnesses.

As humanity progressed in the explanation of disease, more and more was based on information and less and less on superstition. In addition, with the passage of time, humankind developed instruments to help gather information in a more accurate and systematic way. However, the key difference between superstition and science is that humankind, in progressing from one to the other, based conclusions and explanations on observations, aided by instruments or not, rather than on "feelings."

We have considered two illustrations of science in operation. They have some common characteristics, which will be discussed in detail in the following sections. Once examined, these characteristics will provide the themes for the remainder of the book. After this discussion, you will be able to meet the following objective:

- You will understand the nature of science so that, given an illustration, you will identify the characteristics of science shown in it.

Science Is a Search for Regularities

The first and probably most important feature the two illustrations share is that in each *there was a search for regularities.* A regularity is a pattern that has occurred in the past and can be expected to occur again in the future. The world is full of regularities such as:

- The sun rises in the east.
- It gets dark when the sun goes down.
- Winter is the cold season of the year.
- Like poles of a magnet repel while unlike poles attract.
- Plant roots grow toward the center of the earth.

In our second example, humankind first attempted to find a pattern in the causes of disease by suggesting that sickness was the result of evil spirits and demons. This is a belief that we reject today, but that at one time was an authentic attempt to explain and understand the world. Because this explanation was not firmly founded in observable information, it ultimately had to be rejected. Later, people began to rely more heavily on observations and found the following patterns:

- Physically fit people are less susceptible to disease than unfit people.
- People who keep their windows closed at night don't get malaria as often as those who don't.

This attempt to explain events in the real world continued as the current wisdom suggested, "Disease is caused by microorganisms." Each of these statements is a search for some regularity in the world, and each was an attempt to find patterns in that same world. Today we are still involved in trying to find regularities in the occurrence of such hard-to-understand diseases as cancer and mental illness. Some reg-

The Characteristics of Science

regularity

ularities that have been tentatively established regarding cancer include:

- Cancer is more common in highly industralized areas.
- Cigarette smokers have a higher incidence of lung cancer than nonsmokers.
- Some cancers may be linked to heredity.

The woman growing plants attempted to form regularities when she decided, "Ivy needs a moderate amount of sun" and "Jade plants can't tolerate too much water." She arrived at these generalizations by observing her plants and seeing what effect different conditions had on their growth. Like the people who attempted to discover patterns in the occurrence of disease, the woman in her search for regularities was doing science.

The Dual Nature of Science

Defining science as a *search for regularity* implies a dual nature of science, and we will stress this duality in describing teaching procedures for elementary science classes. On the one hand, science is a *search*, which implies a continuing activity. This is the *process* aspect of science; in searching for regularities, people engage in certain processes, such as observing and inferring. The other dimension of science is the product of that search—the facts, concepts, and generalizations that scientists have formed. These are called the *content* of science. (Facts, concepts, and generalizations will be described in detail in the next chapter.) The two aspects of science are so interrelated that they are often confused.

One way to distinguish between process and content is to think of the process dimension as involving *doing* something. For example, Ms. Williams was involved in the process of science when she observed the bad smell of the plant and formed the idea, "Too much water isn't good for jade plants." The actual *forming* of this regularity involved the process nature of science while the regularity—once formed—is called the product or content of science. Similarly, when people observed that closing windows at night prevented malaria and suggested that malaria was caused by "bad air," they were involved in the process of science. The generalization they formed, "Night air causes malaria," was the product of their efforts.

We cite these examples to show how interrelated process and content are and how difficult they are to separate. Unfortunately, teachers often cover only the content aspects of science; they fail to provide their students with experience in the search or the way the regularities are found. Science instruction that attempts to provide students with an accurate view of science needs to provide experiences that include both process and content. We hope you will be prepared to do both when you finish this book. Process and content will be discussed in more detail in chapter 2, and later chapters will provide strategies designed to teach both aspects of science.

Science Is a Naturally Occurring Part of Our Lives

The dual view of science as process and product or content often escapes people for several reasons. Perhaps foremost among these, as noted in the beginning of the chapter, is that the process aspect is often neglected in typical science instruction, particularly at the college level. The majority of instruction has students memorize facts, concepts, and generalizations—the content of science. It is not surprising that students think that science is something to read about rather than do.

Another reason that people find it hard to understand science as a search for regularities is that this same search for understandable patterns is a common part of everyday life. For many, science is something performed by experts in lab coats who work in polished chrome labs, rather than something that all of us do. The tendency to structure our experience, to search for and impose patterns on the world around us, begins at a very early age and continues through life.

Babies, as they play with crib toys and crawl around the house "getting into everything," are attempting to establish patterns they can understand (figure 1–1). The preschooler who constantly asks questions is involved in the same search. As children develop, what seems to us as play or recreation is actually a part of establishing and verifying regularities about the world. Discovering mundane, everyday patterns is an important part of the child's life.

A Search for Permanence

A weary couple get home from work at 5:30 p.m., wanting nothing more than relaxation, peace, and quiet. They are greeted by an equally weary baby sitter, who sighs, "Am I glad you're home! Billy (the two-year-old son) about drove me nuts today. I read *Robert the Rose Horse* four times in a row this morning and now he wants it read again. I thought I'd skip a few pages the third time and put him down for a nap, but he stopped me and said, 'Nana, we didn't read this part.' Worse than that, every time I read even one word wrong he corrected me on it. It's your turn!"

The father, seeing the determination on the sitter's face, reluctantly takes the book, puts his son on his lap and begins reading. As he did with his sitter Billy also corrects his dad's mistakes.

Almost anyone with children has probably had similar experiences. Billy, listening for the story to sound the same way every time, is establishing one very important generalization about the world: "Objects and

Figure 1–1
A Search for Permanence

events remain the same, time after time." Psychologists call this idea *object permanence,* and it is a concept that children and adults form through repeated interactions with their environment. People aren't born with this idea, but develop it after a number of experiences.

Adults, too, form regularities as a natural part of their lives. For example, shoppers will often go to several stores, stopping at each for particular items. Through their experience they learn that certain stores have better produce, others have better meats, and still others have cheaper canned goods. These conclusions are reached through observations the people make as they shop. From these observations, regularities are formed which are used to guide future shopping behavior.

Science is a naturally occurring phenomenon and people often act as scientists without even knowing it. A person is doing science, for example, when he or she varies a recipe slightly and notes the change in the final product. It also happens when someone attempts to change his or her behavior and watches what effect this new behavior has on other people, or when a teacher uses a new teaching technique and observes what effect this technique has on student performance. Each of these people is attempting to find patterns in his or her world by shaping their observations into recognizable forms.

Before proceeding, respond to the following exercises, which illustrate elementary school children doing science in the classroom.

Read the following anecdote and identify the regularities being taught in this lesson.

Exercise 1.1

Mr. Smith was teaching his third grade class about mammals. He brought into the classroom a number of animals, such as mice, gerbils, and hamsters. On the day of the lesson he even brought in his dog with her new puppies. He began his lesson by saying,

"Look at these animals. They're all mammals. What do they have in common? Johnny?"

"They all have fur."

"Good, and what about the color of the fur? Is it the same in each case, Nancy?"

"No, some is brown, some is black, and some is even white."

"Fine, Nancy. Who else can tell me something about all these animals? No one? Why don't you pick them up and tell me how they feel. Jerry?"

"Mine feels warm."

"Martha?"

"This hamster is warm too."

"And how about dogs? Are they warm, too? Jim?"

"Yes, this one is, and my dog at home is too."

"What else can we say about these animals? Jill?"

"When my dog had puppies, she would feed the puppies milk."

"Good! Do any of you have a cat? They're mammals too. How do they feed their kittens? Joey?"

"My cat nursed its babies."

"Fine! Now let's summarize what we've found so far by completing this chart."

Things all mammals have

Things some mammals have

List three regularities discovered in their lesson on mammals.

_____

_____

_____

(If you wish, you can check the answers to this and all the other exercises in the feedback section at the end of the chapter.)

Science Is Based on Observable Data

So far we have said that science is an attempt to form patterns and that it is a natural activity for people. A third characteristic is that the regularities formed are based upon observable data. This is in contrast to nonscientific activities in which people form conclusions on the basis of opinions, feelings, superstition, or authority.

Let us return to the illustrations at the beginning of the chapter to contrast the two approaches. Ms. Williams, concluding that too much sunlight was not good for some plants, was doing science; her conclusion was based on the observations she made of her plants. She had seen that the ivy flourished when the sun was not directly on the plant, declined when subjected to direct sunlight, and flourished again when put in the shade. From this she concluded that Swedish ivies grow best in moderate amounts of sunlight. Her conclusion could be considered scientific because it was based on the information available at the time.

By contrast, the people who described illnesses in terms of evil spirits were not involved in the process of science, because their conclusions were based on superstition rather than observable data. Later, when people formed the generalization, "Disease is caused by bad air," the process they followed could be considered scientific—even though it is not currently accepted; the regularity formed was based upon the evidence that closing the window at night prevented the sickness. From this observation they concluded that sickness was something caused by the air itself.

In time, however, the idea of humours became harder and harder to accept because it failed to explain these other observations: mosquito netting prevents malaria, physically fit people are less susceptible to disease than unfit people, and people who keep themselves clean are sick less often than their dirtier counterparts. Because the idea of humours was unable to account for all the observations, a new explanation was sought and the germ theory of disease was born. This theory is accepted today not because it is inherently "right" but because it explains our observations better than any other competing theory.

For example, the idea of disease-causing humours was unable to explain why mosquito netting prevented a person from catching malaria. However, the germ theory of disease explains this because the netting prevents mosquitoes from transferring malaria organisms to people. Also, the humour theory of disease was unable to explain why cleanliness and good hygiene were effective means of preventing disease (humours would be present whether a person was clean or not) something which the germ theory readily does. Washing would remove or kill germs. So, the humour idea was modified because of the observations people made, and the notion of germs was accepted. The critical factor here is *not* that we believe in the idea of germs today (which we do) but is the fact that the germ regularity is more consistent with observation than any other explanation. (This is why we believe in it.) If it were not, we would abandon it in favor of a pattern that would be more consistent with our observations.

We can see that in order for an activity to be called science there must be a search for some pattern or regularity and this search must be based on information rather than intuition or superstition.

The dividing line between science and nonscience is thin, and areas of research where little evidence exists are often controversial. In the absence of sufficient information, scientists form tentative generalizations anyway, and the validity of these regularities is often questioned. Examples of these areas include the current controversy over the merits of Vitamin C in preventing colds, the debate over the relative contribution of heredity and environment to intelligence, and the Laetrile controversy in the treatment of cancer. The reason for the controversy in each case is the lack of sufficient data to prove or disprove a particular position. Again we can see the importance of observable information in the formation of valid and widely accepted scientific statements.

Perhaps a better way of thinking about the distinction between scientific and nonscientific statements is that they are points along a continuum, rather than separate categories. In identifying these points, we might visualize this continuum as in figure 1-2.

Nonscientific		**Scientific**	**Figure 1-2** **A Continuum**
←		→	
Disease is caused by evil spirits.	Disease is caused by humours or "bad air."	Disease is caused by organisms called germs.	

The three regularities were placed along the continuum according to the degree to which they were based on information rather than superstition. The regularity describing germs is located at the far right not because we believe in it at present but because it is based primarily on evidence rather than intuition, superstition, belief, or authority.

Defining science in this way takes science out of the laboratory and places it as a central part of our everyday lives. We are all scientists when we search for regularities that are based on our observations. The example of the small boy and *Robert the Rose Horse* is consistent with this idea. When he hears his book read he is searching for patterns, and every time the story sounds the same it shows him that the pattern he's formed is correct. When an adult skips some words or passages his observations (hearing is a form of observation) suggest the pattern is incorrect and he tries to correct it.

What distinguishes professional scientists from other people is not so much what they do as how they do it. Scientists are more efficient in finding regularities because they have developed conscious, systematic ways of attacking problems. The woman attempting to discover how to grow plants could have made an organized effort to gather data by systematically varying the conditions in which she grew her plants. One implication of this statement is that we could probably make people more efficient problem solvers if we gave them some training in these activities. Helping teachers develop techniques for doing this with children is the primary goal of this book. This will be covered in detail in later chapters.

Before continuing, please complete the following exercise.

Exercise 1.2

The following exercise describes a situation involving two cities. Read through the description and answer the questions that follow. Figure 1–3 is an outline map of a fictitious country (not to scale).

Figure 1–3
Metropolis and Environs

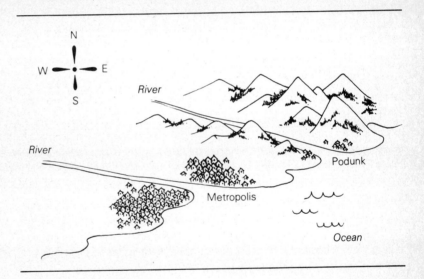

Both cities are on the coast and exist at the mouth of rivers. Metropolis is large and a busy transportation center, while Podunk is smaller. Two explanations are offered below to explain the difference in sizes in the two towns.

A. While both Metropolis and Podunk are on the coast and are at the mouths of rivers, Podunk's harbor is smaller than Metropolis', and the winds and tricky local currents around Podunk made entrance dangerous in the early years when sailing ships were used.

B. The coast range of mountains isolated Podunk but became foothills by the time they reached Metropolis, leaving it (Metropolis) accessible to overland shipping.

The following additional observations were made in reference to the cities. Based on the observations, decide which regularity is best supported and carefully explain your choice.

1. The current along the coast runs from north to south.

2. Metropolis has more roads leading inland than Podunk.

3. As many (approx.) ships ran aground near Metropolis as ran aground near Podunk in the sailing days.

4. Metropolis and Podunk are over 100 miles apart.

5. The mountains around Podunk are more rugged than the mountains around Metropolis.

6. The local winds around Metropolis are more variable than they are around Podunk.

_____

_____

_____

Science Is Information Processing

We have now seen that science is characterized by a search for regularities or patterns based on observable data; in order for the process to be considered scientific, people must form the patterns on the basis of information rather than intuition or superstition. In doing so they take single items of information, summarize the information, and transform it into regularities that are more usable than the isolated pieces themselves. This activity, called *information processing,* is a fourth major characteristic of science.

As an example of information processing, examine the following list of observations and see if you can find a pattern.

Date	Time of Moonrise
June 8	8:25
June 9	9:20
June 10	10:15
June 11	11:10

If you come up with the generalization, "The moon rises fifty-five minutes later each successive evening," and had not known this regularity before, you processed information. In doing so you took the separate items, the moon rose at 8:25 on June 8, at 9:20 on June 9 and so on, and summarized them in the pattern that was the general statement.

As another example of information processing consider the following exercise.

Figure 1–3
Which Are Wogs?

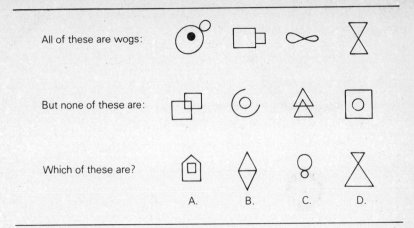

All of these are wogs:

But none of these are:

Which of these are?

A.   B.   C.   D.

If you answered B., C., and D., you correctly processed the information that was provided and formed a concept of wogs. In doing so you had to examine discrete bits of data (the examples and nonexamples of wogs) and put these observations together in a pattern (the concept "wog"). In the illustration at the beginning of the chapter people processed information when some suggested, "Disease is caused by bad air," in that this statement was based on observations (information) about how closing windows could prevent malaria and about the seasonal frequency of this disease. Information processing occurred when these separate observations were summarized in a generalization. Ms. Williams processed information when she concluded that some plants can be overwatered and some plants don't need too much light. On the other hand, no information was processed in forming the conclusion "disease is caused by evil spirits" because the conclusion wasn't based on any information.

People learn to process information through practice, which is the way any skill is learned. Unfortunately, in our schools students are often required to learn regularities (concepts and generalizations) through rote memorization rather than being allowed to form the patterns through their own processing. The following incident, reported by Ralph Tyler, illustrates the problems involved when memorizing is stressed rather than information processing.

> John Dewey reports visiting a class in the vicinity of Chicago which was studying the way the earth was probably formed. Mr. Dewey asked the students whether, if they were able to dig down to the center of the earth, they would find it hot or cold there. No child could answer. The teacher then said to Mr. Dewey that he had asked the wrong question. She turned to the children and said, "Children, what is the condition at the center of the earth?" The children all replied in chorus, "In a state of igneous fusion." (Tyler 1949, p. 27)

Because the children merely memorized the regularity describing the center of the earth, it became a meaningless string of words, and they were unable to respond when the question was phrased a bit differently.

The purpose of forming regularities and processing information is to help children develop the capability to understand and cope with their environment. This is especially critical now, when leaders in education are finding that high school graduates can't fill out a simple form or determine which of two canned goods is cheaper. Having children memorize meaningless facts rather than practice processing information to form their own regularities can only increase this problem. Teaching strategies designed to provide children with practice in processing information and forming meaningful regularities will be described in chapters 4, 6, and 8.

How well did you process the information provided in this chapter? Complete the following exercise before continuing.

Exercise 1.3

Read the following story and identify the information processing that is occurring. Do this by identifying the data that is being used and the product of the processing.

A. Mr. Webb had been given some carrot, celery, and bean seeds by a friend, but the friend had forgotten to tell him how to plant the seeds. In thinking about the problem, Mr. Webb decided to check the seed packages he did have. He noted that lettuce seeds, which were quite small, were planted one-eighth inch below the surface; that radish seeds, which were three to four times the size of the lettuce seeds, were planted one-half inch below the ground; and that squash seeds, which were the largest of all, were planted one inch below the ground, and on the basis of this information he estimated where he should plant his carrots, celery, and beans.

What data did Mr. Webb use in his processing?

_____

_____

What regularity was the product of his processing?

_____

_____

B. The children in Ms. Hill's kindergarten class were working at the water table. In planning for her lesson she had assembled a tray of objects for the children's use in the activity. Her directions to the class were to place the objects in the water one at a time and then to group them according to whether they sank or floated. After the activity the class discussed what they had found.

Figure 1-5
**The Four Major
Characteristics of Science**

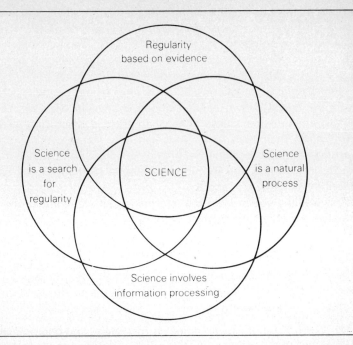

Three conclusions they reached were:

1. Wooden objects float.
2. Metal objects don't float.
3. Some plastic objects float while others don't.

What data did the children process?

_____

_____

What was the product of their information processing?

_____

_____

Summary

In summarizing the material we have discussed so far, we see that science has four major characteristics, which we will use as themes throughout the book. These characteristics are:

- Science is a search for regularities.
- The search for regularities is based on information.

Figure 1–6
Two Fishbowls

- Science is a naturally-occurring process, which can be made more systematic with training.
- Science involves the processing of information.

These four characteristics are obviously not exclusive of each other but rather are closely interrelated. This relationship is diagrammed in figure 1–5.

An excellent book for those wanting to read more about science and the activities of scientists is McCain and Segal's (1973), *The Game of Science.* This book is not only readable, but entertaining. Other recommended sources on this same topic are Conant (1951), *Science and Common Sense,* Kuhn (1970), *The Structure of Scientific Revolutions* and Watson (1968), *The Double Helix.* All these books reinforce the idea that science is a human endeavor engaged in by people trying to establish regularities through the processing of information.

Read the following exercise and answer the questions that follow.

Exercise 1.4

Ms. Jay wanted her students to know that temperature affects the respiration rate of cold-blooded animals. To teach this generalization, she brought out two fishbowls, containing fish as shown in figure 1–6.

Each bowl held a gallon of water and a little imitation reef through which the fish could swim. The children looked at the bowls excitedly and began making comments.

"There are no striped fish in the bowl on the left," Mike said.

"There's five striped fish in the bowl on the right," Ella added.

"The fish in the left bowl are tired," John suggested.

Ms. Jay then queried, "Why do you say that, John?"

"Those fish aren't moving as fast as the ones in the right bowl," John responded.

"What kind of things do you see that make you say that?" asked Ms. Jay.

"Well," replied John, "their fins aren't moving as fast and their gills don't go in and out as often." Ms. Jay then explained how the gill covers of fish are used to move the water over the gills and that by counting the number of times the gill covers opened and closed the class could measure how fast the fish were breathing. When the class counted the gill movements of the fish in the two different bowls, they found that the fish in the right bowl were breathing much faster than those in the left.

In an attempt to explain this difference Martha asked, "Did you put the fish in the right bowl before you put those in the left bowl?"

"They were put in the bowls at the same time," Ms. Jay explained.

"There are more fish in the right bowl than in the left bowl," Beverly noted.

"I know," Rosemary said, waving her hand excitedly. "If the number of fish were the same in both bowls, they would move around in the bowls the same."

"Go ahead and check that, Rosemary," Ms. Jay urged. (Rosemary stuck a small net into the right bowl and took out one of the striped fish, which she dropped in the left bowl. The class watched the fish for a few moments.)

"The fish in the left bowl are still breathing slowly, so it isn't the number of fish that makes them move slowly," Peggy noted.

"The left bowl has a film on the outside," Marcia commented.

"I'll bet the bowl is cold," Dorothy noted. (Dorothy checked the bowls with her fingers.) "The water in the left bowl *is* cold," she stated.

"If we put ice cubes in the right bowl, the fish would slow down," Mary suggested.

"That's a good idea, Mary. Why don't we try that out?" Ms. Jay asked.

"I'll get some ice," Marva suggested, and she jumped up and went to the refrigerator. Several ice cubes were put in the right bowl, and the class waited a few moments.)

"The fish in the right bowl are breathing slowly now, too," Vivian exclaimed.

"Can anyone think of a statement to describe what we just saw?" asked Ms. Jay.

"Cold water makes fish breathe slowly," Jim replied.

"Anything else?" the teacher prompted as she wrote the statement on the board.

"Oh, I know. Warmer water makes fish breathe faster!" shouted Sarah.

"Now, who can put the two together?" asked Ms. Jay, as she wrote the second statement on the board. "Anyone? Why don't you try, Judy?"

"Hmm. How about, the higher the temperature the faster the breating rate for fish."

The class then looked at other cold-blooded animals, such as lizards and toads, to see if this generalization would hold true for these animals as well.

A. What regularities were formed in this science activity?

_____

_____

B. What evidence or data did the class use to form these regularities?

_____

_____

C. Describe how information processing was involved in the activity.

_____

_____

Exercise 1.1

The three regularities that Mr. Smith's class established were: 1) Mammals have fur; 2) Mammals are warm-blooded; and 3) Mammals nurse their young. They formed these regularities by observing the animals in front of them and generalizing from these examples to all mammals.

Exercise 1.2

The regularity best supported by the data is B. To see why, look at each of the additional observations:

1. The current direction is irrelevant to the problem and neither supports nor detracts from either regularity.

2. This observation is consistent with regularity B.

3. This observation is inconsistent with regularity A because a similar number of grounded ships at each harbor implies that one isn't more dangerous than the other.

4. This observation is also irrelevant to the problem.

5. This is consistent with regularity B.

6. This is inconsistent with regularity A, which suggested that the winds were trickier around Podunk.

From this we see regularity A does not account for observations 3 and 6. Because it fails to account for all the relevant observations, it is rejected in favor of regularity B. In the event that additional observations are made for which B cannot account, it too would be abandoned or revised until a regularity is found that can account for the observations.

Feedback

Exercise 1.3a

The data that Mr. Webb used in his processing were the information on the seed packages. The result of his processing was the generalization, "Larger seeds are planted deeper than smaller seeds."

Exercise 1.3b

The information processed by the children was the observations they made of each individual item placed in the water. When they processed this information, they formed the following regularities: 1) Wooden objects float; 2) Metal objects don't float; and 3) Some plastic objects float while others don't.

Exercise 1.4a

The class actually formed one major regularity or generalization that summarized two other generalizations. First, the class concluded, "Cold water makes fish breathe slowly." Next they decided, "Warmer water makes fish breathe faster." They then combined the two to form the generalization, "The higher the temperature the faster the breathing rate for fish."

Exercise 1.4b

In forming these regularities the class observed the breathing rates of the fish in different temperatures of water. Breathing rates were the data they used to form the generalization.

Exercise 1.4c

In forming the generalizations the students made a number of observations. They used these observations as data to form their abstraction. This process can be diagrammed as shown in figure 1-7.

Figure 1-7
The observation process

Data	Abstraction
Observations of fish breathing rapidly in warm water.	The higher the temperature the faster the respiration rate.

Processing

Observations of fish breathing slowly in cold water.

References

Bridgewater, W., and Kurtz, S. eds. *The Columbia Encyclopedia.* New York: Columbia University Press, 1968.

Clark, D. "Teaching Concepts in the Classroom: A Set of Teaching Prescriptions Derived from Experimental Research," *Journal of Educational Psychology* 62, 3:253–278.

Conant, J. *Science and Common Sense.* New Haven: Yale University Press, 1951.

Einstein, A. "Considerations Concerning the Fundamentals of Theoretical Physics." *Science* 91: 487–491.

Guralnik, D., ed. *Webster's New World Dictionary.* 2nd ed. New York: World, 1972.

Kuhn, T. *The Structure of Scientific Revolutions.* 2nd ed. Chicago: University of Chicago Press, 1970.

McCain, G., and Segal, E. *The Game of Science.* 2nd ed. Monterey, Calif. Brooks/Cole, 1973.

Sund, R., and Trowbridge, L. *Teaching Science by Inquiry in the Secondary School.* Columbus, Ohio: Merrill, 1973.

Tyler, R., *Basic Principles of Curriculum and Instruction.* Chicago: University of Chicago Press, 1949.

Watson, James D. *The Double Helix: A Personal Account of the Discovery of the Structure of DNA.* New York: Atheneum, 1969.

Winslow, C. *The Conquest of Epidemic Disease.* New York: Hafner, 1967.

We will begin this chapter with a brief review. In chapter 1 you saw science described as having four major characteristics:

- It is a search for regularities.
- Regularities are formed on the basis of observable information.
- Science involves information processing.
- People are naturally inclined to be involved with science.

It was also noted in the first chapter that these characteristics will be the organizing threads for the remainder of the book. We will develop these themes in detail as we go along.

With this background in mind we are prepared to move forward. We now want to use the characteristics of science as a basis for viewing the goals of elementary science and the elementary science curriculum. These goals can be outlined as follows:

Chapter 2 Science in the Elementary School

- To teach children the facts, concepts, and generalizations that make up the content of science
- To help students develop process skills
- To develop an understanding of science and its role in our everyday lives

In this chapter we will develop these goals in detail and show how they relate to the basic themes of our text. By way of introduction, we will look at a teacher involved with a lesson on animals.

Ms. Lincoln, knowing her second-grade students were fascinated with animals, wanted to teach a lesson to capitalize on this interest. She prepared for the lesson by cutting and mounting a variety of pictures taken from wildlife magazines. She began the activity by displaying the first two pictures, one of an elephant and the other of an insect nearly hidden inside a flower. She then asked the children to describe the pictures. Initially they didn't see the insect in the flower. Here are some of their comments.

"I see an elephant," Sandra said.

Tommy added, "It's really big."

"He's standing by a tree," Robin observed.

"His trunk is wrapped around some leaves," Russ noted.

The teacher smiled and said, "Very good. Now, how about the other picture?"

"Well," Shawn hesitated, "the flowers are yellow."

"There are four flowers in the picture," Jan added.

The class was silent for a moment. Ms. Lincoln finally prompted by pointing at the picture and saying, "Look closely at this flower."

"Aha!" Sandra jumped up. "There's a bug in there."

"He looks just like the flower," Cindy stated.

"What do you mean?" Ms. Lincoln questioned.

"He's the same color," Cindy responded.

"He's sort of round, too, just like the flower," John added.

"Do you know a word that describes it when you say he's sort of round like the flower?" Ms. Lincoln asked. When no one responded the teacher said, "We call that *shape*. The bug is shaped like the flower."

She then went on to ask the children to compare the elephant and the insect. In comparing the two, the children noted such things as:

"The elephant is much bigger than the insect."

"They're both animals."

"The insect is harder to see. We almost didn't see him."

"The elephant is grey and the insect is yellow."

Ms. Lincoln praised the class: "Excellent, everyone! Let's look at some more pictures." She showed a picture of a bison standing on the prairie and a small fawn nearly hidden in the bushes and shadows of a forest. These were put next to the elephant and insect, and again the children were asked to tell what they saw. They responded with the following comments:

"The bison is brown."

"He's very big."

"The fawn has spots on his back."

"He's very hard to see."

"There's his nose."

"The bison is much bigger than the fawn."

Ms. Lincoln then encouraged the class to comment on all four pictures.

"The elephant is hungry," noted Kathy.

"Why do you say that?" asked Ms. Lincoln.

"His trunk is wrapped around the leaf."

Gene added, "The fawn is asleep. See, his eyes are closed."

"Compare the fawn and the insect," Ms. Lincoln encouraged.

"They're both animals," offered Terry.

"They're both hard to see because they look like the flower and the bushes that they're in," Ken added.

"Do you know what we call it when animals are hard to see?" Ms. Lincoln queried. (No response.) "We say that animals that are hard to see because of color or shape are *camouflaged.* Later we'll learn other ways animals can be camouflaged, but for now we'll concentrate on color and shape."

She then continued with the lesson by showing the class other examples of animals camouflaged by shape and color. When she sensed that the students' attention span was nearing its limit, she asked them to compare the size of the camouflaged animals to the size of the uncamouflaged animals.

With some prompting, Karla finally said, "The big animals were easy to see and the small ones were hard to see."

Ms. Lincoln continued by asking if this pattern was always true. In responding, the class studied the pictures and concluded that the statement was generally true, but there were some big animals who used camouflage in their hunting. When asked to explain why smaller animals were more likely to be camouflaged, the class offered the following explanations:

"So they won't get eaten."

"Because they can't run as fast as bigger animals."

"They need camouflage because they don't have big teeth and claws to fight."

The class continued to discuss the pictures until the teacher felt they had completed their analysis, then ended the lesson.

Now, let us look at this lesson and see how it tried to achieve the goals of an elementary science program. As stated earlier, these goals fall into three main categories, as shown in figure 2-1.

Figure 2-1
Goals of an elementary science curriculum

	GOALS	
Teach content	Develop process skills	Form an understanding of science

The relationship of the teaching episode to each of these goals will be discussed in the sections that follow.

Content: The Regularities Formed by Science

One of the major goals of an elementary science program is to help students acquire a knowledge of facts, concepts, and generalizations in science. These forms of content help the students to understand the world around them and to explain, control, and predict events in their environment. This section is designed to help the reader identify and understand these basic forms of knowledge.

After reading this section of the chapter you will be able to meet the following objective:

■ You will understand the forms of science content so that, given examples, you will classify them as facts, concepts or generalizations.

We said that one goal of an elementary science curriculum is for children to learn content—the regularities of science. This content, the result of information processing, exists in the form of *concepts* and generalizations. Concepts and generalizations are the regularities of science (figure 2–2).

Before concepts and generalizations are formed, a learner must have an experiential background to draw from when processing information. This background exists in the form of facts.

Facts: The Basis for All Regularities

Facts are the form of content that is acquired through our five senses, and we form facts whenever we make observations of the world around us. We gather facts in two ways, either through our own direct, sensory experiences or through the experiences of others. People are constantly collecting facts when they read, listen to conversations, or watch TV. The children in Ms. Lincoln's class acquired factual information when they made statements such as:

"The insect is the same color as the flower."
"The elephant is larger than the insect."
"The elephant has his trunk wrapped around the leaves."

All of these statements are reports of the observations the children made in the course of the lesson. An alternative way for students to gather facts would be to hear or read about the observations of others. For example, a person gathers facts when he or she reads that the sun came up at 7:15 a.m. or hears that the air temperature is 78 degrees.

Facts are important because they provide the information necessary to form the regularities (concepts and generalizations) that make up the major content of science. Without a sufficient number of facts students

Figure 2–2
**Concepts and
Generalizations: The
Regularities of Science**

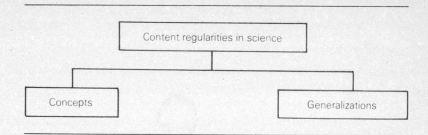

may not be able to form regularities at all. They may only memorize strings of words that are unrelated to experience. The incident in chapter 1 involving John Dewey illustrates this point. Without an adequate background of concrete experiences in the form of facts, students' understandings of concepts such as *igneous fusion* are obscure, if not totally absent. Facts form an important link between the learner and the surrounding world. Because facts are reports of sensory experiences, they provide reference points for the concepts and generalizations students form.

Another problem that arises when one tries to teach concepts and generalizations in the absence of factual information is that students are given an incorrect view of science itself. Without sensory experiences, students may view science as a game of words rather than as a human struggle to find patterns in our experiences. Ms. Lincoln prevented this possibility by providing students with sensory experiences (facts they gathered from the pictures) and allowing them to process this information into regularities (the concepts and generalizations they formed about camouflage).

One way of visualizing the relationship between these various forms of content is shown in figure 2–3.

In the diagram, elementary science content can be viewed as a hierarchy in which facts are the most numerous and least abstract, being grounded in direct experiences with the environment. Not until facts are gathered and analyzed do they become concepts and generalizations.

Concepts: Regularities in the Form of Categories

Concepts are abstractions or ideas that people form to simplify their environment. They do this by grouping their observations into categories, temporarily emphasizing the similarities between the members of the category and ignoring the differences. For example, *dog* is an example of a concept. In forming the concept we focus on similarities found in most dogs such as hair, four legs, and barking. By emphasizing similarities we sometimes ignore other characteristics such as size, color, presence or absence of a tail, and sound of the bark. In forming concepts we typically see a number of examples and nonexamples of the concept and mentally pull out the essential characteristics of the con-

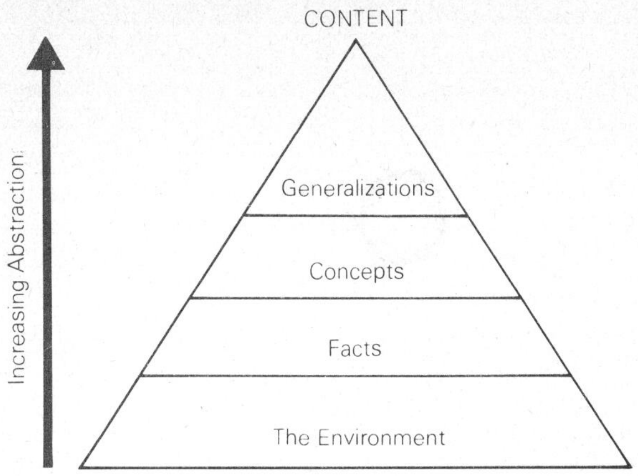

Figure 2–3
The Content of Science

cept. Concepts are called abstractions because they represent this process of abstraction of our actual concrete experiences. Based on facts
(our observations), they go beyond facts. The concept is a mental image
compiled from all the concrete examples we have seen.

Concepts differ from facts in several ways. First, facts can be directly
seen, heard, tasted, felt, or smelled; concepts, though based on observation, go beyond that process. In other words, you do more than simply
observe to form a concept. You gather those observations to create a
category. Second, concepts summarize our observations into patterns.
In Ms. Lincoln's activity the children formed the concept *camouflage,*
which summarized individual bits of information: the insect was hard to
see; the fawn faded into the grass. In both cases there was a form of
blending: rather than viewing each case separately the children grouped
the individual observations together and formed the concept *camouflage.* For them, the concept represented a pattern and summarized their
observations; *the concept was a regularity.* That is, camouflage is a
recurring pattern that can be found in other animals.

The essence of concept learning is the grouping of dissimilar items on
the basis of some similar characteristics. In the lesson on animals the
students grouped their observations of two seemingly dissimilar animals. They were forming a category, grouping the two together because
each was hard to see because of color, shape, or both. Being hard to see
because of color and shape are characteristics of the concept *camouflage.* The concept summarizes information and forms a regularity because all similar instances would be classified as camouflage. In another
case—the concept *mammal*—the defining characteristics are warm-
blooded, has hair, and bears live young. The concept *mammal* represents a pattern or regularity because all mammals have these characteristics, and any animal that has these characteristics can be
classified as a mammal.

This summarizing capability is a critical asset to the human mind, which is responsible for storing the vast amount of information a person gathers. Without concepts the task would be overwhelming. For example, scientists tell us that the human eye can discriminate nearly seven million different shades of color. To remember each of these with a name would leave little room for other information. Therefore we form categories or concepts, grouping together similar shades into colors such as *red, blue,* and *green.* Similar summarizing occurs in all areas of science. We think of animals in terms of broad categories such as *protozoans* (one-celled animals), *mammals,* or *amphibians,* each category being a concept. This not only allows us to summarize our experiences but also provides us with a means of storing information for later use.

Other examples of concepts found in the elementary science curriculum include:

reptile	protein	star
animal	cell	sedimentary rock
plant	dissolve	fish
electricity	heavy	energy
evaporate	fruit	lever

Each of these terms is an abstraction. It can be described using key characteristics and it is used to summarize large amounts of information.

Before continuing, complete the following exercise designed to reinforce your understanding of concepts.

Exercise 2.1

Read about the following description of a concept-centered lesson and answer the questions.

Mr. James was teaching a unit on physical changes. He began this particular lesson within the unit by bringing the class to the front of the room. Then, he took a wet sponge and ran it over the chalkboard. As the class watched, the water left on the board slowly disappeared. He encouraged the students to do the same and to feel the board as the water was disappearing. Then he had members of the class wet their hands and dry them by holding them still, shaking them and placing them in the air in front of a fan. After discussing what happened, the class decided to do two other activities. In the first, they poured water in a number of jars, some of which were placed in the sun and others in the shade. Still others were covered with lids, and the remaining ones were left open. The class also wet paper towels. They hung some over railings in the room and left others wadded in plastic bags. The next day they observed what happened to the water in the jars and on the towels, and compared this to water disappearing on the chalkboard.

Identify:

A. The concept being taught.

_____

B. The facts used by students to form the concept.

_____

C. The characteristics of the concept.

_____

If you wish, you can check your answers in the feedback section at the end of the chapter. Then go on to the next section.

Generalizations: The Patterns of Science

We have just described concepts as abstractions or mental images that are based on patterns we find when making observations. Generalizations further serve to summarize our experiences by relating concepts to each other.

As an example of this process, let's look again at the camouflage activity. Students formed the generalization, "Small animals are more often protected by camouflage than are large animals." While the concept _camouflage_ summarized observable facts, the generalization went further by relating camouflage to _animal size._ By forming this relationship, students summarized large amounts of information related to protection, color, and size of animals into one general statement. Generalizations are even more useful than concepts because they are capable of summarizing more information and describing the environment even more accurately. This process is diagrammed in figure 2–4. As another example, consider this generalization: The higher the temperature, the faster the speed of evaporation. Evaporation is a concept that summarizes facts such as the water drying on the board, on the students' hands, and on the paper towels. The generalization links the concept _evaporation_ to another concept, _temperature,_ and describes a relationship between the two. A person who knows this generalization has a means of organizing and storing information related to these concepts, of explaining observations such as why boiling water evaporates quickly, and of predicting future occurrences, such as the relative drying times of two liquids at different temperatures.

Sometimes people mistake generalizations for facts. For example, the statement, "Full moons occur every 28 days," is a generalization and not a fact for several reasons. First, we haven't formed the statement from observation alone, because we have not seen all past or future moonrises. Also, information in the statement was a summarization, not a report of a single occurrence. To illustrate this difference compare the

Figure 2–4
Forming generalizations

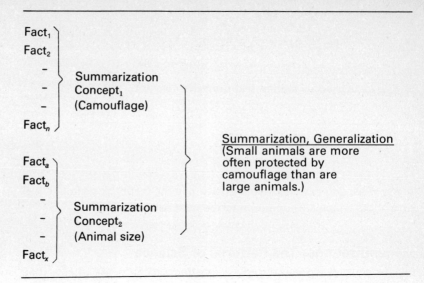

statement, "There are 28 days between full moons," to "It was 28 days since the last moon was full." We could directly observe the second statement—a fact—but must summarize information to form the first—a generalization.

It is a common notion in reference to facts and generalizations that if exceptions to a statement can be found, it's a generalization; if not, it's a fact. We want to dispel this notion right now. We believe the generalization about full moons just as we believe the statement, "Like poles of magnets repel," which is also a generalization. The statement about magnets is a generalization because it relates the concepts *magnetic poles* and *magnetic attraction.* It summarizes observations we have made of magnetic poles and attraction/repulsion rather than being based on observation alone. Because we have not seen all possible cases of magnetic poles and attraction or repulsion we generalized from what we did see to make the statement. For that reason it is a generalization. We believe the statement because we've never observed a contradictory case. This belief in correctness, however, in no way changes the statement from a generalization to a fact.

In addition to acting as storehouses for facts and concepts, generalizations also allow us to predict events. This has important implications because much of education in general, and science education in particular, is preparation for the future. We are concerned not only with what students can do now but with what they will be able to do later in life. If they know generalizations, they can use them to predict and control events in the environment. Fishermen have found, for example, after observing bass over a number of years, that these fish like to feed at around sixty-six degrees (F) (Gibbens 1977). Knowing this generalization allows the fisherman to predict when bass will be feeding, or even where in the different temperature layers of water to look for bass. It also helps conservationists determine what streams and rivers would be best for planting bass. The generalization, which was based on and formed from past observations, can be used to the fisherman's and conservationist's advantage to find fish and to control events in their environment. Similarly, knowing that a full moon occurs every twenty-eight days and remembering when the last full moon occurred would allow a romantically inclined young couple to plan for a canoe ride or moonlit walk on the beach. Again, we can see how the regularities we form help us deal effectively with the world around us. Similar instances could be provided for other areas—gardening, hunting, cooking and car maintenance—in which knowledge of generalizations differentiates the expert from the nonexpert.

We have described content as the regularities of science that form an important goal of the elementary science curriculum. To reinforce your understanding of this dimension of science instruction, complete the following exercises related to facts, concepts, and generalizations.

Examine the examples below and determine if the statement is a fact, defines a concept, or is a generalization. Mark each F, C, or G respectively. In the blanks below each generalization, write the two key concepts being related.

Exercise 2.2

1. A dog is an animal that barks and has four legs and canine teeth.

_____

2. The first manned airplane flight took place at Kitty Hawk, North Carolina.

_____

3. High tides along the Atlantic coast typically occur six hours after the last low tide.

_____

4. Magnets pick up objects made of iron, nickel, or cobalt.

_____

5. A star is a sphere of burning gas that is composed of hydrogen and helium.

_____

6. The longer the vibrating column, the deeper the pitch.

_____

7. The chemical symbol for oxygen is O.

---

8. Sugar is an organic substance that is composed of the elements carbon, hydrogen, and oxygen.

---

9. The Salk polio vaccine was discovered in the 1950s.

---

10. A plant is a living organism that manufactures food through the process of photosynthesis.

---

11. The higher the elevation above sea level the lower the boiling temperature of water.

---

12. Galileo was tried as a heretic when he defied Church authority.

(If you wish you can check your responses in the feedback section at the end of the chapter.)

This concludes our discussion of the content goals of the elementary science curriculum. A major way that these forms of content are taught to young children is through the processes of observation and inference. These processes and their relationship to the different forms of content will be discussed in the next section of this chapter.

Process Goals as Intellectual Skills

After reading this section of the chapter you should be able to meet the following objective:

■ You will understand the processes of observation and inference so that, when given a list of statements, you will identify the process as observation or one of the forms of inference.

In the last section we discussed content as an interrelated set of goals in the elementary science curriculum. When students learn content by processing information through observation and inference, they do more than acquire concepts and generalizations, the regularities that help to simplify the world, they also learn *how* to learn. By processing information, students practice learning skills that aid them not only in science but in all other areas of curriculum. These skills are called *processes,* and the development of process skills is a second major goal of the elementary science curriculum. We'll begin our discussion of process with observation—the starting point for all science.

Observation: The Student's Link with the World

Our first contact with the external world is through our senses. We are deluged with a variety of stimuli from the day we are born, and we continue to have sensory experiences until the day we die. We are continually bombarded on all sides by sights, sounds, tastes, tactile sensations, and smells. Our senses are our first and most basic mechanism for gathering information. Items of information acquired through the senses are called observations; the process of *observation* can be defined as the gathering of information through our five senses. It is through observation that we acquire all the facts we know about the world.

Because science is an attempt to form regularities in the natural world, observation serves as a critical link between the scientist and the environment. Through observation, facts are gathered that can then be processed to form concepts and generalizations. Without the process of observation there would be no starting point for forming regularities nor would there be a way of verifying the validity of the concepts or generalizations formed. Figure 2-5 adds observation to the content pyramid first seen in figure 2-3.

Observations come to us in two ways. One is direct and immediate: we observe that it is raining outside, that a dog is barking, or that something smells sour. The other is vicarious or indirect: we observe on a printed page (read) that Galileo made the first telescope. In this case we observe vicariously the direct observations of those who were alive in Galileo's time. Such observations form a very important part of our learning because they broaden the scope of our experiences to encompass the experiences of people in other times and places.

The process of observation can take many forms. The geologist who lifts and feels rock samples is making observations, as is the chemist who notes the smell of a particular formula. Zoologists use the process of hearing to gather information about the animals they're studying, and taste, too, is an important observational tool for many scientists. The most common type of observation is that of sight.

Scientists' heavy reliance on the process of observation is sometimes obscured by the machines and devices they use to extend the range of their observations and to make their observations more precise. For example, astronomers use telescopes that allow them to see stars hidden to the naked eye and to measure distances between stars accurately. Biologists using radioactive isotopes can "look" into the human body and through the use of instruments like the X-ray machine and the Geiger counter can observe the functioning of the body in ways that would be impossible with the naked eye. But it should be remembered

Figure 2–5
The Content of Science

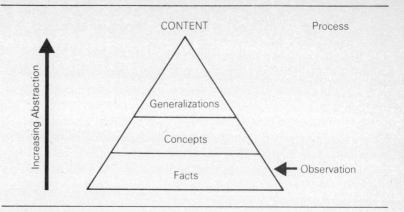

that all of these sophisticated techniques are designed to extend rather than replace the five senses, and all are designed to help scientists make more accurate observations.

The process of observation is also important in the elementary science curriculum. Observations provide the starting point for activities in the elementary school by bringing students into contact with their world. Observations provide the facts needed for subsequent information processing. Students cannot process information in a void; the process of observation allows them to gather the data needed to initiate their own information processing activities. In addition, students who have the opportunity to make observations are practicing a skill that will be useful throughout their lives.

Ms. Lincoln's students made observations when they said things such as:

"There's a yellow flower in the picture."
"There's a bug in there."
"The bug is sort of round."
"The elephant is grey and the insect is yellow."

These observations provided the facts the students needed to form the regularities that resulted from the lesson. The kinds of observations elementary students make are probably as varied as those of the scientist. Opportunities to allow students to practice this skill abound in the elementary school. Measuring, weighing, tasting, feeling, smelling, and hearing take place in virtually any activity-oriented lesson. Students, like scientists, also use instruments to make their observations more precise. Magnifying glasses, tape recorders, clocks, rulers, and scales all help to produce data that are more accurate and precise than they would be otherwise.

Providing students with opportunities to make many observations in their learning activities is important for two reasons. First, through the process of observation students are able to gather facts that can be

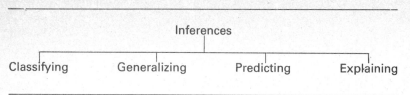

Figure 2–6
Four types of Inferences

processed into concepts and generalizations. Second, observation-oriented learning activities provide the opportunity to practice and develop observational skills. Teachers often mistakenly assume that all students are good observers. Our lessons, reflecting this assumption, provide few opportunities to gather sensory data or to learn how to become better observers. In chapters 4, 6, and 8 we will describe and illustrate activities that promote practice in observation.

As important as the process of observation is to elementary science, it forms only the beginning point in that curriculum. Cramming facts into students' heads will not make them knowledgeable science students unless they are helped to process this information into storable and usable information. Teaching students to make accurate observations is an important starting point, but to help them process their observations into concepts and generalizations we need to teach them to make inferences.

Inferences: Going Beyond the Information Given

We gather information through the process of observation. Through information processing these observations are summarized and made more useful. In doing this, individuals go beyond immediate observations to construct patterns, to predict future observations, and to explain the events we observe. These extensions and interpretations of observations are called *inferences,* and it is through the process of inferring that much of our understanding of the world is accomplished. Because of the importance of inferences in helping us understand and interpret the world, the ability of a person to make inferences and to decide on the validity of others' inferences is an essential thinking skill. The remainder of this section is devoted to a discussion of the process of inference and the relationship between inferences and observations.

Inferences are statements that are based upon observations but include more than just the observations themselves. As such, inferences are extensions of observations and serve to group together (classify), summarize (generalize), predict, or explain. Each of the different functions that inferences perform can be considered to represent unique skills in the individual. These four forms of inference will be described as distinct processes, but the four are closely related and this relationship will be emphasized.

Figure 2-7
Three Coins

Penny   Nickel   Dime

Classifying Inferences

Classifying inferences involve grouping together two objects on the basis of some similarity. Classifying inferences occur frequently in our lives. For example, a young girl at the seashore makes a classifying inference when she makes piles of shells on the basis of color, shape or design. Another form of classification occurs when children group baseball cards on the basis of league, team, or position. Adults make classifying inferences when they notice that two records sound alike or two foods taste alike. In all of these examples there are two common characteristics. The individual first encounters an array of uncategorized objects and then places them in groups on the basis of some commonality.

Classification activities can vary in their difficulty, depending upon the number of objects to be classified and the thoroughness of the classificatory scheme required. For example, three objects are easier to classify than ten because the individual needs to observe only three objects and find a commonality between two of them. An individual who encounters ten objects and is required to make only two classes has an easier job than someone who has to make three or four. (The making of two classes is the most basic of all classification schemes and is called *dichotomous classification*.)

For the most part, classifying is an arbitrary process, with no one classificatory scheme better than the other. For example, consider three coins in figure 2-7. These three coins can be grouped in a number of ways. The nickel and dime could be grouped on the basis of monetary value or on color, the penny and nickel on the basis of nonserrated edges, the penny and dime on the basis of the short hair of the figures; the dime and nickel on the basis of clean-shaven figures, and so on. The point of this is that with any array of objects any number of groupings can be made all of which are "correct." The only criteria that should be used in judging a classifying scheme is whether it is logically consistent.

We're now ready to turn our attention to another, similar type of inference, the generalizing inference. More will be said about classificatory inferences when we discuss developmental differences in chapter 3 and the experiential model in chapter 4.

Generalizing Inferences

Generalizing inferences are statements that summarize and extend a large number of discrete observations. Generalizing inferences serve two complementary functions. The first is to summarize data to simplify it and make it easier to remember. The second function is to extend the summary to include cases not yet observed. In other words, a generalizing inference is used to condense a set of observations into usable form and extend this summarization to a larger set of observations.

Generalizing inferences differ from classifying inferences in two ways: they extend beyond the immediate objects at hand and they are often nonarbitrary. To illustrate these differences, consider a father trying to teach his preschooler the concept of the color blue. The father has gathered a number of toys around them on the floor. He starts out by placing several blue toys together and saying, "These toys are blue; can you find any other toys that are blue?" Slowly, through the process of trial, error, and feedback from the parent, the child starts to get the idea: the concept blue has to do with color, not with the size or shape or function of the toy. For the most part the concept that the child learns is nonarbitrary; that is, most people will agree that a given object is blue or not blue; further, the definition for the concept, whether verbalized or not, is commonly shared by most people in our culture. The nonarbitrariness of the concept is also reflected in the fact that the father wasn't teaching just *any* concept. Rather, he had a specific concept in mind and chose his positive and negative examples accordingly. In addition, this concept, once learned, could be used in the future to describe other objects. So a major function of generalizing inferences is to form concepts and generalizations that can be used in later life to describe and explain the world around us.

The elementary science teacher plays a vital role in this process by selecting important science concepts and generalizations to teach and by providing students with selected data to process in forming these abstractions. Ms. Lincoln did this in the introductory episode when she chose different pictures of animals to illustrate the concept of camouflage and the generalization linking camouflage to animal size.

Parents, too, help their children form generalizing inferences about the world by pointing out situations in which patterns occur. For example, a small boy and his father were feeding their dog when the father noted, "Look, son, the dog likes his food. He's wagging his tail." By calling attention to this aspect of the environment, the parent has set the scene for further learning in which the boy can determine whether this statement applies to other dogs besides his own. In noticing other dogs wagging their tails he first summarizes the information by noting that other dogs also wag their tails when they eat, and finally concludes "All dogs wag their tails when they eat." From a number of discrete observations he has generalized to all possible cases. In other words, from observing a number of dogs wag their tails while they eat he has inferred

Figure 2–8
The Generalization Process

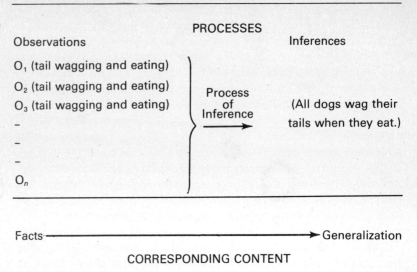

PROCESSES

Observations   Inferences

O_1 (tail wagging and eating)

O_2 (tail wagging and eating)

O_3 (tail wagging and eating)   Process of Inference   →   (All dogs wag their tails when they eat.)

—

—

—

O_n

Facts ———————————————→ Generalization

CORRESPONDING CONTENT

that *all* dogs wag their tails while they eat. In making this inference the child processed information to form a generalization that not only summarized his past observations but extended this summary to all dogs. This process is illustrated in figure 2–8.

Because the boy generalized from a few observations to all members of the class, we call this a generalizing inference. We use the term to refer to the process of extending observations of events or characteristics to include those that have not yet been observed; the process of generalizing transforms facts into concepts and generalizations.

In Ms. Lincoln's activity the children were making generalizing inferences when they concluded, "Small animals use camouflage as a form of protection more than large animals do." In forming this inference the students observed the pictures of different animals and summarized their observations in a statement that included all animals.

The process of generalizing (forming generalizing inferences) is common in our everyday life. It is a critical skill because it is the process through which we form not only generalizations but also concepts about the world. In forming concepts we infer characteristics to a total category on the basis of our observation of a subset of that category. For example, the small boy who encounters his and other children's dogs observes characteristics such as fur, four legs, tail wagging, barking, hand licking, and so on in these dogs. His concept of dog then includes those characteristics and he will expect other dogs that he encounters also to wag their tails, bark, and lick his hand; that is, he has inferred these characteristics to exist in dogs he has not encountered. The concept he has formed summarizes his past observations and extends these observations to examples of the concept not yet encountered.

Predictive Inferences

A major value of concepts is that they allow us to infer characteristics of the concept to new examples that we meet. The boy will, when encountering a new dog, expect that dog to lick his hand. In doing so the child has formed a predictive inference that involves using past observations to suggest what a future observation will be.

Predictive inferences are related to generalizing inferences in several ways. First, predictive inferences are based upon generalizing inferences. In the previous example, the boy could not have predicted that the dog would lick his hand had he not already generalized that dogs are hand lickers. People make predictive inferences based upon other inferences so often that the difference between the two types of inferences is often obscured. For example, the person who throws a ball up into the air and then extends the hand to catch it is performing an action based on a predictive inference. The inference that the ball will come down is based upon the generalizing inference, "What goes up, comes back down." Countless human activities are predicted on just such a relationship between generalizing and predictive inferences.

An important difference between generalizing and predictive inferences should be noted. Generalizing inferences refer to or summarize classes of observations, while predictive inferences refer to singular observations. For instance, the generalizing inference about dogs referred to all dogs; the predictive inference referred to the specific dog encountered by the boy.

In Ms. Lincoln's lesson the children could have formed a predictive inference (prediction) by saying, "When the fawn is bigger, it won't depend so much on camouflage for protection." This prediction would be based on the generalizing inference that related camouflage to animal size.

Explanatory Inferences

A fourth type of inference used by people to process information and, consequently, to help make the world around them comprehensible, is the explanatory inference. As the name suggests, an explanatory inference is used to explain observations. As a simple, commonplace example of this process, consider the case of a small girl who daily is observed watching *Sesame Street* on television. Through our observations of her daily viewing habits we could infer that the child likes the program. Our inference that the girl likes the television program explains why she is watching it.

Scientists frequently use explanatory inferences to help them understand events they encounter. For example, scientists at the Dinosaur National Monument in Utah encountered literally tons of dinosaur bones on an arid hill in the mountains and attempted to explain how they got there. In doing so they observed that fresh-water clam shells were mixed with the bones. They explained this observation by inferring that at one time the area was under water. (Being under water "explains" why the clam shells were there.) They also observed that the sandstone that held the bones existed in layers with rippled surfaces and was embedded with small pebbles. From this they inferred that a stream had flowed through the area depositing the small stones and causing the layers of sandstone to have rippled surfaces. (A gently flowing stream explains both the ripples and the small stones. A fast-flowing river would carry larger rocks.) They also observed that the sandstone layer containing the bones was from eight to twelve feet thick. From this observation they inferred that the bones had been deposited over a period of time rather than at one time. (Deposition over time explains the layer being thick.) The composite picture the scientists painted was that the bones were deposited there over a period of time by a flowing stream that carried the bones for a while and then covered them with sand to preserve them for millions of years. Later, some of the sand slowly eroded, exposing the bones. All this was explained through the process of inference, based upon observations they had made.

Children engaged in process-oriented science activities have a number of opportunities to make explanatory inferences. In Ms. Lincoln's activity, for example, the children made an explanatory inference when they said, "The elephant is hungry." They observed that the elephant had its trunk wrapped around the leaves of a tree and explained this observation by inferring that the elephant was hungry. Being hungry would explain *why* the elephant had its trunk around the leaves. An explanatory inference is used to help understand *why* a particular event occurred. For example, the teacher in the anecdote might have asked, "Why isn't the elephant the same color as the environment in which it lives?" To answer this question students would need to form an explanatory inference to explain the observation that the elephant's covering doesn't match its environment as well as some smaller animals' covering does.

The two examples of the professional scientists and the small children have two characteristics in common. First, an event was observed; second, an explanatory inference was proposed to account for the observations.

Like observing, inferring is a natural process, but that does not mean that people form inferences efficiently or that the inferences they form are accurate. People commonly tend to make inferences based on inadequate data. For example, a person is misusing the process of inference when he says, "Make X cars are lousy. I owned one and I had

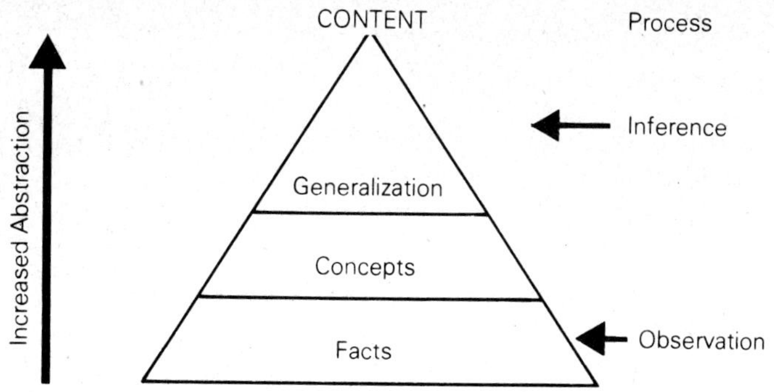

Figure 2-9
The Content of Science

continual trouble with it." Here the person made observations (the trouble with a car) and, based on one instance, formed the generalization, "All cars of Make X are trouble prone."

This problem also occurs in elementary students, who at times seem too eager to make inferential leaps in the absence of sufficient data. The ability to base inferences on sufficient data and to distinguish a valid from an invalid inference is a powerful thinking skill; it is an important goal for elementary science. One way of helping children to learn to do this is to give them opportunities to make their own inferences and to judge the validity of the inferences that others have made. The teaching strategies discussed later in part 2 of the book are designed to provide students with opportunities to practice these skills.

In summary, the process of inference is a skill that involves establishing patterns or regularities in the observations we make. The most basic type of inference, the classificatory inference, groups objects together on the basis of some similarity. Generalizing inferences, which form concepts and generalizations, summarize information and extend this summary to instances not yet encountered. Explanatory and predictive inferences are based upon generalizing inferences and are used to explain or predict events. The relationship between these forms of process and content can be seen in figure 2-9. To reinforce your understanding of the process skills involved in information processing, complete the following exercises.

Exercise 2.3

The following are comments made by a young boy watching some people at a dinner party given by his parents. In front of each statement, write O if the statement is an observation, P if the boy is predicting, C if the boy is classifying, G if the boy is generalizing, and E if the boy is explaining.

1. Mr. Johnson is still eating.

2. The people in the room are happy.

3. There are eighteen people in the room.

4. Mr. Jones eyes are closed.

5. People get sleepy after they eat.

6. Mr. Johnson's and Mr. Jones' pants look similar because they're the same color.

7. The people standing by Mr. Smith are all laughing. The rest of the people at the party aren't.

8. Mr. Smith must be a funny person.

9. Mr. Smith is over six feet tall.

10. Mr. Jones is asleep.

11. If Mrs. Jones sees Mr. Jones she'll wake him up.

12. Adults laugh a lot at parties.

13. My mother will be tired tomorrow.

14. Mr. Johnson must be really hungry.

15. Most of the people at the party aren't smoking; only the two by the window are.

16. Mrs. Smith is moving away from one of the smokers and making a face.

17. She must not like the smoke.

Exercise 2.4

Look at the illustration in figure 2–10 and the two inferences. Based on your observations of the picture decide which inference is better and explain your choice.

Understanding Science: A Curriculum Goal

So far we have discussed two important goals for the elementary science curriculum: process skill development and content acquisition. A third major goal of the curriculum is to help students understand what science is and how it proceeds. Much misunderstanding exists in our society about what science really is. Typically, people think of science as something to memorize that exists in a science textbook, and science instruction has not done much to dispel this image. Too often, elementary science instruction has consisted of occasional teacher demonstrations, periodic reading assignments, and memory-level tests. The overall effect is to create the impression that science consists of facts that are to be memorized but not utilized. To paraphrase Marshall McLuhan, the medium of instruction becomes the message, the message being that science isn't something people do, but rather something people read about.

Figure 2-10
Testing Inferences

Inference 1: It is winter.
Inference 2: The tree is dead.

By contrast, consider the science lessons illustrated so far. In each case, children were involved in making observations and transforming their observations into concepts and generalizations through the process of inference. They processed information to form regularities. These activities capture the essence of science by allowing students to experience science directly. As children acquire more experience in *doing* science, they begin to form a concept of science: that science is an active rather than a passive activity. In other words, the effective way to teach elementary students *about* science is to have them actively involved in *doing* science. Through active involvement students not only gain an overall picture of what science is but also become proficient in the skills that scientists have. Through practice, students begin to recognize when a statement of inference is supported by observations and when a regularity such as a generalization is based on data, not on bias, superstition, intuition, authority, or belief. A student who can do this is becoming "scientific."

We can see that the three goals of an elementary science curriculum we are discussing separately are actually closely interrelated. A major goal of the science curriculum is to develop in students an understanding of the nature of science by placing them in situations where they have the opportunity to act like scientists, posing questions, gathering data, and analyzing this data into concepts and generalizations. These students are not only forming an overall concept of science but are also developing their process skills and learning science content at the same time. The teaching models in chapters 4, 6, and 8 were chosen for two reasons: they have proved their effectiveness with elementary school children, and they have the capacity to integrate all three goals of an elementary science program.

Summary

This chapter described the relationship of science to the elementary school curriculum. In this chapter we listed the major goals of an elementary science program:

- Content acquisition
- Process skill development
- Understanding science.

The most important types of content to be learned in elementary science classrooms are concepts and generalizations. These two types of abstractions are valuable because they summarize our experiences and allow us to predict and explain events in our environment. Facts, while an important part of the information-processing sequence, are not major goals in and of themselves.

Process skills can be divided into two major areas, observation and inference. The process of observation is the major way that we gather information about our environment and the products of this process are facts. The process of inference refines these observations into concepts and generalizations.

There are four types of inference; classifying, generalizing, explaining and predicting; each processes information in distinct ways. Classifying inferences group data into discernable categories while generalizing inferences are used to form concepts and generalizations. Predictive and explanatory inferences then use these concepts and generalizations to predict or explain additional observations.

The third major goal of the elementary science curriculum is understanding science. A major way of accomplishing this goal is by involving students in the activities of scientists. These activities include the processes already described as well as defining problems, forming hypotheses, gathering data, and analyzing that data.

While described separately, each of these goals is closely interrelated. Content cannot be effectively learned in the absence of processes, and processes require content to give them substance. In addition, in an optimal learning environment students learn about science by focusing on specific content and processes. Ways of integrating these three interrelated goals are described in chapters 4, 6, and 8.

Exercise 2.1

The abstraction being taught by Mr. James was the concept *evaporation.* **Feedback** Some characteristics of the concept are: 1) Evaporation involves the drying out of a liquid; 2) Air makes water evaporate faster; 3) Containers prevent water from evaporating. The facts used to form this concept were observations the students made of the water drying on the board, on their hands, in the jars, and on the paper towels.

Exercise 2.2

The following statements are facts: 2, 7, 9, 12. Statements 1, 5, 8, 10 are concepts. The generalizations are 3, 4, 6, 11. The concepts included in each of these generalizations are listed below:

  3. High and low tides; time of occurrence
  4. Magnetic attraction; type of metal
  6. Length of column; pitch
11. Elevation; boiling temperature

Notice that in each of the concept definitions the concept to be described was first linked to a superordinate or more inclusive concept and then further described in terms of additional characteristics. Logically, this appears to be an optimal way of describing concepts for teaching purposes. Textbooks are often remiss in this respect; consequently, teachers must often provide students with this additional amount of structured information.

Exercise 2.3

  _O_   **1.** Mr. Johnson is still eating.

  _E_   **2.** The people in the room are happy.

O   **3.** There are eighteen people in the room.

O   **4.** Mr. Jones' eyes are closed.

G   **5.** People get sleepy after they eat.

C   **6.** Mr. Johnson's and Mr. Jones' pants look similar because they're the same color.

C   **7.** The people standing by Mr. Smith are all laughing; the rest of the people at the party aren't.

E   **8.** Mr. Smith must be a funny person.

O   **9.** Mr. Smith is over six feet tall.

E   **10.** Mr. Jones is asleep.

P   **11.** If Mrs. Jones sees Mr. Jones she'll wake him up.

G   **12.** Adults laugh a lot at parties.

P   **13.** My mother will be tired tomorrow.

E   **14.** Mr. Johnson must be really hungry.

C   **15.** Most of the people at the party aren't smoking; only the two by the window are.

O   **16.** Mrs. Smith is moving away from one of the smokers and making a face.

E   **17.** She must not like the smoke.

Let us look at each item briefly.

1. This can be observed.

2. This may appear to be a generalizing inference but the statement is limited to the people in the room as opposed to people in general and would serve to explain some observations, such as laughter and smiles.

3. This is an observation of the number of people in the room.

4. Again, this could be directly observed.

5. This is a generalizing inference about people. This statement could also be used to explain the observation in item number 4.

6. This is a classifying inference. The boy grouped the pants together on the basis of color.

7. This is another classifying inference. The boy classified people as to whether they were laughing or not.

8. This is an explanatory inference which explains why all the people were laughing.

9. This is an observation involving numbers.

10. Mr. Jones being asleep would explain why his eyes are closed.

Sleep cannot be observed but rather must be inferred from observations such as regular breathing, snoring, body position, unresponsive behavior, and so on.

11. This statement refers to a specific person rather than people in general and suggests what a future observation will be.

12. The statement refers to *all* adults and is therefore an inference.

13. This refers specifically to the boy's mother and suggests a future observation.

14. Mr. Johnson's hunger would explain why he's still eating (the observation in item 1).

15. This is a classifying inference that groups people on the basis of smoking or not smoking.

16. The boy was observing Mrs. Smith's behavior.

17. This statement attempted to explain the observation in number 16.

Exercise 2.4

Inference 1, "It is winter," explains why there are no leaves on the tree, which can be observed. This is supported by the observation that there are no leaves on the trees in the background. Other observations, however, such as the child in a short-sleeved shirt, or the bicycle with the baseball glove on it, suggest that it is not winter. Inference 2, "The tree is dead," would explain why there are no leaves on it and the inference also explains why the branch might be easily broken. The reason there are no leaves on the other trees remains uncertain unless they, too, are dead.

When explaining observations, there is often some uncertainty, and students who understand science learn to cope with uncertainty and maintain a tentative attitude in forming conclusions. With all this in mind, Inference 2 is probably better.

References

Bourne, L.; Ekstrand, B.; and Dominowski, R. *The Psychology of Thinking.* Englewood Cliffs, N.J.: Prentice-Hall, 1971.

Clark, D.C. "Teaching Concepts in the Classroom: A Set of Teaching Prescriptions Derived From Experimental Research," *Journal of Educational Psychology,* 62, 3: pp. 253–278.

Commission on Science Education. *AAAS Science—A Process Approach,* Hierarchy Chart, Inference Section. New York: Xerox Corporation, 1967.

Eggen, P ; Kauchak, D.; and Harder, R. *Strategies for Teachers.* Englewood Cliffs, N. J.: Prentice-Hall, 1979.

Gibbens, J. "Plugging Away," *American Way,* 30: pp. 33–36.

Herron, J.; Cantu, L.; Ward, R.; and Srinivasan, V. "Problems Associated with Concept Analysis," *Science Education* 61, 2: pp. 185–199.

Hurd, P., and Gallagher, J. *New Directions in Elementary Science Teaching.* Belmont, Calif.: Wadsworth, 1969.

Klausmeier, H.; Ghatala, E.; and Frayer, D. *Conceptual Learning and Development.* New York: Academic Press, 1974.

Markle, M., and Tieman, P. *Really Understanding Concepts Or in Frumious Pursuit of the Jabberwock.* Champaign, Ill.: Stipes, 1970.

Martin, M. *Concepts of Science Education.* Glenview, Ill.: Scott, Foresman, 1972.

Martorella, P. *Concept Learning.* San Francisco: Intext, 1972.

Smith, F. *Comprehension and Learning.* New York: Holt, Rinehart and Winston, 1975.

Victor, E., and Lerner, M. *Readings in Science Education for the Elementary School.* 3rd ed. New York: Macmillan, 1975.

Anyone who has ever worked or talked with children realizes that there are significant differences between younger and older students. Besides the quite obvious differences in size and appearance there are also differences in how they think. Differences that can be attributed to maturational levels are considered to be *developmental*, because they develop during the process of growth.

This chapter will focus on developmental differences and their effects on elementary science instruction. The major source of ideas for this chapter came from Jean Piaget, who has worked with children and their reasoning processes for over fifty years. We will not attempt to describe all of Piaget's ideas, however, but will select the ones most instrumental to implementing an elementary science curriculum. In doing so we will be simplifying, possibly clarifying, and probably distorting some of his ideas. We hope that the product that emerges—a better understanding of how to teach science to elementary school students—will justify the interpretations we have made.

Chapter 3   Science and the Elementary School Student

After reading this section of the chapter you will be able to meet the following objective:

Piaget: An Introduction

- You will understand the concepts of organization, adaptation, assimilation, and accommodation so that, given anecdotes illustrating these concepts, you will identify examples of these processes in them.

The Quest for Equilibrium

In the first chapter we introduced the idea that all of us are scientists to some extent; we all attempt to make sense out of the world around us by processing information into regularities. By forming these patterns we attempt to make the world understandable, changing the old structures if they don't work well and forming new patterns or regularities when the old ones don't fit. When the regularities we have do an adequate job, that is, when they allow us to describe and explain what's going on out there, we are in a condition Piaget calls *equilibrium.* It exists when our mental structures are adequate to understand the world around us. When these regularities or structures are inadequate, people are motivated to search for ways to revise them. Quizzical looks, frowns, and exploratory or manipulative behavior are all evidence of this imbalance.

Organizing Information

Piaget calls these processes adaptation and organization. *Adaptation* is the individual's constant effort to understand the surrounding world. In terms we have used previously, the individual is constantly processing information. In doing this, the regularities already formed are often adequate. For example, if you looked up from this page to the room around you and saw familiar sights and objects, the regularities that you have would be adequate to describe or explain these sights. If something that you saw is out of place or strange, however, (if there were an elephant in the room) then your mind would attempt to form an explanation to account for this discrepant information. Adaptation is Piaget's term for these attempts. Adaptation occurs when the individual interacts with the environment and either understands that environment (achieves a state of equilibrium) or tries to figure out why he or she does not.

Piaget uses the term *organization* to refer to the products of adaptation. When we "learn" something new, we can say that the organization of our mind has changed. This change might consist of the addition of a new fact, concept, or generalization, or it could consist of the altering of an old regularity. For example, if a student who has previously thought of mammals as having four legs finds out that whales are mammals, the concept of mammal changes and a change in organization occurs.

To illustrate, take an example from everyday life. A person who has always driven a car with a stick shift on the floor has a certain organizational structure in the mind. We know this 'because the individual knows what to do when he or she gets into the car. The organizational structure allows the driver to start the car and operate it smoothly. Take that same person, put him or her in a car with an automatic transmission on the steering column, and watch the person reach for the clutch and the stick shift. The existing organizational schemes are no longer adequate. Consequently, adaptation or change in the structures must occur.

A second example of the interrelationship of organization and adaptation comes from the science curriculum. A student who has had a number of experiences with different kinds of fruit will often think of the concept as including only things that are sweet and that grow on trees or bushes. In other words, experiences have been organized on the basis of the examples that have been encountered. But the concept of fruit will have to be reorganized or adapted when additional examples, like tomato and avocado, are presented. Since these aren't sweet, and because tomatoes don't grow on trees or bushes, the student's organizational structure for fruits would have to be adapted or changed.

One aspect of both examples has its central importance in science instruction. In each of these examples both organization and adaptation occurred because of experiences the individual had with the environment. An important idea of Piaget's, and a central notion to our idea of science instruction, is that people form structures and change them through an active exchange with the environment. The focus of the elementary science curriculum, then, should be to place students in situations where they can experience the world about them, rather than only reading about it. Science lessons should be structured so that children have ample opportunity to experience and manipulate the objects they're learning about.

Adaptation: A Process of Assimilation and Accommodation

Central to the whole idea of cognitive growth or learning is the concept of adaptation. If the individual's organizational structure (his or her ideas about the world) do not change, cognitive growth cannot occur. The notion of change is central to the ideas of learning and growth. But how is it that adaptation occurs?

Piaget describes adaptation as occurring through two complementing and reciprocal processes, assimilation and accommodation. *Assimilation* refers to the process of interpreting or viewing the external world according to structures (regularities) that we already possess. For example, when a small girl eyes a four-legged animal and says, "Doggie," she is assimilating the information she is receiving about that animal (four legs, small, brown and white fur) into her existing cognitive structure. Everything is fine for the child until the animal walks up to her and meows. Then accommodation must occur.

Accommodation refers to the processes of changing existing mental structures or patterns in response to the realities of the environment. Accommodation occurs when we learn something new, when we change our minds on a position because of new information, or when we change our attitudes about a person or groups of people because of experiences we have had. When accommodation takes place, the content of our minds—concepts, generalizations, attitudes, and views—change to make them more in line with the real world around us.

The young child encountering the animal had to do this when the "dog" meowed. According to past experiences, dogs bark, and don't meow. In attempting to reconcile or accommodate her mental structures or ideas with this new experience, she had two options: to conclude that dogs do indeed meow or to conclude that not all small, four-legged animals are dogs. With some help from adults around her, the child will be able to accommodate or change her structures to bring them more in line with the environment.

Summary

We have presented a view of learning that has a number of implications for teaching in the elementary science classroom. First, we restressed the idea that people are natural inquirers, who continually try to make sense of the world around them by processing information into patterns, structures, or regularities. Piaget calls these patterns the *organizational structure* of the individual. In organizing the structures the individual maintains a close contact with the environment. Contact is easy for the young child as he or she walks, crawls, smells, touches, and listens his or her way through the world. Later, when children are forced to sit quietly in desks and listen passively, adaptation cannot occur as efficiently. Adaptation implies an active interchange between the person and the environment. Under these conditions new information cannot be assimilated into previously formed structures. Accommodation, the restructuring of these patterns into newer, more realistic, patterns, is also made difficult.

To correct this situation we suggest that science teachers construct their lessons so that students can actively interact with the world around them. This structure allows them to practice and strengthen the process skills and the concepts and generalizations they already possess. It provides them with new data to build new process skills and form new abstractions by interacting with new data and shaping it into patterns and regularities.

In the process of adapting to the environment and organizing and reorganizing cognitive structures, children often exhibit characteristic reasoning patterns and encounter some unique learning problems. In other words, children adapt to the environment in different ways at different ages. (Of course all children are unique in their own ways of adapting, but patterns have been found at different ages.) Piaget has identified unique characteristics of the adaptation process at different age levels and has identified what he calls four stages of human intellectual development through which all children pass. These stages will be discussed in the next section. Before turning to this section, please complete the following exercises. They are designed to reinforce your understanding of the material just covered. The feedback for all exercises in this chapter will be found at the end of this chapter.

Exercise 3.1

Directions: After reading each of the following examples identify the mental organizational structures operating, then describe the adaptation that occurs. In describing this process use the terms assimilation and accommodation.

1. A driver who had been driving in the United States for a number of years had an excellent driving record. In fact, she enjoyed driving because it provided her with an opportunity to think about things and work out problems in her head. In England, however, she almost gave up driving altogether, as she couldn't get used to driving on the left side of the road.

    a. Organization _____

    _____

    _____

    b. Adaptation process

        1. Assimilation _____

        _____

        2. Accommodation _____

        _____

2. Babies' first encounter with solid food is often a humorous event. Expecting liquid nourishment from a nipple, they don't seem to know what to make of this new kind of food.

    a. Organization _____

    _____

    _____

b. Adaptation process

    1. Assimilation _____

    _____

    2. Accommodation _____

    _____

3. People from western or Occidental cultures often have a difficult time understanding or appreciating Oriental music because it is so different from ours. However, once they learn about the subtleties and intricacies of this different type of music, they appreciate it more.

    a. Organization _____

    _____

    _____

    b. Adaptation process

        1. Assimilation _____

        _____

        2. Accommodation _____

        _____

4. Freshman entering college for the first time often encounter all kinds of difficulties in learning how to succeed at the "college game." Unaccustomed to the autonomy and personal freedom, they often don't realize that the extra time away from classes is to be spent in studying and preparation.

    a. Organization _____

    _____

    _____

    b. Adaptation process

        1. Assimilation _____

        _____

2. Accommodation _____

_____

How Developmental Stages Affect the Learning Process

After reading this section of the chapter you will be able to meet the following objective:

■ You will be able to understand the four major stages of developmental growth so that, when given the proper materials, you will be able to administer and diagnose a developmental test for these stages.

In the previous section we discussed the basic concepts Piaget uses to describe the process of cognitive growth. We said that people continually interact with their environments and process information in an attempt to understand the world around them. In doing so, people at all ages attempt to achieve some type of equilibrium between the organizational structures they have formed and the stimuli they receive from their environment. If these organizational structures are adequate, new information from the environment is assimilated into their existing cognitive structures. Sometimes these structures are inadequate. Accommodation involves either the modification of old structures or the development of new ones. The name for this whole process of attempting to understand the surrounding world through the use and refinement of one's mental structures is *adaptation.*

The Learning Process and the Science Classroom

A similar analysis can be done for the elementary science classroom. Children, in their attempts to understand the world around them, process information into regularities or patterns. In this way students are attempting to develop structures that adequately represent, describe, or explain the world around them. When these structures are adequate to the demands of the environment, a condition of cognitive equilibrium occurs: the individual is able to assimilate new information into these structures. We can think of this process as one in which existing structures are exercised or reinforced. When accommodation takes place and old, inadequate structures are replaced by more efficient ones, we can say that learning has occurred. Elementary science teachers facilitate this process by providing students with experiences that will allow them to strengthen previously existing structures and to form new ones.

For example, consider the child who sees a picture of a snake and is told that the snake is a reptile. On the basis of this example he or she forms a structure (regularity)—reptile. At this time, snake and reptile are the same regularity. Seeing a picture of another snake, the child *assimilates* this example into the existing structure of *reptile.* The concept has not been appreciably altered. When the child sees a picture of an alligator, however, and is told it is also a reptile, the structure (concept, regularity) must be altered. In other words, the child goes through the process of *accommodation.* This process continues constantly with slight accommodations being made as experiences cause the structure to come closer and closer to approximating "real" reptiles. For instance, snakes are often considered slimy; upon touching them we find that they are not slimy at all. Therefore, a child who experiences a live snake can form a more valid structure than one who merely sees a picture or reads about reptiles in books. This example shows how the adaptive process works as described by Piaget, and it illustrates the importance of encounters with the environment that are as realistic as possible.

Children at all ages don't assimilate or accommodate information in the same way, according to Piaget. Small children aren't developmentally capable of forming structures for abstract ideas such as *energy* or the *atom,* neither of which can be seen. Nor are they capable of certain forms of abstract reasoning. In saying this, we want to differentiate clearly between development and intelligence. Because a child of two is incapable of forming a structure (regularity, concept) for *atom* doesn't imply any lack of intelligence. Rather, it means that developmentally the child is not yet ready to form the structure.

Instruction Keyed to the Developmental Stages

In observing the process of cognitive adaptation in children, Piaget noted certain stages or levels. These stages refer to the types of problems children find meaningful (that is, they understand what the problem is asking them to do) at different levels as well as the kinds of solutions they find to these problems. For example, a child of three will not find the following type of problem to be meaningful, but a seven or eight year old probably will.

> John and Bill and Sam are brothers. Sam is taller than John and John is taller than Bill. Is Bill taller than Sam?

The reason such stages are important to the elementary science teacher is that they help to explain the workings of young children's minds, as well as suggesting things that children at different stages will find either interesting and meaningful or uninteresting and downright confusing. So by understanding these stages science teachers will be able to make better judgments about what and how to teach.

Developmental psychologists have defined these stages by making a number of observations of children and by processing these observations into regularities—the concepts of the four stages. The concepts represent general descriptions of how children act at different age levels. Similarly, our concept of a teenager is a generalized notion of how kids act at that age. There are, however, large individual differences within that category and huge differences between the extremes of that category. As you read about these stages, keep in mind that they are merely attempts to describe general patterns of behavior and that individuals within a given stage or level may exhibit considerable variance. Also try to remember that human beings change in gradual ways. Movement from one stage to another is more a slow change over an extended period of time than a dramatic jump from one stage or step to the next.

The Sensorimotor Stage (approximately 0-2 years)

The stage of development that occurs from the time of birth to approximately two years is called *sensorimotor* because the individual's attempts at adaptation are primarily concerned with the coordination of tactile, visual, auditory, and muscular coordination.

During this stage of development the infant uses the basic data gathering mechanisms of seeing, hearing, touching, and moving to form structures about the environment. The direct relevance of the development of these structures to science teaching is probably not as important as some in later stages. Consequently, our treatment of this early stage will be somewhat cursory. Nevertheless, the sensorimotor stage is of interest because it illustrates Piaget's basic concepts of organization, equilibrium, adaptation, assimilation and accommodation and sets the stage for development in the next stage.

Early Changes Are Dramatic.

Anyone who has watched a child grow from a point of relative helplessness at birth to the actively inquiring child of two will appreciate the dramatic changes that occur during this stage. At birth the child is essentially helpless, armed with little more than a few reflexes and the tendency to grow and adapt to the world around it. At the risk of oversimplification we can say that the young child's mind is relatively devoid of organizational structures of either a content or process nature. In other words the child does not have many concepts or generalizations in the cognitive repertoire nor does he or she possess effective observational or inferential skills. Basic skills, like being able to reach for an object and grab it, are absent at the beginning of this period but are well represented at the end. How does this change occur?

The Natural Tendency to Adapt

As stated previously, children at this stage, as well as all other stages, possess a natural tendency to adapt to the environment. They do this by gathering information about the environment and by processing this information into organizational structures. What characterizes this stage of development are the kinds of structures formed and the limitations placed on the individual by physical conditions.

At birth children are for the most part immobile and must be content with processing information that happens to come to them. Consequently much of their cognitive energy during this period is aimed at developing better ways to process information. The way they develop these skills is by processing information that comes to them in their cribs and playpens.

Changes in Child Rearing

An interesting sidelight to this idea is the profound influence developmental psychology has had on child rearing practices. A generation or two ago parents were encouraged to keep their infants quiet and still in a crib with white or plain colored sheets and *avoid* stimulating them. Today parents are encouraged to keep colorful objects such as toys, mobiles, pieces of cloth and so on in or near the infant's crib *in order to* stimulate them (White 1975). This marks a turnabout in the experts' position. We now know the stimulation small children receive aids them in developing their information-processing abilities.

Development of Selectivity

Flavell (1975) described this developmental process in infants as one of learning perceptual-attentional selectivity. Initially the young baby's attention seems to wander at random, with little success at focusing upon specific aspects of the environment. Anyone who has tried to teach children with short attention spans and wandering eyes and ears will attest to the inefficiency of this type of information-processing system. In order to learn adequately, however, a person must be able to focus on the subject or topic and maintain attention for a certain length of time. The newborn does not seem to have this capacity, although the two year old obviously does. Countless waking hours of watching and listening are instrumental in the development of this capacity.

Development of Object Permanence

Related to this perceptual-attentional selectivity is the development of object permanence, or the belief that an object still exists even though it is out of sight. We infer that babies up to about six to ten months don't have this concept because they fail to look for objects that are placed behind a screen or blanket. The fact that they quickly turn their gaze away from the place where the object disappeared gives new meaning to the saying, "Out of sight, out of mind." Gradually the child develops the ability to continue to fixate on the place where the object disappeared, until finally at about ten months the child will actively seek an object placed under a blanket.

Development of Coordination

A third major dimension of development during this period is in the area of muscular development and coordination. The ability to focus the eyes on an object and follow it through space as it advances and recedes as well as the ability to coordinate eye and hand movements are included in this area. Evidence for the development of the latter cluster of abilities can be seen in the newborn baby's ineffective attempts to reach for and grab objects like a rattle. During this period the young child gradually develops not only the ability to reach for and grab the rattle but also to hold it and shake it, much to the joy of parent and child alike.

Summary

We will summarize our description of growth during this stage by referring to the concepts introduced in the previous section. During this period the child's efforts at adaptation are primarily involved with the refinement of perceptual mechanisms and muscular coordination. Through practice in activities such as watching, listening, crawling, and grasping the young child develops and refines new organizational structures. More often than not, these structures are concerned with sensorimotor activities, hence the name for this stage. Once developed, these structures allow the child to assimilate new information from the environment. In addition, as the child applies these structures or plans to the environment, some of them are found to be inadequate, and the child through trial and error seeks to develop new ones. Thus, cognitive growth occurs.

The Preoperational Stage (approximately 2 to 6 years)

This next period of cognitive growth is called preoperational because it precedes the period of concrete operation which is to follow. Flavell (1975) has noted that all too often the child during this period is compared to the operational child, and made to look wanting or incomplete rather than a distinct entity with strengths and positive characteristics. We agree with Flavell's comments and will attempt to decribe the child not in terms of things he or she can't do, but rather in terms of the significant developmental steps the child takes.

Development of Symbolic Behavior

The child during this period takes monumental strides in the development of symbolic behavior. During this period the child begins to develop the idea that symbols stand for objects and classes of objects. During the initial part of the period the child uses words and symbols as direct referents for objects. The word *cup* is not a name for all containers with handles, but rather a name for the child's own cup. Similarly *dog* doesn't refer to a class or group of animals with similar characteristics but to a particular animal. Later in this period the child begins to understand that the word dog is a generic term that refers to all dogs; that is, he or she generalizes to form the concept *dog.* This significant step forward is a necessary one for students who are to learn concepts and generalizations in the elementary classroom.

Deferred Imitation

Additional evidence for the emergence or growth of symbolic behavior is deferred imitation. Piaget recounts the story of one of his children watching in wide-eyed amazement as another child threw a temper tantrum. The next day Piaget's child acted in a similar way, something he had never done before. Piaget speculated that children during this period must encode events like this through the process of imagery, retaining a picture or image of the previous event. The ability to imitate or model another's behavior is another important step forward for the elementary science student, providing an additional means of learning. A teacher who wants to teach students how to conduct valid science experiments could model this behavior for students and expect them to be able to approximate his or her performance at a later date.

Sorting Out Reality

In addition to the ability to represent events and occurrences in terms of symbols (words or images), children during this period are attempting to distinguish what is real from what is not real. At the beginning of this period children are very susceptible to appearances of reality rather than reality itself. Four year olds, shown a wire that is then bent in front of them, when asked if it is the same wire will assert that it is not.

In another demonstration (DeVries 1969) children were shown a cat and allowed to pet it. Then they were told that the cat was going to change. While they watched, the cat was taken partly behind a screen where a realistic dog mask with bared teeth was placed on it. The rear end of the cat was left in view so that the children could see that it was the same animal. When the cat reappeared, small children believed it had actually changed and refused to pet the "new" animal. Older children (around five or six years of age) asserted that the animal couldn't change. In a similar problem, younger children were more likely than older ones to assert that a boy could become a girl if he wanted to, if he did "girlish" things, or if he wore girls' clothing.

The Power of Selective Focus

The tendency of children to focus on one aspect of the environment and to accept surface appearance as reality are the bread and butter of magicians. They also have direct implications for science instruction. Children at this stage have a hard time understanding that water, steam, and ice are different forms of the same substance, or that pouring a liquid from one container to another changes the shape but not the weight or volume.

An explanation for this type of behavior is that children during this stage tend to focus on one aspect of the environment to the exclusion of others. It is almost as if their newly developed perceptual-attentional selectivity has become too powerful, with the child completely focusing on one part of a problem to the exclusion of other elements. In the wire task, for example, the child focuses on the shape of the wire rather than the fact that the wire is the same color, thickness, and length. In the cat problem the young child focuses on the mask and disregards the fact that the body has remained the same.

To illustrate further, if a child during this stage is shown two identical pencils placed next to each other, the child will agree that the pencils are of identical length. If one is pushed ahead of the other, however, the same child will claim that this pencil is now longer. This child focuses on the extended end rather than the overall length, not realizing that moving the pencil back to its original position would result in the original comparison. This kind of operation, called a reversible action, is one of the benchmarks of the next period of development.

Not to sound too pessimistic, we should reemphasize the significant progress made during this period. The child progressing through this stage has made great strides in symbolic behavior. The notion of an abstraction referring to classes of behavior (concept learning) is now understood. Vocabulary has become impressive, and communication with a six year old can accomplish things impossible to do with a two year old. Both developments have implications for elementary science instruction as they allow for the inclusion of concepts and generalizations in the curriculum and provide verbal means to supplement hands-on experiences. More will be said about this when we discuss teaching strategies in the next section of this chapter.

Concrete Operations (approximately 6 to 11 years)

As in the stages that have preceded it, the name for this developmental stage refers to characteristics of the learner during this period. *Concrete operations* refers to the idea that students in this stage can perform logical operations if these operations are performed on real or concrete objects. A child who has reached this level of development, when asked if there are more boys or students in the class, will be able to think this problem through (with the aid of concrete props in the form of students in the class) and conclude that there are more students. By contrast, a child at the preoperational level might answer something like this, "There are more boys because they're bigger and so there are more boys than girls." Children at this stage are not able to perform logical operations using concrete props, a characteristic of the concrete operational child.

It should be stressed that the concrete operational child needs physical props to perform cognitive tasks successfully. The same child would probably encounter difficulties if asked to solve the following problem:

All A is B.
Some B is C.
Is all A, C?

But this student would probably be able to figure out the following problem:

All mammals are animals.
Some animals are herbivores.
Are all mammals herbivores?

Implications for Science Instruction

These strengths as well as limitations of the concrete operational child have direct implications for elementary science instruction. Students at this stage of development are beginning to learn how to perform logical operations. They can solve problems if tasks are presented in concrete terms, but encounter difficulties in performing the same tasks with abstract, verbal problems. The need for hands-on, experiential activities for students in the first through sixth grades is obvious.

Growth during the period of concrete operations occurs in a number of areas, perhaps the most important of which is classification. The preoperational child, when given an array of blocks of different shapes and colors, will form inconsistent classes, sometimes grouping on the basis of color and sometimes on the basis of shape. In addition, the early preoperational child has trouble with exhaustive sorting in which *all* of the objects that belong in a class are placed there. Instead, the two to four year old will place *some* objects in a class but forget to place others. By the time the child reaches first grade (approximately corresponding to the onset of the concrete operational period) the child can take an array of objects and sort them consistently and exhaustively.

Another classification skill that is added during the concrete operational period is the ability to utilize multiple classification schemes. At the beginning of this period children have difficulty classifying an array of multicolored and multishaped blocks first by color and then by shape. (Kofsky 1966) It appears that these children do not see the first classifica-

Figure 3–1
**A Hierarchial
Classification
System**

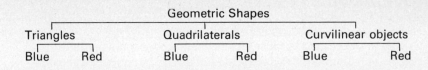

tion system as an arbitrary scheme that can later be rejected in favor of another. Later in this period up to 90 percent of the children are able to classify objects one way and then another, attesting to their newly gained cognitive flexibility and understanding of the arbitrariness of classificatory systems.

Classification Aids Inference

At about the same time the early preoperational child develops the ability to classify objects hierarchically. For example, when given an array of different-shaped and -colored blocks, the concrete operational child can first divide them by shape and then by color, constructing a classification system similar to figure 3–1. In addition, the same child can correctly answer some questions like: "Are there more quadrilaterals or geometric shapes?" and "Are there more red triangles or blue triangles?"

This ability to understand not only the idea that concepts refer to *classes* of objects but also that these classes can be related in a hierarchy provides elementary science students with powerful inferential weapons. For example, once having learned the concept of mammal, students can now infer mammalian characteristics (that is, warm-blooded, fur, live birth, and nursing their young) to any new mammals that they meet in their texts or in the real world. In addition, when learning about new classes of mammals such as canines or ungulates (cows) they can successfully attribute mammalian characteristics to these animals without being told specifically to do so. From these examples we can see that during this stage of development concepts become tools for thinking rather than the names for specific objects or limited classes.

The Concept of Conservation

Another major advance during this period is the development of the ability to conserve. *Conservation* refers to students' ability to understand that certain properties like weight and volume are not changed by operations like pouring and flattening. Two simple experiments illustrate this idea. Children are shown two identical glasses with identical amounts of liquid in them. The liquids are then poured into a short wide glass and a narrow thin glass. When asked if the two amounts (volumes) of liquid are now the same or different, the nonconserver will say there is more in the tall glass. In a similar type of problem with clay or play dough, children are asked to weigh two identical balls of clay. Having determined that they weigh the same, the students then watch as one of the balls of clay is flattened out and made longer. When asked again if the two weigh the same, the nonconserver will say that the longer one weighs more. The conserver, on the other hand, will answer that they are still the same because only the shape has been changed.

One explanation for this difference is focus: the nonconserver focuses on only the salient or obvious aspects of the problem, disregarding other variables. In the liquid volume problem, the nonconserver focuses upon the greater height of the tall, thin glass, disregarding the width of the shorter one. Another explanation is the notion of *reversibility:* the mental ability to invert a sequence of steps to return from the final condition to the initial. In other words, it involves the ability to realize that if the two liquids in the different shaped containers were poured back into their original containers, they would have the same volume.

However the ability to conserve is explained, it constitutes an important skill in the science curriculum. Without it, simple transformations like pouring and shaping are viewed as changing the amount of a substance. Such a view of the world makes accurate observations difficult and makes an accurate idea of measurement impossible. A simple operation like pouring a liquid into a measuring container would be seen as a major transformation. Both processes are important skills in the elementary science curriculum because they provide a major means by which children gather information, and their development or lack of it have important implications for teachers.

In summary, significant progress is made during the concrete operations stage in the development of conceptual thinking and in the specific concept of conservation. It should be stressed, however, that the success of both these advances is dependent upon the existence of concrete props to accompany these cognitive operations. Children at this stage of development are still not able to perform actions on ideas that do not have concrete referents. The need for hands-on experiences and laboratory experiences in science is crucial.

Formal Thought (approximately 11 years on)

This stage of development has been called the period of abstract thinking (Good 1977) and involves the ability to think without the need to refer to concrete objects or directly observable properties. For our purposes, probably the most important advances that mark this stage involve the ability to do theoretical reasoning and to control variables.

By theoretical reasoning we mean that the formal operational child can approach a problem in an abstract manner and mentally consider all the possible solutions before jumping into a problem. Flavell contrasts this with the younger child, who burrows

> . . . right into the problem data as quickly as possible, using his or her various concrete operational skills to order and interrelate whatever properties or features of the situation he can detect. His is an earth-bound, concrete, practical-minded sort of problem-solving approach, one that persistently fixates on the perceptible and inferable reality right there in front of him." (1975, pp. 102-103)

Flavell contrasts this child with the formal operational child, who looks at reality (what is) as only a subset of what might be. In other words, the formal operational child is able to approach a problem systematically and consider all possible alternatives or explanations and then select one for investigation.

Consider some typical responses of students who were asked why certain puppies grow faster and are healthier than others. Younger children are more likely to make comments such as the following:

> Food makes the difference. I had a dog and fed him the right food and he grew up big and strong.

> You have to exercise a dog or else he won't grow up right.

Contrast these statements with the following.

> Hmm, food and water are important, but so are other things, like. . . .

> If we wanted to find this out we should list all of the things that make things grow and see which ones are important for puppies.

The first approach to problem solving was concrete, while the second was more theoretical and more characteristic of the formal operational thinker.

Related to the ability of formal operational students to consider a number of possible explanations is their ability to control variables in an experiment. For example, read the following description of an experiment designed to determine which dog food is better and tell what's wrong with it.

> Two brothers were arguing about the relative advantages of canned and dried dog food in promoting puppy growth, so they agreed to try an experiment. The brother who lived in the city agreed to feed his litter of four Irish setters nothing but canned dog food. The brother who lived in the country agreed to feed his litter of seven golden Labrador retrievers nothing but dried food. They agreed to weigh their dogs at the end of a three-month period and compare results.

The problem with this experiment was that the brothers failed to control variables, that is, they failed to make it a valid test of dog food because other factors that might affect weight were also different in the two conditions. The place where the puppies were raised, the breed of dog, the size of the litter, and the starting weights of the puppies were all

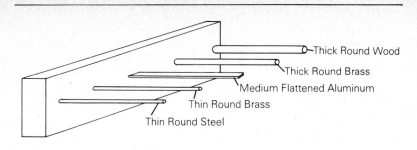

Figure 3–2
A Formal Operational Device

factors that could influence the results of the experiment. A better experiment and one that controlled variables would compare dogs of similar size and breeding from litters of similar size, and would be conducted in identical settings. By controlling these variables, we could then conclude that any difference between groups of puppies was due to the kind of dog food and not other factors.

A second illustration of this capability utilizes the device pictured (figure 3–2) which has a number of different rods embedded in a piece of wood.

In working with this device, students put different numbers of washers at different lengths from the end to determine factors that affect bending. The device as it is set up allows students to investigate a number of factors, but to do so accurately, students must control extraneous variables. To find out whether brass or steel bends more easily, for example, students would have to use the same number of washers and place them at the same distance from the end of the thin, round steel rod and the thin, round brass rod. (What's wrong with using the thick, round brass rod for this comparison?)

Other differences between the formal and concrete operational child aren't as central to science instruction as these two are. These differences, the ability to reason theoretically and to control variables; permit the elementary science student to participate in inquiry activities that are aimed at active experimentation. This important operation in science will be discussed in chapter 6.

The exercises that follow differ from previous exercises in that they are designed to be administered to elementary school-age students. We strongly recommend that you complete these exercises before continuing with the chapter.

Directions: The following tasks are designed to help reinforce the ideas discussed in the previous section and to provide you with some first-hand experiences in working with children at different levels of thought.

Exercise 3.2 Piagetian Tasks

To administer these tasks you'll need several children for approximately fifteen minutes each and the following list of materials.

■ Clay. Four clear (plastic) glasses: two identical in size and shape, one tall and thin, and one short and wide.

■ A dozen pennies or checkers. Two pieces of wire or string, scissors. A wooden dowel, four pieces of string, and a dozen washers or other weights.

The children you choose for these tasks should be around four, eight, and twelve years of age. These ages approximately correspond to the preoperational, concrete operational, and formal operational stages of thought. You should remember that this correspondence is only approximate, however, and that variations can and very likely will occur.

The tasks are designed to be administered individually. As you present each task to a child, you can present it as a game, but stress that the child should try to do as well as possible. As children complete these tasks, listen to the reasons they give for their answers. The reasons may be as interesting and informative as the answers themselves.

Task One: Conservation of Mass

Materials: Two identical balls of clay.

Procedure: Place the two balls of clay on the table and ask the child if the two pieces have the same amount of clay. Let the child touch or feel the pieces if he or she wants to. Then ask the child to flatten one out into a pancake. Now ask the child if the two pieces contain the same amount or if they have different amounts and ask why.

Task Two: Conservation of Liquid Quantity

Materials: Two identical clear plastic glasses, a short wide clear glass, a tall thin clear glass, and pitcher of water.

Procedure: Place the two identical glasses on the table and pour water into them until the child agrees that there are identical amounts in each container. Then have the child pour the contents of each glass into either the tall or short glass. Now ask the child if the two containers have the same amount of water or if they have different amounts. Ask why.

Task Three: Conservation of Length

Materials: Two identical pieces of string or wire, scissors.

Procedure: Place the two pieces of string on the table next to each other so the child can see that the two pieces are identical in length. Before proceeding, make sure that the child believes that the two pieces are identical in length; if necessary, shorten one with a pair of scissors until the child agrees that they are. Then take one of the pieces of string and make it wavy (like this $\sim\sim\sim\sim\sim$). Now ask the child if the two are the same length or if one is longer now and why.

Task Four: Conservation of Number

Materials: A dozen pennies or checkers.

Procedure: Place the dozen pennies in two rows of six each so that the members of each row correspond, or are next to each other (like this, oo oooo / oo oooo). Then ask the child if there are the same number of pennies in each set. If necessary allow the child to manipulate the sets and count the objects. Once equality of sets has been determined spread out the pennies in one set so one line of pennies is about one and a half times as long as the other. Now ask the child if the number of objects in the two groups is the same or different and why.

Task Five: Control of Variables

Materials: A wood dowel (a ruler will do) with four pieces of string tied to it. One of these pieces should be longer, two should be identical in length and one should be shorter. Tie three metal washers (or any other standard weight–paperclips will do) to the long, short, and one of the medium strings. Tie two washers to the other medium-length string.

Procedure: Show the four pendulums to the child and demonstrate how the different ones swing back and forth when released from a single height. Then ask the child how the pendulums could be used to find out if the length of the string or the number of washers affects how fast the pendulum will swing.

Task Six: Control of Variables

Materials: None.

Procedure: This is an open-ended activity to see if the child understands the need for controlling variables in an experiment. Start the activity by saying, "I'm trying to find out which dog food, dog food A or dog food B, is better for making young puppies grow. Tell me how I can find this out." Wait for the child to respond. If the child suggests setting up an experiment, listen for variables in the experiment that are controlled, for example, same amounts of food, same kind of dogs, same amounts of exercise. If the child doesn't suggest an experiment say, "Why don't we set up an experiment and feed dogs the two different kinds of food and see what happens?" If the child agrees to do this, ask him if there is anything special that needs to be done in the experiment. Listen for any mention of attempts to control variables.

The Development Of Science

Often, when students encounter a particular area of science like biology or chemistry, they form the impression that the knowledge in that area has always existed in that relatively sophisticated form and that it was handed down to scientists by someone on a mountain, like Moses and his tablets of stone. As we mentioned, a major reason for this belief is the way science has been taught. Unfortunately, this view of science as something that is chiseled in stone fails to present a true picture of the human element in science. We believe this is a real problem in science instruction because it not only fails to give a realistic view of science and scientists, but also tends to alienate people studying science. Rather than being caught up in the excitement of the continuing search for new knowledge, students are instead frightened off by the demands of memorizing a body of knowledge that appears far removed from human efforts.

In this section we will look at another kind of developmental sequence, the way in which different areas of science grow. The way that science develops is of practical importance to elementary science teachers for several reasons. One is that elementary teachers should have an accurate idea of how science unfolds so they can more accurately transmit to students a valid picture of the nature of science. In addition, parallels between the development of science and the development of the child have direct implications for instruction. These will be discussed in the balance of the chapter. This discussion will form the framework for the remainder of the book.

When you have finished this section of the chapter you will be able to meet the following objective:

■ You will understand the three phases of science so that, given an unlabeled description of these phases occurring, you will identify them.

If we examine the history of most areas of science, we can see that all areas go through three basic stages. Like the developmental stages presented in the previous sections, these historical stages are not sharp, discrete entities with clear boundaries, but are broad descriptive categories with considerable overlap. In addition, the sequence of these stages is not fixed or invariant, but will vary from discipline to discipline. In general, however, we believe that the sequence of these categories as well as the categories themselves provide an accurate picture of the development of a particular area of science. With these cautions in mind let us examine these three stages.

The Experiential Phase

During the first stage of development of any new area of science, there is heavy reliance on the process of observation. Because detailed concepts, generalizations, and theories haven't been formed to guide these observations, the observations serve the primary purpose of data gathering. Because of the emphasis on direct observation of all kinds, we call this the *experiential phase* of science, because the primary focus is on experiencing the world around us.

The Conceptual Phase

Out of these experiences scientists start to see patterns or regularities in the observations they have made. Through the process of inference, concepts and generalizations are formed to help describe and explain the observations that were made. We call this phase of development the *conceptual phase.* The products of this period are concepts.

Astronomy from Experience to Concept

Let us see how science progresses through these two phases with a historical example. In the late 1500s, the Danish astronomer, Tycho Brahe, made significant contributions to astronomy through his observations. With a crude telescope little better than the aiming mechanism of a rifle he made hundreds of thousands of observations of the heavenly bodies, carefully charting their locations in the heavens at different times of the night and different seasons over the years. He devoted his life to this task. Imagine! Here was a man who spent his life making observations without knowing whether anything would come of his work. This immense body of raw data, however, was to lead to a dramatic breakthrough in the development of science. Johann Kepler, a German scientist who worked in the early 1600s, studied Brahe's data and found patterns in it. These patterns, the elliptical orbits of the earth and other planets around the sun, became known as Kepler's laws. Without Brahe's data Kepler would never have been able to form his regularities. In this classic example, the experiential phase of science—Brahe's data—moves gradually to the conceptual phase of Kepler's regularities.

Many people prefer to use the word *invent* rather than *form* to describe the process of establishing regularities because it emphasizes the role that human beings play in the process. There are no patterns and regularities out there for people to "discover," they claim; rather, humans construct these patterns through toil and the power of the mind. Whatever the process is called the end result is the same: the creation of concepts and generalizations to direct research efforts and to order observations.

Scientists soon find that newly formed concepts and generalizations differ in their ability to describe the world accurately. In chapter 1 we saw how the concept of humours was formed (conceptual phase) to describe the phenomenon of sickness. Initially, this concept appeared logical and seemed to do an adequate job of explaining sickness and disease. The concept was ultimately rejected in favor of the germ theory of disease, partly because the humour concept couldn't explain why screens and mosquito nettings prevented malarial disease. Thus, the observations made of the effects of screens and netting helped clarify our understanding not only of malaria, but of disease in general.

The Inquiry Phase

In testing the adequacy of concepts and generalizations, scientists often consciously use the process of experimentation, typically beginning with some problem that needs to be resolved. For example, at one time there were conflicting theories about how life begins. Some believed in spontaneous generation; they thought that life could spring from dead objects and that a process of fertilization and growth was unnecessary. Evidence for their position came from observations. They saw mice growing "spontaneously" from piles of rags and maggots appearing on uncovered meat. Others, disagreeing with the concept of spontaneous generation, said that life could come only from life.

To resolve problems like this, scientists can set up experiments. To test the theory of spontaneous generation, Redi, a famous Italian scientist of the seventeenth century, set up experiments based on two very different predictions or hypotheses. He placed meat in a glass container with gauze netting over the open end. The netting prevented flies from entering the container and laying eggs on the meat. (We now know that maggots are the larval stage of flies.) The spontaneous generation advocates predicted that maggots would grow on the meat anyway; their opponents predicted the opposite. Redi gathered data by observation, watching for the appearance of maggots on the meat. When none appeared, he and his supporters had strong evidence that the concept of spontaneous generation did not explain how life begins.

The previous example was not only a rough description of the process we call experimentation but was also an example of the third stage of the development of an area of science: the inquiry stage. Primary characteristics of this stage are the active investigation and testing of concepts and generalizations through the process of experimentation. The sequence and development of these stages in astronomy can be seen in the following paragraphs.

The Three Stages in Astronomy

Probably since the beginning of time people have gazed at the heavens and tried to understand what the stars were and why they appeared as they did. We could call this the experiential phase of astronomy because the primary emphasis was on the process of observation or data gathering. Through these observations they began to see patterns or regularities in the heavenly bodies. They noticed, for instance, that some of the "stars" moved through the heavens at a faster and more irregular pace than others. They called these "stars" planets, which literally means *wanderers*. (Now we know that the reason that these planets "wander" through the patterns of the stars is that they are revolving around our sun.) When they first formed this concept, they didn't understand why these planets moved as they did in the heavens but only that they did. Early observers were not astronomers by trade; they were craftsmen and artists. They also noticed other patterns: the sun always rose in the east and set in the west, for example. During this time many concepts and generalizations were formed. We call this period the conceptual stage of development in astronomy.

Inevitably in science, however, competing concepts or ideas develop that need to be tested to see which describe the world more accurately. In astronomy, this clash of ideas occurred between the Ptolemaic and Copernican view of the solar system.

Ptolemy, an ancient Egyptian astronomer, observed the sun rising in the east and setting in the west and concluded that the sun revolved around the earth. People accepted this view for well over a thousand years. Early in the sixteenth century Copernicus, a Polish astronomer, challenged this idea. He introduced the notion that the sun and not the Earth is the center of our solar system; the planets, including our own, revolve around the sun. Additional observations and experimentation ultimately led to the downfall of the Ptolemaic view and the acceptance of the Copernican view.

Thus we can see a movement in astronomy from a heavy emphasis on observation, to the formation of patterns and regularities on the basis of these regularities, and, ultimately, to the clash of ideas and the resolution of this clash through experimentation.

The Sequence of Stages in Biology

A second example, from biological science, will further illustrate the progression of science through these phases.

From earliest times people have been interested in animals, as animals have often been a major source of food and labor power. This initial period of interest and observation would be called the experiential phase. On the basis of these observations, animals were grouped on the basis of similarities. One of the first recorded groupings was animals of the air, animals of the sea, and animals of the land.

During the conceptual period a number of ways of classifying animals was offered; each one explained part of the puzzle but none accurately described all the relationships between animals. Controversies arose over the classification of certain animals. Certain people claimed that bats should be classified birds because they flew, and whales as fish because they swam. Structuralists argued that our classification system should be based upon internal organization and structure, not outward appearances.

Upon analysis, the structuralists won out. Whales were found to be warm-blooded, unlike fish, and they breathed with lungs rather than gills. The young of whales were carried inside the mother, while most fishes lay eggs in nests outside the body. Closer examination of bats showed them to be more like mammals than birds. They had teeth, not beaks; they gave birth to live young; and their wings were formed differently than those of birds.

Both these examples show a gradual but perceptible change in emphasis from observation to the formation of concepts and generalizations to the refinement of these abstractions through active inquiry. These three phases describe the way in which scientists operate while a science is developing. They also describe what we feel to be an optimal sequencing of teaching strategies to accommodate the development of children at different stages of cognitive growth. But before we pursue these ideas further, complete the exercises that follow. They are designed to reinforce your understanding of the three stages of science.

Exercise 3.3

1. *Directions:* Read the following description of a scientist at work and determine which of the three phases of science is being emphasized. Substantiate your answer with data from the story.

It was still dark enough to see stars when I arrived at the Amalgamated Clothing Workers of America (ACWA) building near Baltimore. I saw and heard nothing. I left the car, walked around the building, returned, checked the air temperature, and reported my findings into a tape recorder I always kept with me:

2 September 1970, 64 degrees F., clear and slightly windy, 4:20 a.m. No signs, garbage behind homesite from previous day now gone—probably collected. I will now wait for Shag, who I suspect is still in the shrubbery, left side of ACWA, Eutaw and McMechen.

Studying the stray dogs of Baltimore is my thesis project for a doctorate in ecology, and for the next few weeks I would be concentrating on Shag, a large, white shaggy-haired male with black markings. I chose him from the study population because he was a truly ownerless stray. Ordinarily, owned and ownerless strays are indistinguishable, except at moments of owner-dog interaction, and both types serve as the feral dogs of the city environment.

Lately, Shag had been spending his nights in the shrubbery, although earlier in the summer he had found shelter in a house hallway. He would push the front door open to gain access and wait for someone leaving to help him get back to the streets, but his habit of "marking" the inside hall had led to his ouster by the building's residents. During the past two years, I discovered other stray dog den sites—in vacant buildings and garages, under porches and cars, and in garbage dumps. All provide protection against weather and people.

4:50 a.m. Barking now becoming apparent. The area is coming alive, but still no sign of Shag.

Waiting is a very real part of wildlife study. I welcome it, however, as it gives me time to plan future approaches and reflect on aspects just completed. I spent the first part of the summer of 1970 sampling the dog populations of selected areas around the city, mainly by photographing each stray dog and plotting the sighting on maps. One advantage of working in the urban ecosystem is the ability to locate the subject with remarkable precision by using street crossings and house numbers.

Another advantage of studying feral dogs is that their mixed heritage leads to wide variations in morphology and behavior, which enabled me to recognize individuals. I seldom encountered the monotony of pedigree breeds. As part of my studies, I photographed every stray dog I saw while traveling through a neighborhood. A dog photographed more than once is, in the terms of wildlife study, a recapture. Therefore, just as a wild bird population can be calculated from the number of banded birds captured, I was able to compute the city's stray dog population from the number of dogs rephotographed. Photographic recapture and other methods revealed a total population of 100,000 dogs, both owned and ownerless, in Baltimore, which is an increase of 25,000 animals over the city's dog population as estimated ten years ago by Dr. Kenneth Crawford, the state veterinarian.

Cities throughout the world are encountering such dog population explosions, including the half-million dogs each in New York, Mexico City, and Buenos Aires. In many cities, dogs appear to be increasing more rapidly than humans. Such populations have many ecological implications for a city. A study by New York's Environmental Protection Administration noted that the owners of dogs permit them to leave from 5,000 to 20,000 tons of excrement and from 600,000 to over 1 million gallons of urine on the streets each year. Even if Baltimore has only one-fifth of those estimates, what does it mean for this or any city? While my original objective was to establish the life history of the feral urban dog, I had to include such implications, for they are part of the ecology of the animal. . . .

At 5:22 a collie bolts out of an open doorway, which is then closed. Other dogs are now apparent, but still no sign of Shag.

This kind of pet release, before and after the usual workday, is one reason why dog activity is greatest in the mornings and evenings. Ownerless strays are also active during these periods, possibly because dogs are gregarious animals, initiating each other's activity, or because all dogs avoid activity during the heat of the day.

6:00 a.m. The sky is light blue and church bells are ringing. Shag and a male Doberman, Shag's constant companion, appear in the rear view mirror. Where in the hell did they come from? (Beck 1971, 18–21).

Which phase of science was being utilized the most? Why?

_____

2. Read the following anecdote describing the work of Piaget and try to identify the three stages of science in operation.

You've already been introduced to the ideas of Piaget, but the way in which he developed these ideas makes an interesting story in itself. Initially Piaget's interests were in the area of philosophy and biology and it was just by the stroke of fortune that he was hired by people in France who where working on the development of intelligence or IQ tests. The particular tests he was hired to develop and administer were individual IQ tests. In the course of administering these tests Piaget listened to the answers the children gave, both correct and incorrect. In questioning the childern Piaget found the same wrong answers occurred frequently in children of about the same age. At the same time, he found that there were different kinds of common wrong answers at different ages. As he considered these findings Piaget came to the conclusion that the thought of younger children was qualitatively different from that of older children. From these experiences he formed the idea of stages and tried to apply these same ideas to his own children. When these ideas seemed adequate to describe the development of children in general, Piaget put the notion of developmental stages into print. Skeptics doubted Piaget's ideas and much effort was made to disprove them. But cross-cultural studies for the most part reaffirmed Piaget's contention that all children pass through these stages in the order mentioned, and intervention studies aimed at accelerating development through these stages showed this to be a difficult process.

Identify the three stages in the example.

A Developmental Approach To Elementary Science Teaching

In the previous sections we have presented two types of developmental sequences. The first sequence related the stages children go through as they develop increasingly more sophisticated ways of processing information. Piaget named them sensorimotor, preoperational, concrete operational, and formal thought. The second developmental sequence described the phases that individual areas of science go through: the experiential phase, the conceptual phase, and the inquiry phase.

How these two developmental trends relate to each other and what implications they have for science instruction will be the topic of this last section of the chapter.

We will begin by stating an important assumption we have about teaching. We believe that there is no one best way to teach. We see the best teaching strategy as one that matches a particular strategy with the goals of instruction and characteristics of the learners. An effective teacher, we believe, is someone who understands the goals he or she is trying to accomplish and is able to select and implement a teaching strategy congruent with these goals and with the information-processing capabilities of young children.

This approach, the models approach to teaching, was formulated by Joyce and Weil (1972). It has been applied to information processing strategies by Eggen and colleagues (1979). The models approach is a reaction to the assertion that there is one best way to teach; it is an attempt to encourage teachers to consider a number of factors before selecting teaching strategies.

In this section we will describe three teaching strategies we see as appropriate for the elementary science curriculum. Based upon the stages of development in science, these strategies focus upon the goals of the elementary science curriculum and correspond to the stages of cognitive development described earlier. The three teaching strategies are the experiential model, the discovery model, and the inquiry model.

The Experiential Model

The first teaching strategy, the *experiential model,* is designed specifically for the early primary grades. Although it is designed to teach all of the goals of science, its heaviest emphasis is on the development of process skills. As its name suggests, this model corresponds to the first stage of scientific development, in which the primary emphasis is on information gathering. Most children at this age would be in the preoperational phase of development. The experiential model is designed to provide young children with hands-on, direct experiences with their environment. Because of this emphasis, this model is ideal for very young elementary school students and for students at all levels whenever new material is being introduced. This model is described in detail in and provides the focus for chapters 4 and 5.

The Discovery Model

The next teaching strategy is designed for use with more experienced learners. Because its primary focus is the formation of concepts and generalizations, the heaviest emphasis of the discovery model is on content acquisition. Nevertheless, it deals with the other goals of science as well. The discovery model is based upon the second phase of scientific development and builds upon the experiences and information gained in experiential activities. Although this teaching strategy is specifically designed for a learner at a particular developmental phase, the concrete operational child, it can also be used effectively with preoperational and formal operational thinkers. The discovery model is discussed in detail in chapters 6 and 7.

The Inquiry Model

The third teaching model we will present, the inquiry model, involves children in the process of experimentation. Because this process of experimentation is unique to the sciences, we would say that this model, more than the others, provides students with unique insight into the nature of science. The other goals of science instruction are not ignored or considered unimportant; rather, the model is designed to teach students about the nature of scientific experimentation. Like the other models, this teaching strategy is also designed with a specific developmental stage in mind, in this case the formal operational stage.

Table 3-1: **Developmental Models of Science Instruction**

Model	Corresponding Developmental Stage of Science	Piagetian Developmental Stage	Emphasis on goals of Elementary Science
Experiential	Experiential	Preoperational	Process
Discovery	Conceptual	Concrete Operational	Content
Inquiry	Inquiry	Formal Operational	Nature of Science

Applications to Science Teaching

Before discussing implementation of these models in the elementary science classroom, we will briefly illustrate how each of these models mights be used to focus upon the same topic, plants.

Gathering Data

With young children, the experiential model might be used to acquaint students with plants and how they grow. For example, each child is given a seed to plant and water. As the seeds start to germinate, the teacher encourages students to observe them closely, noting the appearance of the first signs of growth. In tracing the continued development of these plants, the teacher has students draw the plants at different stages of development, introducing the terms *roots, stem,* and *leaves.* Some plants will grow faster and some will die, and the teacher encourages students to explore factors like watering and sunlight that affect plant growth. In these activities the primary emphasis is on processing information and providing students with hands-on, experiential activities. These activities and the information that is gained form the basis for thinking that will be used in the next developmental model.

Forming Generalizations

The discovery model is slightly more structured than the previous model. Working toward a specific context goal, it presents to students specific, selected data that allow them, with guidance, to form the concept or generalization being taught. For example, a lesson designed to teach the concepts of coniferous and deciduous trees might use pictures of these different types of trees. Pictures are selected to illustrate essential characteristics of each concept: type of leaf, shape of tree, and kind of fruit or seed, among others. Students are asked to observe these pictures and to identify characteristics peculiar to each of these concepts. While the major emphasis is on content acquisition, students are also provided with opportunities to practice the processes of observations and inference. Like scientists, they experience the process of analyzing data to discover patterns.

Testing the Generalizations

The inquiry model introduces students to the process of experimentation and gives them opportunities to conduct experiments of their own. An inquiry lesson might begin with the problem, "What factors affect plant growth?" Through earlier experiences with plants, students will typically be able to suggest or hypothesize a number of factors. Then students design experiments that investigate the effects of each of these factors. The notion of control of variables enters at this point. Having designed experiments, students then gather data by growing plants under different conditions. They try to conclude from this data how each factor affects plant growth.

These three teaching models are called developmental models primarily because of the differing demands that they place on the learner at each stage. The experiential model requires students to process information in ways that are completely natural for the young child. They use their senses to gather data directly through hands-on activities with concrete objects. The discovery model is slightly more demanding. It requires students to focus their observations on certain aspects of the data and to use these observations to form concepts and generalizations. The inquiry model places even greater demands on the learner. Students are required to analyze a problem and hypothesize possible solutions. Then they must design an experiment with controlled variables to test these solutions. The latter processes, characteristic of the formal operational child, usually do not develop until a student reaches the upper elementary grades.

A Flexible Developmental Approach

We do not suggest that the experiential model should be used only with lower elementary-age students and the inquiry model only with older students. The approach we suggest is a flexible developmental one: age and developmental level of students should influence the choice of a particular model for a given lesson, but the models should not be rigid prescriptions for teaching at different age levels. Instead, a number of factors should determine the choice of a model in a particular situation. These factors include the content to be taught and the developmental characteristics of all the members of the class, as well as the goals of science instruction.

Content Background of Students

A major factor to consider in choosing a teaching model is the experiential backgrounds of students. Developmental researchers have found that the type of content chosen for a particular task will influence people's performance on that task. For example, if we asked you to design an experiment to see which cars got better gas mileage, most of you would be able to do so, because you're familiar with factors that affect gas mileage. If we asked you to conduct an experiment on human memory, however, you might experience difficulty because you're not familiar with the topic.

Two additional problems (Flavell 1975) can serve to illustrate this idea.

Two identical circular wire hoops are lying side by side on a table. Their perimeters are equal and enclose identical areas of table surface. Suppose one of the hoops is now squashed slightly to make it ellipsoid in shape. Are the perimeters still equal? Are the areas?

Two sheets of 8½ X 11-inch typing paper are placed side by side on the table. Everyone agrees that their perimeters and areas are exactly the same. Then a 2 X 11-inch strip is cut off one of the papers and is placed so that its 2-inch base just touches the top edge of the 6½ X 11-inch sheet to make a "house" with a 2 X 11-inch "chimney" on top of it. Is the perimeter of this house-plus-chimney still equal to that of the other piece of paper? Are the areas still equal?

Both problems involve conservation of area and perimeter. Most of you reached the stage of concrete operations and became conservers long ago, but if you're like most of the people we've tried these problems with, you either had trouble with them or got them wrong. (In the wire problem the area changed but the perimeter didn't, and in the paper problem the perimeter changed and the area didn't.) The point is that peoples' ability to solve problems and to use cognitive structures they have developed depends heavily on the content being covered. When new content is introduced, students who were able to perform certain operations with familiar content may be unable to do so with new content.

When applying this idea to the elementary science curriculum, teachers should try to familiarize themselves with the experiential backgrounds of their students and select learning activities accordingly. Inner-city students might have a difficult time designing valid experiments on plant and animal growth if they haven't had any experiences with these topics. Students from farm communities who have grown up taking care of animals and raising crops would be familiar with these topics and more able to design valid experiments in these areas. In general, when new topics are being introduced it is better to use hands-on observational activities to orient students to the new topic and to provide an experiential base. Students can then use this knowledge to form abstractions and design experiments.

Facilitating Developmental Growth

Sensitivity to students' experiential backgrounds can also be useful in sequencing instruction when introducing students to new processes, such as the control of variables. Lawson (1975) showed how familiar objects could be initially used to develop this idea with eleven and twelve year olds. The teacher began the lesson by telling students that the problem was to decide which of three tennis balls was the "bounciest." To find this out, students were to tell the teacher how to perform tests. Typically, students would begin the experiment by asking the teacher to take two balls and bounce them to see which bounced higher. The teacher would then drop the balls, but drop them from unequal heights. Students would then respond that the test wasn't fair because they weren't dropped from the same height. Then the teacher repeated the experiment, this time letting both balls go from the same height but pushing or throwing one of the balls. Again, students would say that this wasn't a fair test.

Following this activity, in which the idea of fair tests (controlled variables) was established, students were asked to apply this idea to the metal rod apparatus discussed earlier (see figure 3-2). The notion of controlled variables was again important but the content was different. Then students were asked to take this same idea and apply it in designing an experiment on plant metabolism. A posttest showed that the students in this class, who were classified as concrete operational at the beginning of the activity, could control variables in the design of experiments.

Several aspects of this research study should be mentioned. First, note how the experimenter used tangible, hands-on experiences to teach an abstract idea. Also, note how the topics varied from familiar to unfamiliar and that this continiuum was consciously chosen to encourage cognitive growth. When introducing a new teaching model to the students, teachers should attempt to use materials that are familiar to minimize any difficulties involved with the model itself. A third notable aspect of this study was that the researchers, through the use of structured activities, were able to teach a process that was supposedly beyond the grasp of concrete operational children. Similar results have been obtained by Case (1974) in work with eight year olds.

The significance of studies like these is that they show that developmental stages need not be viewed as rigid contraints on the kinds of activities that can be used with children. Instead they can be thought of as a flexible categorization system that teachers can use to guide them in their instructional decisions.

Instructional Goals

Another factor that influences the choice of a teaching model are the primary goals of science instruction. If a goal of the elementary science curriculum is to promote developmental change and cognitive growth, one way of achieving this goal is to provide students with experiences that will facilitate that development. To help concrete operational children understand how to conduct experiments and control variables, place them in situations where they can practice these skills and see others use them effectively. The Lawson tennis-ball study mentioned earlier is an example.

We suggest that a teacher may at times intentionally choose a teaching strategy that is beyond the developmental capabilities of the students in order to help these students develop more effective processing strategies. This developmental view of elementary science instruction differs from other interpretations of Piaget, which advocate that the experiences in the classroom should exactly match the developmental level of students. This position is inefficient for several reasons.

First, it doesn't provide for developmental cognitive growth. Growth occurs as the individual encounters problems that current cognitive structures are unable to solve or deal with. When a mismatch occurs, the individual must accommodate these structures; the result is cognitive growth. Elementary science teachers can encourage this growth by placing students in situations that are developmentally demanding and that encourage students to develop new structures for dealing with the environment.

Second, most elementary classrooms are heterogeneous. In the typical classroom a teacher finds one group of students at one stage of development, another group in a transition state, and a third group at a higher stage. The effective science teacher uses this heterogeneity to enhance cognitive growth by selecting activities that more developmentally advanced students can handle. In this way the teacher provides opportunities for other students to see in action the operations of the advanced students and to learn from them. Cognitive growth occurs when less logical and efficient strategies for processing information are compared to more efficient strategies. If students are placed in heterogeneous groups, with some members functioning at a higher cognitive level than others, certain students can act as catalysts for the cognitive growth of others.

The Nature of Cognitive Growth

Cognitive growth, or the transition from one level of thought to another, is a gradual process that occurs over time. It is not a sudden jump; rather, it takes place slowly as the individual tries out new ways of dealing with the environment. Karplus (1977) likened this process to the change that occurs when an individual drives a car with a brake adjustment that differs from the one he or she is accustomed to. Accommodation to this new brake is not sudden. It is rather a gradual process, that occurs through trial and error with feedback from the environment. The change from one level of thinking to the next is a similarly gradual process, in which the individual tries out new processing patterns and sees how they work. Teachers who attempt to facilitate this growth should recognize it as a gradual process, requiring a number of opportunities for trial-and-error, experiential learning.

In order to group students effectively this way, the teacher must measure the cognitive development of different students. One way to measure development is by administering the Piagetian tasks described in Exercise 3.2. Doing the tasks individually, however, is probably too time consuming a task for most elementary teachers. As an alternative, we offer a group test with written responses.

Directions: In administering this test to students, encourage them to do their own work, answer all questions, and try to explain their answers whenever they can. These explanations can provide the teacher with valuable insights into the thinking processes of students.

Part I. These items are to be administered to the group as a whole.

Developmental Test

Item 1: The Conservation of Weight

This item requires two balls of clay of identical size, shape, and weight. Show the students that the clay balls weigh the same by placing them on opposite ends of a balance beam. Flatten one of the balls into a pancake shape and ask the students about the relative weights of the pieces. (Piaget & Inhelder 1962)

Item 2: Conservation of Volume

Start by pouring equal amounts of water in identical containers. Show these to students and make sure that they all know that the amounts are equal. Then pour these into two clear containers, one that is tall and thin, and one that is short and wide. Ask students which container has more water in it.

Item 3: Conservation of Number

Arrange two equal sets of objects on a board for students to see. (This can be done with a flannel board or by placing tape on the back of circles of paper and placing them on the board.) The sets should be arranged so that there is one-to-one correspondence between the objects in the two sets. Make sure that students see that the two sets are equal. Then take one of the sets and spread the objects out. When this is done, ask students which set has more.

Item 4: Displaced Volume

Locate two solid metal cylinders of equal size but of different density. Show the students the level of water displaced by the lighter cylinder and ask them to predict the level of water displaced by the heavier cylinder. (Karplus & Lavatelli 1969)

Item 5: Controlling Variables—1

Construct three pendulums (two of equal length but with bobs of 50 g and 100 g, the third longer with a 50-g bob). Ask the students to select which of the pendulums should be used in an experiment to find out if the variable of length effects the period of the pendulum. (Inhelder & Piaget 1958)

Item 6: Controlling Variables—2

Using the same three pendulums, ask the students to select which pendulums should be used in an experiment to find out if the weight of the bob effects the period of the pendulum. (Inhelder & Piaget 1958)

Part II. These items can be duplicated on a sheet of paper and administered individually to each student.

Item 7: Serial Ordering

Four types of rats were bred for laboratory experiments. Type A rats were found to be more resistant to disease than Type C rats. Type B rats were less resistant to disease than Type C rats and Type D rats were more disease resistant than A rats. Which type of rats were least disease resistant? Explain your choice. (Karplus, et al., 1977)

Item 8: Control of Variables

Fifty pieces of various parts of plants were placed in each of five sealed containers of equal size. At the start of the experiment each jar contained 250 units of carbon dioxide (CO_2). The amount of CO_2 in each jar at the end of two days was as shown in the table. (Karplus, et al., 1977)

Container	Plant	Plant Part	Light Color	Temperature (Celsius)	CO_2 Remaining
1	Willow	Leaf	Blue	10°	200
2	Maple	Leaf	Purple	23°	50
3	Willow	Root	Red	18°	300
4	Maple	Stem	Red	23°	400
5	Willow	Leaf	Blue	23°	150

On the basis of the data in the table, a fair test of the amount of CO_2 used per day at two different temperatures could be made by comparing which jars?

Item 9: Proportional Reasoning

The number of containers of chemicals that a laboratory can produce varies directly with the time available and the number of chemists available. If ten chemists work six hours to produce six containers, how many containers can be turned out by four chemists working for five hours? (Karplus, et al., 1977)

A 2
B 20
C 4
D 3

Please explain your choice.

Item 10: Proportional Reasoning

The Ratio Puzzle

The figure on p. 88 is called Mr. Short. We used large round buttons laid side by side to measure Mr. Short's height, starting from the floor between his feet and going to the top of his head. His height was four buttons. Then we took a similar figure called Mr. Tall, and measured it in the same way with the same buttons. Mr. Tall was six buttons high. Then we measured Mr. Short with paper clips and found him to be six paper clips high. How many paper clips high would Mr. Tall be? (Karplus, et al. 1977)

Evaluating Student Responses

Item 1

Students operating at the concrete or formal operational levels will answer that the weights are the same because only the shapes have changed. Responses indicating a change in weight would indicate a lack of conservation skills, and patterns of thinking similar to the preoperational child.

Figure 3–3
Mr. Short

Item 2

Again, students operating at the concrete or formal operational levels will answer that the volumes are the same, because nothing has changed but the shape. Failure to conserve volume may be a sign that the student is operating at the preoperational level.

Item 3

Students operating at the concrete operational level or above will say that the number is the same and that spreading objects out does not change the number.

Item 4

Concrete and formal operational students will say that the volume displaced will be the same for both objects. Students at the preoperational level may predict differences between the two.

Item 5

Students at the formal operational level will choose the two bobs of equal weight but unequal length to solve this problem.

Item 6

Formal operational students will select the two pendulums of equal length and unequal weight.

Item 7

Concrete operational students will be able to order the rats in this order, D A C B, and will conclude that type B rats are least resistant to disease.

Item 8

Formal operational students will be able to analyze the data and conclude that a valid test of the effect of temperature on the carbon dioxide production would be a comparison of containers one and five.

Item 9

Formal operational students will be able to figure out that it takes ten work hours to produce one jar of chemicals (10 chemists X 6 hours = 60 work hours; 60 work hours ÷ 6 jars = 1 jar per 10 work hours). Four chemists working five hours represent twenty work hours, which would produce two jars.

Item 10

Formal operational students should be able to place the problem in mathematical perspective ($4/6 = 6/X$) and to conclude that Mr. Tall would be nine paper clips high.

Interpreting the Results

As noted in our discussion of the answers, items 1, 2, 3, 4 and 7 are designed to measure attainment of thinking at the concrete level of thinking, while items 5, 6, 8, 9 and 10 are designed to measure attainment of thinking at the formal operational level. If students distributed themselves cleanly into these categories the following results might occur. Students at the preoperational level of thinking would get few if any of these items correct. Students at the concrete operational level of thinking would answer items 1, 2, 3, 4, and 7 correctly but would be unable to answer items 5, 6, 8, 9 and 10; and students at the formal operational level would answer all of the items correctly. However, seldom do we get as clean a differentiation as that.

A more typical pattern is for students to answer some of the items in a group correctly and some incorrectly. For example, consider the data in Table 3–2.

Table 3–2 **Sample Distribution Patterns for Four Different Students**

Student	Number Correct on Concrete Operational Items	Number Correct on Formal Operational Items
A	3	0
B	4	2
C	5	3
D	4	5

Student A's responses would indicate that she is making the transition to concrete operational thought. Grouping her with students already at this level could help her make this transition. Student B appears to be operating at the concrete operational level and attempting to make the transition to the formal operational level, as is student C. Grouping these two students with student D, who is currently operating at the formal operational level, would help them make this transition.

We've designed the following exercises to provide you with practice in interpreting student responses to items like these. We encourage you to complete these exercises before proceeding to the summary section.

Exercise 3.4

Directions: The following are student responses to some of the items described above. Your task is to examine these responses and describe the level of thinking evidenced: preoperational, concrete operational, or formal operational.

A. The conservation of weight problem (see Item 1 under *Evaluating Student Responses above).*

1. "The one on the right has more because it's wider and flatter."

   _____

2. "They're both the same because you've only changed the shape and not the weight. You could make them look the same again and they'd still weigh the same."

   _____

3. "The one on the right has more because now it's bigger."

_____

B. Serial Ordering (see Item 7 above).
4. "Type B rats are the least resistant because they are less resistant than C and C is less resistant than either A or D type rats."

_____

5. "Type B rats are the least resistant because they're less resistant than C."

_____

6. "Type C rats are least resistant because they are worse than A."

_____

C. Control of Variables (see Item 8 above).
7. "Compare containers 2 and 4 because they have the most and least carbon dioxide remaining."

_____

8. "Compare containers 1, 2, and 5 because they all have leaves in them."

_____

9. "Compare containers 1 and 5 because they both have willow leaves in them."

_____

10. "Compare containers 1 and 5 because they both have willow leaves in them, are in the same kind of light (blue) and are at different temperatures."

_____

Summary

The central focus of this chapter has been to look at developmental characteristics of students and of science and to explore the relevance of these characteristics for instruction in the elementary science classroom.

We began the chapter by describing the work of Jean Piaget, a prominent researcher in the area of child development. Piaget's greatest contributions to the elementary science curriculum have been his view of learning and his idea of stages of development. Piaget reconceptualized our thinking about the way that children learn by placing the learner as a central part of the learning process. Rather than being viewed as a passive responder to environmental stimuli, the learner is viewed as an active investigator of the environment. Central to this investigation process are the organizational structures the individual is constantly testing and modifying. When these structures are adequate, the individual assimilates new information through these structures. When they are inadequate, they must change or new ones must be formed. Through the process of accommodation, new concepts and generalizations are formed and older, inadequate ones are modified.

Central to the dual processes of assimilation and accommodation is the idea of adaptation. Adaptation refers to the individual's active attempts to bring cognitive structures in line with the demands of the environment. When the environment makes sense, new information is gained; when it doesn't, the individual actively strives to figure out why.

The picture we are trying to paint for the elementary science teacher is of a child who wants to learn, who has been actively learning for years prior to this class, and who, if given the time and resources, will learn. To help the child in this process, the teacher must be willing to provide opportunities and materials.

The types of learning experiences must match the information-processing capabilities of young learners. Prior to Piaget, most people realized that the reasoning patterns used by young children were not identical to those of adults, but it took Piaget to describe the differences accurately. In working with children, Piaget found that they exhibit characteristic reasoning patterns that can be grouped into stages. These stages not only describe the information processing capabilities of children, but also suggest optimal teaching strategies to match the stages.

In a related vein, the developmental stages of a developing area of science were described. As any area of science begins, there is typically a heavy emphasis on data gathering through the process of observation—hence the name *experiential phase*. As patterns emerge from these observations, concepts and generalizations are formed during the *conceptual phase*. These are refined through active experimentation in the *inquiry phase*. Like the process of development in the child, each phase of science involves increasingly more complex and sophisticated ways of processing information.

These two lines of development were combined in a models approach to teaching science that emphasized selecting specific teaching strategies only after the goals of instruction and the developmental characteristics of learners were considered. The experiential model was introduced as a teaching strategy specifically designed to provide the lower-primary-grade student with hands-on, process-oriented activities. The discovery model builds upon these experiences by encouraging students to further analyze this data into concepts and generalizations. These abstractions are then used to guide the process of experimentation in the inquiry model.

Though ideally suited for lower-, middle-, and upper-elementary students respectively, these developmental models were not described as rigid prescriptions for instruction. Additional factors, such as the backgrounds of learners, the content to be taught, the processes to be emphasized, and the particular goals of science instruction all interact to suggest an optimal teaching strategy for a particular lesson. A teacher might choose to use a simplified inquiry lesson with first graders (How does sunlight effect plant growth?) and another teacher might choose an experiential activity to introduce a new topic to sixth graders.

Factors influencing decisions like these and modifications of these strategies to accommodate characteristics of learners will be described more fully in chapters 4 through 9, in which the individual strategies are discussed.

Exercise 3.1   Feedback

1. The organization implied in this anecdote involves all the habits that the person had developed while driving in America. Most of these habits, such as driving at a safe speed, following at a safe distance, and signaling before turning were useful to her in driving in England. Consequently she used these patterns to assimilate new information and to drive successfully. However, one aspect of the organizational scheme, driving on the right side of the road, had to be accommodated or changed to allow her to survive on the roads.

2. Through their experience with the bottle or the mother's breast, babies form a concept of what food should feel and taste like. This concept constitutes the organization of their minds in this respect. When they encounter solids that taste something like the milk they're used to, they assimilate this new part of the environment as food. But their actions (chewing, or should we say gumming) change to accommodate this new food source, as well as their concept of food.

3. The organization involved here is all the ideas about how music should sound. These ideas are based on peoples' previous listening experiences. Certain aspects of this new type of music are assimilated into these structures (that is, the new sounds are recognized as music) while at the same time certain parts of the person's structure must be changed or accommodated and other new concepts must be formed.

4. When freshmen enter college they bring with them a number of past experiences and future expectations. These are formed from their own experiences in school and as a result of reading about and talking to people who have attended college. This organizational structure is then applied to the new situations encountered at college. When aspects of this structure fit, new experiences are assimilated into it; when parts do not fit, they are either changed, abandoned, or supplemented.

Exercise 3.2

1. The first four tasks were designed to measure whether students had attained the concrete operational level of thought. Students at this level of development would state that the changes made had not altered the mass, volume, length, or number and that the operations performed are reversible. In all four cases, when these tasks are administered to a particular child, he or she will sometimes get two or three of the four correct. This may indicate that the child is in a transitional state between two levels. Also, correct answers but inadequate justification might indicate the same condition.

The last two tasks were designed to measure students' attainment of the idea of controlled variables, a characteristic of the formal operational level of thought. Both of these activities are quite open-ended, so you'll have to listen more carefully for trends or patterns. Try to see if the child has any notion of the idea of experimentation in which two conditions are compared. Also, listen for any statements that reflect a need for controlling variables. If children mention the need for controlled variables (not by that name) listen to see how adequately they perform this operation.

Exercise 3.3

1. The major emphasis in this passage was on the experiential phase of science. Studying feral or wild dogs in the city is a fairly new field of study. Consequently there is a heavy emphasis on data gathering through the process of observation. Note how this scientist had to wait long hours to make his observations and how he used photographs to help him make more accurate observations.

2. The experiential phase occurred here, as it does so often in science almost accidentally. Piaget was observing the reponses of the children as he was testing, but he was not purposefully looking for stages of development. The concept of these stages developed over time as Piaget saw patterns or regularities in the errors that children made on the standardized test. This represents the transition to the conceptual phase of his work. The inquiry phase occurred when Piaget attempted to see if these same stages applied to his own children and when other researchers attempted to determine if these stages could be accelerated and were found in all cultures.

Exercise 3.4

1. This type of response indicates that this student is a nonconserver of weight and is operating at the preoperational level of thought.

2. This student is operating at at least the concrete operational level of thought because she understands to some degree the idea of reversibility.

3. This student would be classified as a nonconserver and is operating at the preoperational level.

4. This student understands the process of serial ordering and would be classified as operating at at least the concrete level of thought.

5. This answer, while correct, is correct for the wrong reason. An incomplete explanation like this might indicate that this student is in transition to the concrete level of thought.

6. Again, this student has a partial idea of the task involved but is unable to fully execute the task. Though not at the concrete level of thought, this student may be in a transitional stage of development.

7. This student is definitely below the formal level of thought because his response indicates a complete lack of understanding of the concept of control of variables.

8. Though not at the formal level of thought, this student has an incomplete but developing idea of controlling variables. This may indicate that the student is in transition between the concrete and formal levels.

9. This student chose the right answer but justified the answer incompletely. (Compare this student's response with that in number 10.) A response like this may indicate a transitional state between the concrete and formal operational thought.

10. This student not only had the right answer but also the right reasons for the answer and would be operating at the formal operational level of thought.

References

Beck, A. "The Life and Times of Shag," in A. Ternes, ed. *Ants, Indians and Little Dinosaurs.* New York: Charles Scribner's Sons, 1975, pp. 18–26.

Case R. "Mental Strategies, Mental Capacity, and Instruction: A Neo-Piagetian Investigation." *Journal of Experimental Child Psychology* 18 (1974): pp. 382–397.

DeVries, R. "Constancy of Generic Identity in the Years Three to Six." *Society for Research in Child Development Monographs.* 34, Serial No. 127, 1969.

Eggen P.; Kauchak, D.; and Harder, R. *Strategies for Teachers.* Englewood Cliffs, N.J.: Prentice-Hall, 1979.

Flavell, J. *Cognitive Development.* Englewood Cliffs, N.J.: Prentice-Hall, 1977.

Furth, H., and Wachs, H. *Thinking Goes to School.* New York: Oxford University Press, 1975.

Ginsburg, H., and Opper S. *Piaget's Theory of Intellectual Development.* Englewood Cliffs, N.J.: Prentice-Hall, 1969.

Good, R. *How Children Learn Science.* New York: MacMillan, 1977.

Inhelder, B., and Piaget, J. *The Growth of Logical Thinking from Childhood to Adolescence.* New York: Basic Books, 1958.

Jaffe, B. *Crucibles: The Story of Chemistry.* 7th ed. Greenwich, Conn.: Fawcett, 1967.

Joyce, B., and Weil, M. *Models of Teaching.* Englewood Cliffs, N.J.: Prentice-Hall, 1972.

Karplus, R., Lawson, A., Wollman, W., Appel, M., Bernoff, R., Howe, A., Rusch, J., and Sullivan, F. "Science Teaching and the Development of Reasoning, General Science," Unpublished paper. Berkeley, Calif.: University of California at Berkeley: Lawrence Hall of Science, 1977.

Karplus, R., and Lavatelli, C. *The Developmental Theory of Piaget: Conservation.* San Francisco: Davidson Film Producers, 1969.

Karplus, R. "Science Teaching and the Development of Reasoning." *Journal of Research in Science Teaching* 14 (1977): 169–175.

Kofsky, E. "A Scalagram Study of Classificatory Development." *Child Development* 37 (1966): 191–204.

Lawson, A. "Developing Formal Thought Through Biology Teaching." *American Biology Teacher* 37 (1975): 411–419.

Mason, S. *A History of the Sciences.* New York: Collier Books, 1966.

McCain, G., and Segal, E. *The Game of Science.* 2nd ed. Monterey, Cal.: Brooks/Cole, 1973.

Piaget, J., and Inhelder, B. *Le développement des quantités physiques chez l'enfant.* 2nd ed. Neuchatel: Delachaux and Neistel, 1962,

White, B. *The First Three Years of Life.* Englewood Cliffs, N.J.: Prentice-Hall, 1975.

Part 2

Teaching Elementary Science in the Classroom

Part 2, composed of chapters 4 through 9, contains three developmental teaching models and three corresponding activity chapters. Each model is founded in one of the developmental phases of science outlined in chapter 3. The models are designed to meet the unique information-processing capabilities of children at different developmental stages and to correspond to the developmental stages of science. Each model is designed to promote content learning and process skill acquisition, as well as help children understand the nature of science.

The activity chapters should fulfill three functions: (1.) provide a source of activities for the teacher; (2.) illustrate further each teaching strategy in an effort to reinforce your understanding; and (3.) show how related learning activities and strategies can be modified and interrelated. Because they are designed to reinforce the themes developed in part 1 and implemented in these teaching models, each activity chapter corresponds with a particular model and serves as a source of ideas for classroom application. Also, as you read chapters 4, 6, and 8 you may wish to scan the corresponding activity chapter as a source of examples of the models in use.

Chapter 4 in this section builds on the themes running through the first three chapters by describing an experiential model, which is designed to provide first-hand, sensory experiences for primary school-aged children. The model is a teaching strategy that provides teachers with a framework for involving children in the learning process through direct contact with their environment. Emphasis is placed on activities in which children are purposely exposed to a variety of sensory stimuli. These experiences form the prerequisite background for the formation of important scientific abstractions and the development of process skills. Lesson ideas corresponding to chapter 4 are found in chapter 5.

A prescriptive teaching model designed to teach concepts and generalizations is discussed in detail in chapter 6. The model is designed to promote maximum participation from students and to develop both content acquisition and process skills. The model uses an inductive approach in the development of major science concepts and generalizations, while at the same time involving students in process skill development. Discovery activities corresponding to this chapter are found in chapter 7.

The inquiry model, discussed in chapter 8, is designed to teach students scientific inquiry, in addition to developing process skills and content acquisition. The chapter describes a four-step inquiry procedure and provides a number of illustrations of the model in classroom practice. Suggestions for implementing the inquiry model are found in chapter 9.

In general, lessons in the activities chapters are organized in the following way. The objective, or purpose, describes the goal of the lesson. Content background discusses science content relevant to the topic. Materials lists the equipment you need to implement the lesson; items listed are those that can easily be found in most homes and communities. We have tried to avoid activities that require specialized or esoteric equipment. The procedures suggest the sequence of activities and some possible questions teachers might ask in implementing the lesson. In each lesson related activities include suggestions for possible lessons that could be used as follow-up for unit planning or integration with other curriculum areas.

All the activities are intended to be flexible and to serve as springboards for the teacher, rather than as highly structured activities that can only be implemented in a certain way. In accordance with this view, you are encouraged to expand, adjust, and modify the activities in any way that your judgment dictates.

The matrix which follows is a classification of all the activities that appear in chapters 5, 7, and 9. They are classified according to *topic* and *phase of science.* The purpose of the matrix is to help you interrelate the activities in sequencing lessons and preparing unit plans. The nature of the topic influences the type of activity to some extent, and for this reason the topics are not equally distributed among the phases of science.

When you have finished part 2, you should have not only the conceptual framework and techniques for teaching elementary science but a catalogue of ideas as well. We hope this information base will give you the ability to develop your own background and teaching style toward the end goal of becoming an independent learner and professional elementary science teacher.

Topic	Experiential Activities	Discovery Activities	Inquiry Activities
Seeds & Plants	5.2, 5.3, 5.16, 5.18	7.7, 7.10, 7.12, 7.20, 7.23	9.7, 9.8, 9.16
Animals and their Behavior	5.1, 5.2, 5.11, 5.15	7.15	9.4, 9.5, 9.9
Electricity and Magnetism	7.9	7.8, 7.9, 7.18	9.11
Heat & Temperature	5.4, 5.5	7.3, 7.6, 7.13, 7.21	9.1, 9.14, 9.15, 9.17
Liquids and Evaporation	5.10	7.2, 7.4, 7.14, 7.16	9.10, 9.12
Vibration and Sound	5.7	7.1	9.6
Combustion	5.7	7.14	9.3
Rocks and Erosion	5.8		9.2
Sun, Moon and Weather	5.4	7.5, 7.24	5.4
Force and Motion	7.19	7.11, 7.17, 7.19	7.17, 9.13
Observation and Senses	5.6, 5.7, 5.12, 5.13, 5.14, 5.19, 5.20	5.6	5.6
Symmetry	5.9, 5.17, 5.19	7.22	
Weighing and Measuring	5.14	5.20, 7.4, 7.16	

Having completed the basic framework for the book, now we are ready to begin a discussion of teaching strategies to implement the ideas discussed so far. These strategies will provide ways of teaching science content (facts, concepts, and generalizations) while allowing student to develop process skills (observation, inference, and classification). In addition, the science activities related to each model should provide students with first-hand experiences that help them understand what science is all about. These activities, using familiar, everyday materials, involve students in attempts to make the world comprehensible. As students do the activities, they process information in an attempt to form regularities based on data. Finally, these activities are matched to the developmental characteristics of the learner. This goal includes efforts not only to ensure that the activities are within the developmental limitations of the learner but also that they will encourage cognitive growth and new levels of development.

Chapter 4 The Experiential Model: Making Contact with the Environment

The teaching strategy we will consider in this chapter is the experiential model. As we mentioned earlier, this strategy is designed especially for younger elementary science students and for older students being introduced to a new area of study. Like all three teaching models described in this book, it aims at accomplishing all three major goals of the elementary science curriculum, but puts particular emphasis on process skill development. The teacher who uses the model also has a number of opportunities to teach science content and to provide students with hands-on experiences with science. The following lesson will illustrate:

Ms. Lee was doing a unit on different types of plants. Monday she asked her students to bring in as many different kinds of leaves and needles as they could from around their yard and neighborhood. She told the children to put the leaves in a sealed plastic bag to prevent them from drying out and said the class would do an activity with the leaves on Tuesday.

The next day Ms. Lee had the students gather in a semicircle and they all took out the leaves. For the first five minutes she let them look at their leaves and share their observations with each other. To help them make observations she handed out a number of magnifying glasses and let the students use them to look at their leaves. After students had acquainted themselves with the leaves, she called the class back together. She asked each student to hold up one kind of leaf or needle and began a discussion.

"Kim," she began. "Describe what you have for me."

"Well, I have three pointed things here," holding up some needles.

"Tell us about them."

"They're pointed on the end."

"What else?" Ms. Lee smiled.

"They're sort of greenish brown."

"Yes they are, aren't they? Class, look at Sarah's leaves. What color are they, Tom?"

"They're brown."

"Good, and now let's look at Jim's leaves, class. What color are they? Mary?"

"They're really green."

"Hmm? Why do you think these leaves are all different colors? Can anyone tell? Well, maybe if we felt the leaves. How do yours feel, Jim?"

"Mine feel soft."

"And, Sarah, how about yours? How do they feel?"

"They're dry and crinkly. Look how one just crumples up when I touch it," Sarah replied.

"Hmm, that's interesting. Where did you find yours, Sarah?"

"They were lying on the ground in my front yard."

"Okay, now can anyone tell me why some of our leaves are brown and some are green? Gerry thinks she knows. Do you, Gerry?"

"Oh, it's because some came right off the trees and some had fallen on the ground. The ones on the ground are all brown and dried."

"What do you think, class? How can we check? (pause) Think back to where you got your leaves. If they're brown, were they on the ground? Cynthia?"

"Yes. Mine came from the ground and they are brown and Sandy's were from a tree and they're green. See, they're still on the branch."

"So what do you think will happen to these green leaves? Does anyone think they know? Cami?"

"They'll turn brown."

"Does everyone think so? How about you, Ginger? Don't you think so?"

"No, not if they stay attached to the plant and the plant is in the ground." Ginger replied.

"That's an interesting idea. Why do you say that?"

"Because look at the plants in the windows. Their leaves don't turn brown."

"That's right. And how are all these leaves attached to plants? Look at the leaf that each of you has. Can you tell which end was attached to the plant? Annette?"

"This end," replied Annette, holding it up for the class to see.

"Good, now can all of you find the end of your leaf that was connected to the tree? (pause) Does anybody know what that's called? Joey?"

"Stem."

"Fine, Joey, and here's how we spell that word."

With that she turned around and wrote the word on the board. Then she continued:

"Can everyone find the stem on their leaf? Yes, on some of them it's hard to find. Oh, and class, look what Kim has attached to some of her leaves. Does anyone know what they're called? Theresa?"

"Those are cones. We have some on the tree by our house."

"Good, Theresa, and what are cones for? Does anyone know? Jeb?"

"They're the seeds to make new plants."

"Good, Jeb. The cones have seeds in them and these seeds make new trees. I think I'd better put this new word on the board too."

Ms. Lee continued with the description of the leaves until everyone had made several observations about their leaves. When they had finished she brought out several colored pictures of leaves from trees not native to their area. Between the pictures and the leaves the children brought in, the class had samples from nearly every part of the country.

"Now, I'd like you to find two other partners to share your leaves with, and I'd like you to put all your leaves on the floor between you. Then I want you to see how many different groups you can make with your leaves, and later we'll come back and share what we found."

The class then broke up into groups and discussed and classified the leaves in front of them. As they did, Ms. Lee walked around the class, discussing with each group of students the categories they had formed and the basis for these groupings. After the class had done this for a while the teacher called them back together again.

Figure 4-1
**Groups of Leaves and
Needles**

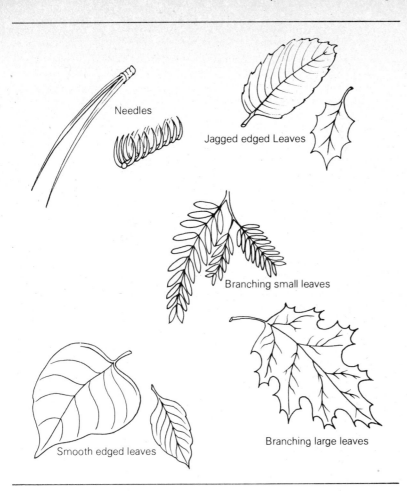

Needles

Jagged edged Leaves

Branching small leaves

Branching large leaves

Smooth edged leaves

"Now everyone," Ms. Lee said, "I'd like you to choose one leaf from your collection and put in the center of our circle for everyone to see."

The class did so, and she continued:

"Let's look at all these leaves and try to decide which ones go together. Any ideas, Linda?"

"We could put all the sharp pointed ones together," Linda said enthusiastically.

"Also, the lines on some of the leaves sort of spread out, and on others they don't," Ricky put in.

"Excellent everyone! Now bring up the leaves that have branching lines and we'll put them together. Also bring all the sharp pointed ones and we'll put them together."

The class did this, continued grouping and finally had each group labeled with a term of their choice. A sample of the groups appears in figure 4-1.

As the class was discussing the groups they had formed, Ms. Lee asked if anyone knew the name for all the needly leaves. When no one answered, Ms. Lee wrote the word "conifers" on the board. She asked if anyone knew why they were called that and when she got no reply she held up a branch with needles and cones on it. At that several students raised their hands and one of them explained how all the needle-bearing trees had cones on them and the word conifer is sort of like cone. The class continued analyzing all the examples of conifers and agreed that each had needles, cones, and a sticky, funny-smelling sap.

After the class had grouped all the leaves by shape, Ms. Lee asked if there was any other way to arrange them. After some discussion the class decided that the size and color could also be a basis for grouping. They then separated the leaves according to these schemes and discussed how the leaves could be grouped in more than one way.

Ms. Lee then suggested to the students that they glue their leaves on pieces of poster paper and hang them on the bulletin board for display. The children decided on how they could arrange the leaves to be most attractive, glued them on the paper and hung them up. The next day, to evaluate her students' classification skills, Ms. Lee gave each student a small assortment of differently formed buttons on a paper tray. She asked the students to group the buttons into four groups, explain the basis for their grouping in writing, and bring the materials to her. Having done this, she moved on to another activity.

Ms. Lee's lesson is an example of the experiential model. It provided the students with first-hand, sensory experiences and opportunities to practice their process skills. In Piagetian terms, the primary goal of the model is to provide students with opportunities to exercise, expand, and change their cognitive structures. Through the processes of observation and classification of concrete objects, the child adapts his or her cognitive structure to deal with the data presented in the activity.

We said in chapter 1 that science is an attempt to find patterns in the world. The elementary teacher in an experiential activity brings a small part of the world into the classroom and focuses students' attention on it. In interacting with this data the student learns things, that is, strengthens or modifies the structure already present. The children who already knew that pine needles were kinds of leaves were assimilating the newly encountered pine needles into their presently organized structures. Other students, who did not realize that pine needles were types of leaves, came away from that lesson with their concepts of both pine needles and leaves changed—they accommodated. In addition, students who were not familiar with the concepts of stem, cone, and conifers added these new concepts to their cognitive structures. So, in addition to gaining direct science experience with the environment and practicing their process skills, students also had an opportunity to learn new content in the form of concepts.

Turn now to a more analytical look at the lesson's procedure and the characteristics of the experiential model. After the discussion you should be able to meet the following objective:

Three Steps to Learning

- You will understand the phases of the experiential model so that, given an illustration, you will identify the phases of the model shown in it.

- You will understand processes, so that given illustrations, you will demonstrate the processes of observation and the four forms of inference.

There are three basic teaching and learning steps in the experiential model:

- Open exploration.
- Teacher-guided exploration.
- Classification.

We will discuss these steps in the pages that follow.

Open Exploration

In this first phase of the lesson, students are provided with data and allowed to explore that data on their own. Ms. Lee's students were involved in *open exploration* when they were encouraged to look at their leaves, make observations, and share their observations with their neighbors. This step gives students time to familiarize themselves with the data and provides a stepping stone to the second phase.

Teacher-Guided Exploration

After students have had time to explore the data individually and have acquainted themselves with it, the teacher expands this process by asking questions. Notice that the initial questions ask for observations. This gives students a chance to share the information they have gathered and to acquaint themselves with each other's data. After doing this the teacher might continue by asking for a variety of inferences. In Ms. Lee's activity, the students were encouraged to make explanatory inferences when she asked them to explain why some leaves were green while others were brown. She also asked them to suggest what would happen to the green leaves over a period of time. These statements are predictive inferences.

During this phase a teacher could also encourage students to make generalizing inferences. As we said, the products of a generalizing inference are either concepts or generalizations. While content goals aren't the primary focus of experiential lessons, teachers may find opportunities to introduce concepts and generalizations during the course of the lesson. Ms. Lee did this when she taught her students the concepts of stem, cone, and conifers, using examples that members of the class had brought in. After students have had an opportunity to make observations, share them with each other, and process some of them through inference, the lesson can move to the third and final stage of the activity.

Classification

In the final stage of the model, students are provided with opportunities to practice their classification skills. Ms. Lee's students did this in several stages, first in groups of three students. In this activity all the children got a chance to practice classification skills and to share their classification schemes with other students. Next, Ms. Lee made classification a large-group exercise, giving students an opportunity to share their ideas with the whole class.

Finally, Ms. Lee asked her students to develop new classification schemes. This is an important part of experiential activities because it teaches students that classification schemes are not absolute or inflexible. Instead, by seeing that objects can be classified in more than one way, students learn that the classification systems that they make are tools that people can change and adapt to fit their needs and circumstances. This is in sharp contrast to the way classification schemes are presented in typical science textbooks. The classification of the animal kingdom, for example, frequently appears in textbooks as a tool devised and organized by scientists in an effort to understand animals and patterns in their characteristics. Here it is presented in a way that leads students to believe that some system exists in nature; people discover the system rather than *devising* it. The difference between discovering and devising is an important one. Helping students to recognize this difference is an important outcome of experiential activities. Teachers can develop this insight by providing students with opportunities to try out a number of classification activities in the classroom. Later in the chapter we will discuss some relevant strategies.

Ms. Lee concluded her lesson by incorporating the science lesson into an art activity. While this is not an explicit step in the procedure, we encourage blending other areas of the curriculum. It provides opportunities for *reinforcing* learning from different areas of the curriculum. In working with leaves in an art project, the students not only had a chance to continue practicing observing and classifying but also were provided with an opportunity to learn about concepts such as color, form, and design. This encourages students to see relationships among different areas of the curriculum. It facilitates adaptation, expanding and reorganizing their cognitive structure. If the school curriculum is chopped up into discrete periods, in which students are asked to "think arithmetic" and "think reading," the students are not shown how all these areas relate as an integral whole. This practice robs students of a chance to expand and exercise their cognitive structures. Also, the integration of science with other areas provides the teacher with a vehicle for planning a series of cohesive learning experiences. We will discuss this process in more detail later in the chapter.

There are three essential characteristics of activities used in the experiential model:

- They emphasize sensory experiences for each child that are concrete and manipulative.
- They place primary emphasis on process goals.
- They have no specific content objective.

Each of these characteristics has been implicitly discussed in the previous section. We will discuss them further in the following pages.

Characteristics of the Experiential Model

Sensory Experiences That Are Concrete and Manipulative

Concrete and *sensory* describe the tangible nature of the items that the children can experience with their senses. *Manipulative* simply means that they can handle them. The children in Ms. Lee's class had the actual leaves as opposed to pictures or verbal descriptions of the leaves. They could feel, see, smell, taste, and even hear them when the leaves were rustled or moved in some way. Although Ms. Lee supplemented the activity with pictures, the children had a chance to work with real leaves before pictures were used.

The reasons for using concrete, sensory materials relates to the themes introduced earlier in the book. In chapter 1 we described science as an everyday occurrence in which people try to find patterns in their environment. As teachers, we can help reinforce the idea of science as an integral part of our lives by providing children with objects and events that come from their own experience and by helping them find patterns in these experiences. Ms. Lee did this when she asked the students to bring in leaves from around their homes and neighborhoods.

In chapter 2 we stressed that science is a search for regularities, characterized by processes that lead to forming concepts and generalizations. Teachers can facilitate the development of students' process skills by allowing them to work with tangible objects. In addition, students need concrete referents to give meaning to the concepts and generalizations they form.

In chapter 3 we said that processing unfamiliar information is a difficult operation, particularly for children in the preoperational and concrete operational stages of development. These two stages approximately span the ages from two to eleven, the years most children are in preschool and the elementary grades K-6. While children in these stages of development can classify and form concepts, they need concrete, tangible props to aid them.

Sometimes concrete referents are simply impossible. When compromises are necessary, the teacher has two options: to defer the topic until later when children can more adequately deal with it in the absence of examples, or to use photographs, slides, or pictures. If there is no zoo nearby it is certainly better for children to study pictures of animals than to skip the activity entirely. In that case, the more lifelike and realistic the pictures, the better the experience will be for the children. For young children, they should be in full color.

The notion of manipulative activities is closely related to these concrete, sensory experiences. *Manipulative* means that the children can handle the objects and play with them, instead of having the teacher demonstrate for them. As children actively interact with data, they involve their sensory channels in the learning experience. Allowing children to see, touch, smell, hear, and (sometimes) taste the objects they're learning about is better than just having them passively look at them. In addition, manipulative activities are motivational. Children generally prefer doing something to watching someone else do it. Clearly, allowing students to "tinker" with the objects they're learning about provides a realistic experience with science. Although demonstrations are certainly better than reading a book and answering the questions at the end of the chapter, children in such a lesson are not really involved in "doing" science.

An important characteristic of experiential activities is that, if at all possible, *each child should have his or her own material to work with.* When compromises are absolutely necessary, teacher demonstrations are certainly appropriate. Exclusive reliance on teacher demonstrations, however, should be avoided.

Emphasis on Process Goals

Another characteristic of experiential activities is that they have their primary emphasis on process. Remember that process and content were described as being closely interrelated and literally inseparable. This means that experiential activities are not (and should not be) content free, but rather that the activities are designed primarily to teach the children intellectual skills and processes. For example, in Ms. Lee's lesson the primary emphasis was on the processes of observation and classification. During the lesson, however, Ms. Lee encountered and took advantage of a number of opportunities to introduce ideas and to teach concepts. For example, the class considered why some leaves were brown while others were green and tried to figure out why this occurred. Also, Ms. Lee introduced the terms stem and cone and taught the concept conifer using the examples that the students had brought to class. Nevertheless, while she taught some content, Ms. Lee's primary focus was on process development.

Many different kinds of activities can emphasize this process development. For example, the teacher could have each child bring in a different vegetable or fruit, make a large number of observations of each, and then compare and group all observations of the fruits and vegetables, finally labeling each group. As another example, a field trip to the zoo could be followed by having the children recall as many observations of the animals as possible and then classify their observations in a way similar to that described for the fruits and vegetables. This kind of observing/grouping/labeling activity could be used with other materials such as rocks, shells (if you live near a coastline), seeds, grains, bones, or even buttons, blocks, pieces of cloth and so on. With each of these topics, other inferential activities could follow.

No Specific Content Objective

A related idea that we have already mentioned is that experiential activities have no specific content objective. This means that when a teacher begins to plan for and implement experiential activities, he or she does not explicitly focus on certain concepts and generalizations. Rather, as opportunities to teach content unfold within the course of the lesson, the teacher can take advantage of them. This orientation provides teachers with flexibility and allows them to adapt their lessons to the backgrounds, interests, and needs of their students. In chapter 6, we will discuss a more structured teaching model, especially designed to teach science concepts and generalizations to elementary students.

Directions: Read the following description of a teacher using the experiential model and identify the three phases of this model as described in the previous section. Feedback for this and all other exercises will be found at the back of the chapter.

Exercise 4.1

Mr. Keith wanted to do a lesson on foods to familiarize students with the sources of different foods as well as develop their process skills. To do this, he distributed magazines to his first-grade students and asked them to cut out pictures of food and mount them on construction paper. After they had done this, he asked the students to share their pictures with their neighbors in preparation for large-group sharing. During the large-group sharing he had students bring their pictures to the front of the room and tape them to the chalkboard. As they did this, he asked each student to tell about his or her own picture. The teacher supplemented this description by asking questions of the whole group. This initial sharing process took several days, but Mr. Keith wanted to give everyone a chance to speak in front of the class.

After this activity was completed, the teacher chose ten of the most interesting pictures and pinned them on a flannel board. He asked the class to look at the pictures and tell him which ones went together. The first grouping scheme was on the basis of taste, but with some prompting the students came up with alternate schemes based on source, meal typically eaten at, color, and whether they were cooked or not.

As a final exercise to evaluate students' ability to classify, the teacher passed out a duplicated sheet with different foods sketched on it and asked students to draw circles around the foods that went together. As students handed their papers in, each was asked to explain the basis for his or her groupings.

Planning Experiential Activities

After completing this section you should be able to meet the following objective:

- You will understand the goals of experiential activities so that given a series of goals, you will identify those appropriate to the experiential model.

The planning phase of any teaching strategy involves everything a teacher must consider prior to actually doing a lesson in the classroom. For experiential activities, this involves considering the goals of the activity and providing the materials that will be used during the activity. Each of these topics will be covered in the sections that follow.

Goals of Experiential Activities

Planning begins with a consideration of the teacher's goals, and the goals for an experiential activity are quite simple: the teacher wants students to develop their process skills and gather a body of information. For example, here are three possible goals.

- A teacher wants students to understand that "Animals that use *running away* as a means of protection from predators are light-bodied and long-legged."
- A teacher wants students to determine what factors influence the amount gerbils will grow over a period of time.
- A teacher wants students to group a number of insects on the basis of appearance.

Each of these is an important and worthwhile goal for science teaching, but they differ in their appropriateness for a particular teaching model.

In the first goal, the statement, "Animals that use *running away* as a means of protection are light-bodied and long-legged" is a generalization. It is a particular form of content. This goal could be reached in a discovery activity, such as those discussed in chapter 6.

In the second goal, the teacher wants students to be involved in determining what factors influence growth in gerbils. This teacher has an inquiry activity in mind for the students. Inquiry activities are the subject of chapter 8.

Goal three, on the other hand, is directed at developing students' ability to make observations and classify objects on the basis of these observations. Emphasis on the processes of observation and classification is characteristic of the experiential phase of science as well as the experiential model.

In reality there is considerable overlap among the processes used in each of the strategies, and the difference between each of them is primarily one of emphasis rather than exclusive use of a particular technique. For example, in goal one, students would be observing and then inferring in order to reach the generalization that compares body structure and forms of protection. These processes would also be used extensively in goal two, where students would attempt to determine factors that influence gerbil growth. Students in the second activity would need some prior knowledge of factors that influence the growth of animals. But compare the fundamental purposes of these models. In the first case the primary purpose is learning the generalization; in the second case the purpose is understanding science through inquiry; in the third goal the primary purpose is development of students' process abilities. When the primary focus of the lesson is process, it is characterized as experiential.

One way to understand the differences between the three models is to think of them as sequential learning strategies that build on the goals of the previous models. In the experiential model the primary emphasis is on process skill acquisition and the gathering of information that results. Discovery activities also use processes but explicit emphasis on process development is reduced. Instead, the processes are used to form concepts and generalizations. In inquiry activities, both content and process are used in the structuring of science experiments. These relationships are diagrammed in figure 4–2.

The purpose of this analysis is twofold. First, it reinforces our conception of the phases of science and how science develops. Second, and more practically, as you study this material and do activities with children you may think to yourself, "I am doing an inquiry lesson, but the students seemed to be involved heavily in processes." Our reaction would be that this is as it should be, because *process* is an integral part of all three phases of science and their corresponding teaching models. On the other hand, you might say to yourself, "I am doing what I think is an experiential activity but the children are learning a concept." Again, this is perfectly appropriate. The phases are neither distinct nor mutually

Figure 4-2
The Phases of Science Hierarchically Represented

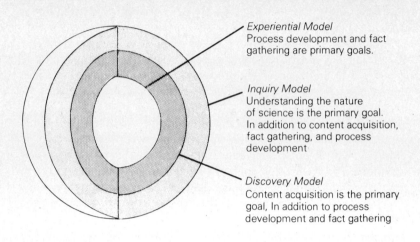

Experiential Model
Process development and fact gathering are primary goals.

Inquiry Model
Understanding the nature of science is the primary goal. In addition to content acquisition, fact gathering, and process development

Discovery Model
Content acquisition is the primary goal, In addition to process development and fact gathering

exclusive. The key is in the major focus of the goal. Goals that aim primarily at process skill development and fact gathering are experiential goals.

Now complete the exercises below, then proceed to the next section, which deals with the preparation of data for experiential activities.

Exercise 4.2

Directions: Look at each of the activities below and identify those appropriate as experiential activities.

1. A teacher wants students to use objects and mirrors to make images of the objects appear in different forms.

2. A teacher uses beans in a shoebox to help students understand radioactive decay.

3. A teacher has children observe an aquarium closely and list all the objects in it as to whether they are living or not living.

4. A teacher has the children work on an activity to determine what affects the burning rate of a candle.

5. A teacher wants her students to understand the difference between deciduous and coniferous trees.

6. A kindergarten teacher brings in a bag of soda pop bottle caps and has her students sort them into groups.

7. A teacher has children cut open lima beans, look at their structure, and see the seed embryo inside.

Data Preparation: Materials for Process Skill Development

Because experiential activities have process skill development as their primary focus, the teacher must provide data to be used in the activity to fulfill that purpose. For the most part, this simply means the activity must be planned and materials made available for each student or each pair of students. A simple way of handling this is to have the students bring their own materials. For example, Ms. Lee had each student bring in his or her own leaves to observe and classify. As another example, students could be asked to bring a small toy to class. Toys would be classified as to color, shape, or function. Again, with the example of fruits and vegetables, each student could be asked to bring in one fruit or vegetable and share it with the class. In this example, experiential activities could tap a new sensory dimension by having students smell and taste the vegetables and fruits and classify them as sour, bitter, sweet, or salty.

This abundance of individual data is desirable because it makes direct individual involvement possible. Sometimes data is not available for the whole class, but the teacher still wants to involve the students in an experiential activity. If one child brings in a branch covered with caterpillars, it provides an opportunity for all the members of a class to experience and learn about these interesting creatures. A teacher who wants students to learn about different tools might bring a variety of tools into class and place them on a table for all to share.

A practical way of allowing all children access to the data is to set up a corner of the room as a science learning center. Students can visit it before class, on breaks, or during individual work periods. The teacher can encourage process development by having work cards at each table that ask students to answer questions such as the following:

- What's happening here?
- Make a list of everything you see and then split this list into two lists, then four.
- Which objects go together?
- Has anything changed here since yesterday?
- How do these work?

Teachers can then discuss these questions during a group discussion.

A third alternative for data gathering is to use media such as slides, pictures from magazines, or cassette tape recordings of various sounds, distributed either as a group activity or in the learning center. Although they are not concrete, forms such as pictures provide opportunities to bring large segments of the world into the classroom that would otherwise be inaccessible.

Another consideration to be made in selecting data is the grouping arrangement of students. Experiential activities usually work equally well in large groups, small groups, or learning centers. Classroom management problems you may encounter are unique to the grouping arrangement and are not a function of the activity. For example, it is much easier to provide materials for a learning center or a small group than it is for a large group. On the other hand, activities requiring observation and description require that the description would have to be in writing if a learning center arrangement were used. If you want information on learning centers or grouping arrangements, you may wish to read one of the sources cited at the end of this chapter.

Implementing Experiential Activities

Having considered the goals of the lesson, gathered the materials, and reviewed the grouping arrangements, the teacher is now ready to implement the activity. Let us review briefly the three steps of the implementation phase:

- Open exploration (student observations)
- Teacher-guided exploration (observation and inference)
- Classification.

You will recall that the processes of observation, inference, and classification are emphasized in an experiential activity.

Because some teachers who have tried experiential and other process-oriented activities with their students have encountered initial difficulties, we will discuss how these processes can be developed in students. Typically, difficulties arise when students or teachers do not understand exactly what to do in these activities. Practice through some of the activities listed below is usually all that is needed to correct this problem.

Observation

Experiential activites, like most science lessons, begin with the process of observation. This is a logical starting point since all the information we receive about the world comes to us through our senses. When first introduced to the process of observation, students may approach it casually or not understand what is being required of them. Most of them have not been encouraged to be careful and conscientious observers, either in school, at home, or at play. They accept their surroundings without comment. One way of teaching this new skill is to provide everyone with a common object like a pencil, paper clip, or coin. Ask them to make as many observations as possible. Our experience has shown that students are surprised when they learn that they can make dozens of observations from just one object.

Variations on this activity include dividing the class into teams and having contests to make the most (and most accurate) observations. Another variation is to have students make their observations from memory. Students are allowed to observe the object for a minute or so; then it is put away and they recall as many observations as possible. A third kind of observational activity employs a picture or slide as the stimulus object.

To reinforce your own understanding of the process of observation and to provide you with first-hand experience with the process, complete the next exercise. This exercise can either be done by yourself or with a group of students.

Directions: Obtain a simple household candle (one larger than a birthday candle is preferred), place it in a candlestick and light it, and *make as many observations of the candle as possible.* You should be able to make *at least thirty observations* of the candle. Some of the observations we made are found at the end of the chapter.

Exercise 4.3

Inference

Besides the process of observation, experiential activities offer opportunities to practice inferential skills. For example, Ms. Lee had students making explanatory and predictive inferences when she had them explain why the leaves were brown and predict what would happen to the other leaves over time. Another opportunity for the development of process skills could occur with unusual or distinctive leaf patterns. For example, the leaf pattern shown in figure 4–3 might prompt a teacher to ask, "Why do you suppose the holes and the notch appear in the leaf on the left?"

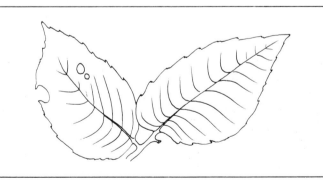

Figure 4–3
An Opportunity for Explanatory Inferences

The children could suggest that an insect has eaten the leaf or the trees that the leaves came from were diseased, among other suggestions. The children could then be prompted to consider how long the leaf had

Figure 4-4
**Development of
Inferential
Skills**

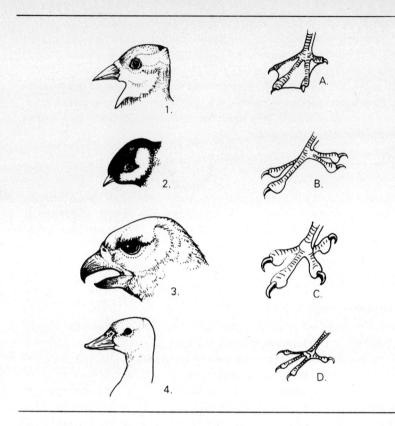

looked like this and why the second leaf shows no notch or hole. Seizing on this opportunity when it arises is one characteristic of a teacher who is artful in the classroom compared to one who is merely mechanical. (Incidentally, this example again shows the inseparability of process and content. Neither inference would be possible without some knowledge of insects or the way trees look when they are diseased.)

As another example of an activity that can be used in the classroom to develop inferential skills, consider the pictures in figure 4-4. After examining the pictures, students could be asked to suggest which heads go with which feet and explain why (they must infer the relationship). Discussion could occur in a large or small group. Note here that this type of activity could be extended to other animals and their parts. For example, students could be given a worksheet or overhead transparency showing the picture in figure 4-5. They could be asked to match the skeletons or skulls with the heads of animals shown. Students could then be asked to make inferences about the function of different parts of the skull, such as the length of the jaw, the teeth, and so on.

Activities such as these could be designed as worksheets. Elementary

Figure 4-5
**Development of
Inferential
Skills**

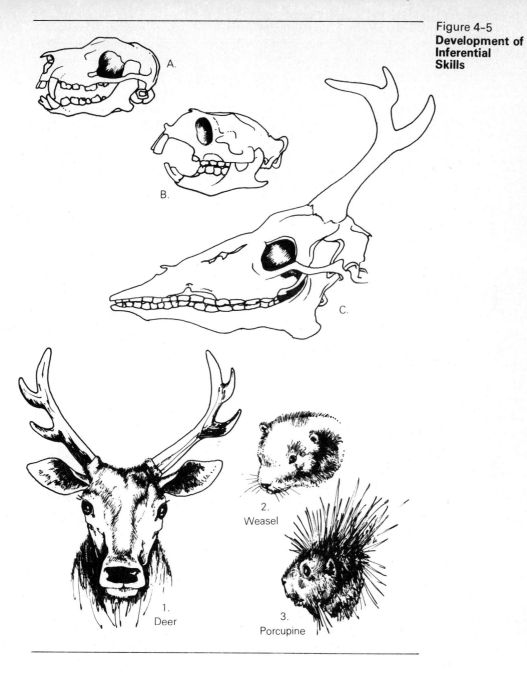

A.

B.

C.

1.
Deer

2.
Weasel

3.
Porcupine

school children spend a considerable portion of their time working
individually at their desks. Worksheet activities emphasizing inference
would be a welcome change from those that emphasize repetition and
drill.

Finally, some activities may emphasize process in a less explicit sense. For example, children could be asked to mold clay until it floats and then see how many marbles it will carry before it sinks. The same could be done with aluminum foil, and students could compare the flotation property of clay to that of aluminum and so on. Experienced students could even be involved in a discussion of density and specific gravity.

Three Stages of Classification

Another process employed in experiential activities is classification. There are several kinds of classification; the particular form chosen should be based on logical and developmental considerations. One way to sequence classification activities in a lesson is to follow the developmental sequence in which these skills occur in the child. Kofsky (1966) notes three levels of classification skill as they typically emerge: consistent sorting, exhaustive sorting, and hierarchical classification. *Consistent sorting* occurs when students adopt a particular classification strategy and use it without changing over to another system. *Exhaustive sorting* occurs when students use a classification system to sort all of the objects. *Hierarchical classification* is the process of creating groups within groups.

When initially introducing the process of classification, the teacher should not assume that since students are in second or third grade, they automatically know how to classify. All children may not yet have achieved this understanding. One way to teach this skill is by modeling: actually performing the activity in front of the class while explaining what is happening and why. This modeling can be followed by an individual or small group activity monitored by the teacher, to make sure the students understand both consistent and exhaustive sorting.

When introducing the process of classification, it is a good idea initially to use small numbers of familiar objects. By making the classification easier, the learning task for students will be simplified.

After students feel comfortable with the sorting task and the groups they have formed, the teacher can encourage students to regroup or resort the objects. Initially this may be difficult, because some students tend to view the classes they have formed as the only ones possible. They may feel that after spending so much time and effort building something—forming the original classes—they are reluctant to destroy the system. To help them in this process the teacher should praise the groups that were formed, but encourage students to form new and different ones. Again, the teacher might have to model this process initially, explaining what is being done while performing the activity.

The final stage in the classification sequence, hierarchical classification, is the creation of groups within groups. For example, all the students in the room can be divided by sex and then again by hair color. The product of this system is diagrammed in figure 4–6.

Figure 4-6
**A Hierarchical
Classification System**

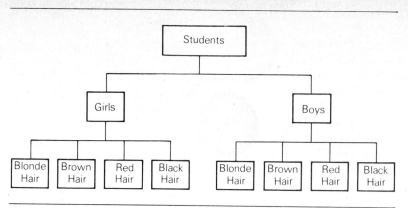

This process could be extended by dividing the hair color groups by eye color or size.

Ms. Lee could have told her students to take their leaves and develop a hierarchical classification scheme to categorize each leaf instead of grouping them the way she did. Figure 4-7 shows one possible classification hierarchy.

In addition, the unbranched leaves formed in that activity could be further subdivided hierarchically. Figure 4-8 shows how the unbranched leaves would appear. These two figures show a complete classification for unbranched leaves. The same could be done for branched leaves, as well as needles.

As another example of hierarchical classification, consider five animals, horse, cow, deer, alligator, and snake. A classification scheme based on their observable characteristics might appear as in figure 4-9.

Remember, this scheme is merely an illustration. There are certainly other ways of classifying the animals; for example, on the basis of size, kind of covering, or what they eat. The particular classification is not important as long as it is based on observable characteristics and applied logically and consistently. Now take a moment and do the following exercise, which is designed to reinforce your notion of hierarchical classification.

Directions: Take a penny, nickel, dime, quarter, and half-dollar and devise a hierarchical classification scheme that will allow each coin to be separately classified.   **Exercise 4.4**

A Classroom Example

Mr. Peterson, a fourth-grade teacher, was beginning a unit on soils. Since his students were inexperienced in this area, he decided to use an experiential activity.

Figure 4–7
A Hierarchical Classification System for Leaves

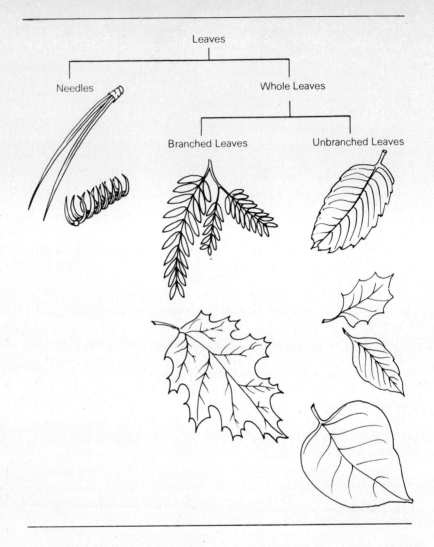

He began the lesson by dividing the class into groups of three and passing out pieces of screen and magnifying glasses. Then he said: "Today we're going to start our unit on soil. I've brought in four buckets of dirt from different places near here. Rather than tell you where they come from, I'd like you to see if you can find out. So, now I want you to come to the front of the room, take four of these small containers, and pick up a sample of soil for your groups. Then I'd like you to make as many observations of each of these as you can, and we'll compare notes in about ten minutes."

The class then broke up into their small groups and began their observation task. They put the dirt on small pieces of screen, sifted the contents, and examined the results with a magnifying glass. Different

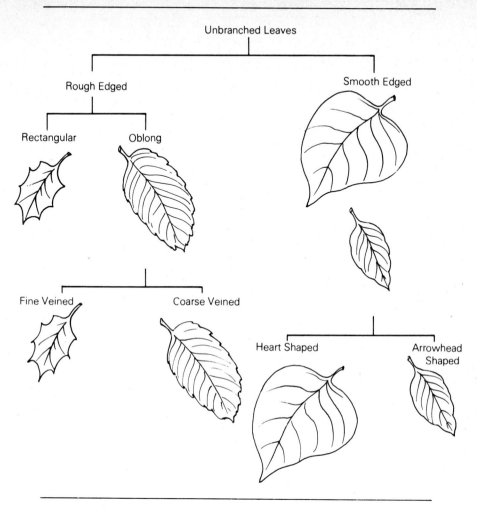

Figure 4-8
**An Elaborated
Classification Scheme**

groups recorded their information in different ways. Some elected one person to examine each bucket. After they had had an opportunity to make their observations, Mr. Peterson continued.

"Now let's see what the different groups found, by comparing the observations we made for each of the buckets starting with number one. What did you find, Bonnie?"

"Mostly sand, it was really light colored."

"Anything else, Kathy?"

"Some leaves and stuff, but not much."

"Kerry?"

"We found some plants in ours."

"Could you tell what kind?"

"Mainly they looked like tall grass."

Figure 4-9
A Hierarchical Classification

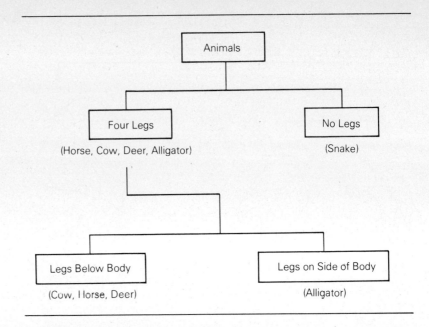

"And what else, Jeb?"

"There was some black or dark dirt around the roots of the plants."

As the students described each of their observations, Mr. Peterson wrote them on the board in a list under the heading, "Bucket 1." When they finished they had the lists shown in table 4-1.

Table 4-1 **Results of Student Observations**

Bucket 1	Bucket 2	Bucket 3	Bucket 4
Mostly sand (light colored)	Really dark	Reddish Color	Blackish colored
Some leaves, not much	Lots of bits and pieces of leaves and twigs	Lots of small rocks	Dusty, fine particles
Plants (grass)	Not very heavy	Rocks mainly look alike	Gravel and broken glass
Black dirt around roots of plants	Some small animals a) worm b) insects	Some leaves and twigs	Paper in it
Some broken shells	Some seeds	Dry	Really dry
	Wetter than others		Few leaves and twigs

Mr. Peterson then went on. "Let's look at the observations we've made. Can anyone make a guess where these different buckets of dirt came from, Ronnie?"

"Well, we're pretty sure that number one came from the beach, because it's sandy and has broken shells in it, and two could come from anywhere. It looks like the dirt in my dad's garden."

"Do the rest of you agree?" queried Mr. Peterson. "And what about the other two buckets? Any ideas?"

"Bucket four has a lot of junk in it so it could be from a junky lot or some place in the city?"

"That's interesting. Anybody else?"

"I think George is right," added Mindy, "because there aren't many leaves and stems in it. And that means that there aren't many plants growing in it."

"Okay, and what about bucket number three? Where do you think it came from? Any ideas?"

"I think it came from a pretty rocky area because of all the pebbles and rocks in it," replied Shawn.

"Any other clues? Jan?"

"Well, our dirt from bucket three didn't have much plant material in it and it was a funny red color."

"Okay, let's leave that question for a second and instead focus on another question. What if you had to group these samples of dirt into two groups. Which ones would go together, Ted?"

"I think two and four would go together because they both are kind of black and the others are kind of light-brown colored."

"Any other ways we could group them together, Sarah?"

"Well, we could group one, three, and four together because they didn't have much organic material in them."

"Another way would be to group three and four together because they have rocks and other big things in them."

"All right, let's leave that question for a while and look at the things you found in each of the buckets. Why don't you just tell me and I'll write them on the board. John, why don't you start?"

"Okay, how about rocks, twigs and leaves?"

"Kerrie?"

"We found broken shells and pieces of grass."

"Mike?"

The listing continued until the board looked like this:

rocks	sand	gravel
twigs	roots	bugs (insects)
leaves	piece of bone	seeds
broken shells	broken glass	bottle cap
pieces of grass	dirt	earthworm

Then Mr. Peterson continued, "Look at the words that we have on the board. Which of them go together? Anyone? Jan."

"Well, we could put twigs, leaves, and pieces of bone together because they all come from living things."

"Okay, I'll put an 'A' by each one of them. What else? Tony?"

"Broken glass, paper, and bottle cap could also go together because they're manufactured."

"All right, I'll put a 'B' by each member of that group."

"And bugs and earthworms could go together because they're alive," added Sherry.

"Or we could put shells in that group and call it animals and animal products."

The lesson continued, with the class grouping and regrouping the items, until everyone was satisfied with the classes that were produced. After discussing these groupings the class focused again on the buckets of soil. The question of why some of the buckets of soil were wetter than others was considered. Some suggested that they had been watered recently, while others claimed that they just held the moisture better. So the class decided to try an experiment the next day to see if the different buckets of soil did hold water at a different rate. With this, the class ended for the day.

Let us consider what makes this activity an experiential lesson. The lesson began with the *presentation of data.* Mr. Peterson had planned for the lesson by gathering the buckets of soil, the pieces of screen, and the magnifying glasses. An alternate but perhaps less systematic way of providing for the data would be to ask each student to bring in a sample of soil. The choice is a matter of judgment. Notice that the teacher chose this type of lesson format for his fourth graders because for them, the topic was new and unfamiliar. As we noted earlier, the experiential model is an excellent strategy for use in introducing a topic to students at all levels.

After the teacher presented the data, students were allowed to engage in open exploration, phase one of the model. This phase allows students to familiarize themselves with the data while they practice the process of observation. These observations provide the basis for the other processes that occur later.

After the students had become familiar with the data, the teacher guided the investigation (phase two) by having the class *list their observations* of each soil sample. During this phase the teacher also probed the students for explanatory inferences by asking where the different buckets of soil came from.

In phase three of the model, the teacher asked the class to *group the kinds of soil* according to their similarities. Several alternate classification schemes were suggested before Mr. Peterson asked the class to list and categorize the content of the buckets.

So far we've encountered all of the phases of the experiential model. The teacher chose to extend this lesson by going back to phase two and asking the class to list the components found in each of the buckets, another example of teacher-guided exploration. He then continued by asking the students to classify these observations. In doing so, he put letters by each of the members of the group as a short-hand way of keeping track of the groups.

The lesson concluded with the class deciding to do an experiment on water content the next day. One activity can serve as a springboard to other activities frequently in science lessons. This type of piggybacking should be encouraged because it provides students with a realistic picture of how science and scientists operate. Seldom does a scientist plan a series of experiments without adjusting these plans on the basis of findings. As much as possible, classroom lessons, like the plans of scientists, should be flexible enough to accommodate student interests and meaningful "research problems" that arise.

Variations in Experiential Activities

Now that we have discussed procedure in some detail, let's look at some variations the teacher might consider. It may be appropriate to emphasize some phases of the model more than others or do an activity with affective or attitudinal considerations in mind. The content or the materials involved in the lesson will often influence these decisions. For example, in the activity relating the beaks and claws of birds, the first two phases of the experiential model can be covered very nicely. The students can make and verbally state observations about the pictures. The teacher can request a large variety of explanatory inferences, such as comparing the function of different claws, the birds' typical habitats, or diet—whether they're herbivorous or carnivorous. The teacher-guided exploration phase of the activity could be very involved, limited only by the teacher's imagination and insight, while the classification phase would be brief and quite sketchy, amounting merely to classifying the feet and heads together. The teacher could supplement the materials with additional pictures. Experiences could be planned in which students observed additional birds, either outside the window, on a nature walk, or on a trip to a zoo or aviary.

As another illustration, consider the burning candle exercise you did earlier in this chapter. In this exercise the emphasis was primarily on observation. It could have been expanded to include inferences explaining certain observations and the observations could have been categorized into groups. The relative emphasis on each phase is a matter of the teacher's judgment, relating to the curriculum goals.

As a third example, consider the activity in which students are asked to mold clay until it floats and see how many marbles it will hold. This activity is manipulative and fun for students. Typically it is a high-interest activity. A variation might be to place the emphasis on the teacher-guided exploration phase. After the students had constructed the different boats, and described the designs that would carry the most marbles (phase one), the teacher could ask questions such as:

"What does this tell us about the design of large ships?"

"If a rounded design is best for floating marbles, why are ships long and thin?"

"What does the placement of marbles tell us about how ships are loaded?"

"Did you notice the 'stretching' of the surface of the water as the 'boat' was about to sink? What is this called?"

In this activity the classification phase of the model might be eliminated entirely. On the other hand, a teacher might want students to make a number of observations as they build the boat and classify these observations, or classify the different boat designs. As with other examples, the emphasis in the activity would depend upon the teacher's goals for the lesson.

Before concluding the discussion of the implementation phase of the model, we want to make several additional comments about teacher actions during experiential lessons. Because these lessons are for the most part unstructured, the teacher must be flexible and responsive to the questions and answers of students. This is not easy. It requires a skilled, sensitive, and insightful teacher to respond to an opportunity to probe students through questioning to practice their thinking skills. For example, it is strictly a function of the teacher's skill *at the instant it takes place* to ask the student to give a reason for a certain fact he or she observes. When students make observations about leaves, for example, one student might state that one leaf is notched. A skilled teacher would immediately ask why he or she thinks the notch exists. After the student responds that an insect probably ate it, the teacher would continue to probe. Leading questions would be: "Why do you say that?" or "Were others leaves from the same tree also notched or did they have holes in them?" This discussion could continue until the topic was exhausted or the students' interest began to wane. A less skilled teacher might miss the opportunity to probe altogether or might ask only the "why" question. The skilled teacher provides the children not only with some valuable practice in developing thinking skills but also with equally valuable practice in verbalizing their ideas, thereby developing language ability.

Before moving to the next section, complete the exercises that follow.

Exercise 4.5

Read the example below, then answer the question.

Ms. Cole was starting a unit on animals with her second-grade class. She began the lesson by passing out magazines, construction paper, and paste. She asked each student to find a picture of an animal in the magazine, cut it out, and paste it on the construction paper. As the students did this they were encouraged to discuss their pictures with the people next to them. When they were finished she asked each of her reading groups, consisting of about ten students each, to come up and discuss the pictures with her. She started the small group activity by

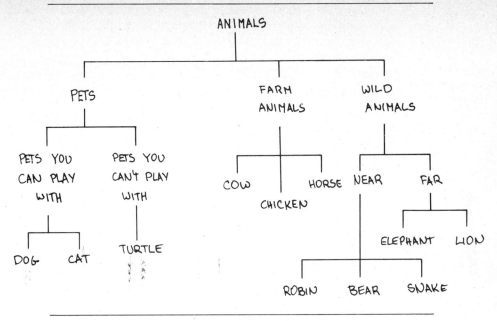

Figure 4-10

having each student describe the animal they had cut out. As they talked about the animal she asked the following questions.

"What kind of animal is that?"

"What color fur or skin does it have?"

"How big is it?"

"Where does it live?"

These questions were designed to develop verbal fluency, as much as to acquaint the other students with the picture.

After the students described their pictures, Ms. Cole put adhesive tape on the back of each and put them on the board. Then she said, "Look at the pictures we have on the board. Which ones go together? Jim?"

"Mary and Jan's go together because they're both dogs."

"Missy?"

"And we could put Sandy's animal in that group, too, because it's a cat. Then the group would be pets."

As the students mentioned each of the groupings, the teacher placed the pictures in each class together.

"Okay, does anyone else see any more pets? Kim?"

"I have a picture of a turtle, and sometimes they're pets."

"All right," agreed Ms. Cole. "Does anyone see any other pets? No? Can you see any other animals that go together? Marie?"

The classification exercise continued until the pictures were sorted into the groups shown in figure 4-10.

Ms. Cole then asked if there were any other way to group the animals. When there was no reply, she asked if they all ate the same kind of food. With that, several members of the group raised their hands and suggested alternate grouping patterns. After the group considered and discussed the alternate groupings, Ms. Cole asked the students to go back to their seats and write a story about two of the animals.

1. Identify in the anecdote where each of the following phases occurred.

   a. Open exploration _____

   _____

   _____

   b. Teacher-guided exploration _____

   _____

   _____

   c. Classification _____

   _____

   _____

2. Identify in the anecdote where each of the following types of classification occurred.

   a. Exhaustive sorting _____

   _____

   _____

   b. Reclassification _____

   _____

   _____

   c. Hierarchical classification _____

   _____

3. List at least five alternative classification schemes that students could have used.

Since the primary focus of experiential activities is on process skill acquisition, our discussing of evaluation techniques in this chapter will be limited to the process dimension. Measuring students' content acquisition and evaluating their understanding of the nature of scientific experimentation will be discussed in chapters 6 and 8 respectively.

Evaluating Experiential Activities

A Taxonomy of Skill Objectives

Learning to perform a skill can be described as a hierarchical series of steps. It begins with knowledge of the skill, progresses to comprehending its use in science activities, and culminates in its application in scientific settings, either in the classroom or in the world at large. This hierarchy is based on an organizational structure of educational objectives developed by Bloom (1956).

At the first level of this hierarchy or taxonomy students can provide a definition of a process skill or can recognize a correct definition when they encounter one. Simply being able to cite a definition does not ensure that the student understands the skill or could recognize its occurrence in a scientific experiment (Anderson 1972). At the next level, comprehension, students are able to discriminate between instances and non instances of the skill being performed. This level is a critical interim step in the mastery of skills, for without comprehension of the skill there is little chance that it can be applied in a systematic way in science activities. At the third level, application, the student is able to perform the skill in real life or in simulated settings. The hierarchy is summarized visually in table 4–2.

Table 4–2 **A Conceptual Model of Skill Learning**

Level	Learner Behavior
Application	The learner can utilize the skill in either real life or simulated settings.
Comprehension	The learner can recognize a skill being correctly applied.
Knowledge	The learner can produce or recognize the correct definition of a skill.

This hierarchy is based on a conceptual view of skill learning. It views skills as actions based upon concepts, which are classes or categories that are defined by essential characteristics (Klausmeier 1974). Skill-related concepts in the science curriculum include observing, inferring, classifying, and controlling variables, among others. Each of these skills can be thought of as a category of behavior. Performance of the skill is dependent upon an understanding of the concepts involved. For example, the process skill of classifying is based upon students' understanding of the concept of this skill. To be able to classify, students must first understand what classifying is.

This hierarchical model of skill learning has several implications. First, it suggests an optimal series of steps in teaching these skills; the learner must first know and understand a skill before he or she can apply it. Related to this is the idea that failure to perform at one level may be traceable to a lower level; that is, a student's lack of comprehension of a skill may be the reason he or she cannot apply a skill. Consequently, adequate instruments to measure students' comprehension of different skills must be a component of every science teacher's repertoire.

In the final analysis, evaluating students' acquisition of process skills involves measuring their ability to *do* something, whether this be forming hypotheses, controlling variables, or interpreting data. But as we have said, students' inability to perform a certain skill may arise from their lack of knowledge about that skill. For example, students who do not know what hierarchical classification is would not be able to take an array of objects and classify them hierarchically. This suggests a two-step method of evaluation in which the teacher measures students' understanding of a skill before asking students to apply the skill itself. A typical question might be: "What do people do when they classify?"

Although measuring each individual student's ability to perform a process skill can be a cumbersome activity, requiring expendable or expensive equipment, we believe that it is essential for students to perform these skills with real objects. Nevertheless, the teacher can gather valuable information about student capabilities through paper-and-pencil measures that are easy to construct, administer, and score.

An excellent way of measuring students' understanding of a skill is to present examples and nonexamples of the skill being used and ask students to classify these examples. As an example of this type of item, consider the following exercise, which describes an activity designed to measure students' understanding of the skills of observation and inference. We encourage you to complete this exercise to reinforce your understanding of these processes as well as to give you a first-hand experience with this type of evaluation item.

Exercise 4.6

Directions: Read the following description of a science class and identify the statements made by students as being either observations (0), generalizing inferences (G), predicting inferences (P), or explanatory inferences (E).

Mr. Jones's class was discussing some fruits and vegetables they had in front of them. Mr. Jones began the lesson by asking: "Look at the vegetables. What do you notice about the watermelon, cucumber, and yellow squash?"

1. _____ "The watermelon is big."

2. _____ "The cucumber is long and thin."

3. _____ "The yellow squash has seeds inside of it."

4. _____ "So does the watermelon."

5. _____ "And the cucumber, too."
"Feel the insides of all of them. How do they feel?" asked Mr. Jones.

6. _____ "Vegetables are moist inside."
"Now feel their coverings," said Mr. Jones.

7. _____ "Why, they're all waxy!"
"Why do you think the covering feels that way?" asked Mr. Jones.

8. _____ "To keep in the moisture."
Mr. Jones asked, "What kind of coating do you think a honeydew melon would have?"

9. _____ "I think it would be somewhat waxy also."
"How about this vegetable?" (Mr. Jones shows them a zucchini squash.) "What will its insides look like?"

10. _____ "If the outside was waxy then it will be moist inside."
"Why do you say that?" asked Mr. Jones.

11. _____ "Because plants that have waxy coatings have high moisture content."

Another important dimension to measure is students' ability actually to apply the processes in new situations. This can be done in a number of ways, including paper-and-pencil items or with students in realistic settings. Each of these measurement formats has advantages and disadvantages. Paper-and-pencil items are more convenient; actual lab settings are more valid. We recommend a combination of the two, with paper-and-pencil measures preceding the testing in realistic settings. We will discuss in this section some examples of paper-and-pencil measurement items that tap students' ability to apply process skills.

Evaluation of ability to apply process skills requires that you place students in situations where they can utilize these skills on selected data. For example, after having done the animal classification activity described earlier, the teacher who wished to evaluate ability to classify might present a second set of animals and ask the children to classify them. This set would be unrelated to the first to prevent the students from merely recalling the previous system. The item could appear as follows:

Look at the pictures of animals below. Devise a classification system with at least three categories. Describe these categories and explain why the animals belong in them.

Criteria for an acceptable classification would be factors such as:

- Is the classification based on observation?
- Are the categories discrete?
- Are the different animals correctly classified in each?

Figure 4–11
Making Inferences

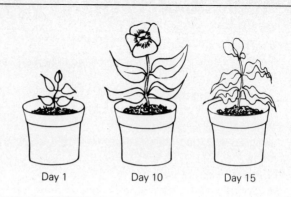

Day 1   Day 10   Day 15

Evaluation of other process abilities, such as observation, can also resemble the learning activities they are based on. An item to measure the process of observation might appear as follows:

Look at the pencil and make as many observations of it as possible. Be sure to give only observations.

Criteria for determining success on the item would be the number of observations and the extent to which the list was limited to observations.

One reason for limiting the students to observations is to determine if they comprehend the difference between observations and other process skills. Another is to prevent the list from becoming unwieldy. The list of inferences could go on and on.

Measuring students' ability to make inferences requires that you place students in situations where inferential processes are called for, then evaluating their ability to perform. This measurement also requires the teacher to select and supply data to process. For example, consider the item in figure 4–11. Look at the picture of the flowers. Based upon what you observe, which of the following inferences is better?

a. By day fifteen, the flower is past its prime and no longer is in bloom.
b. The pictures show three different flowers.

Explain your choice by citing observations.

Exercise 4.7

Before continuing this chapter, complete the following exercise.
In the flower example just given, select the better inference (above) and explain your choice.

Students' process skills can be measured as an individual or group activity. Both have advantages. Group evaluation can occur as activities in which the whole class offers and discusses answers. This format

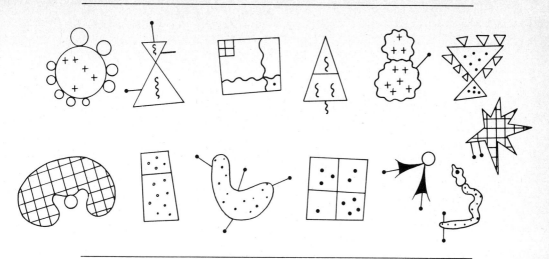

Figure 4–12

allows the teacher to gather considerable information in a short time and also provides the students immediate feedback. Group evaluation tends to mask individual differences, however, and students who are not performing successfully tend to recede in the group. Individually administered items can identify problem areas and provide a basis for remediation.

To summarize our discussion of evaluation procedures, please complete the following exercises.

Exercise 4.8

Directions: Read the following case study and answer the questions that follow.

Mr. Knox wanted to do an activity with his students in which they practiced developing thinking and discrimination skills. He had done a number of experiential activities with familiar concrete objects and now he wanted to see if students could work with unfamiliar abstract objects. He drew some abstract shapes on a piece of paper, then made an overhead transparency and some handouts. The shapes are illustrated in figure 4–12. He began the lesson by flashing the figures on a screen.

After handing out a sheet of these figures to each student, he asked them to draw a figure that was like one of those on the sheet but unique. When they were finished, he had individual members of the class share their drawings; the rest of the class had to guess which figure it was most closely related to. Lively discussions ensued.

Then Mr. Knox asked a dozen class members to tape their figures on the board and had the entire class discuss different ways to group them. After doing this Mr. Knox told them to look at the classes and try to

Figure 4–13.

incorporate additional figures into the classes they had formed. These figures are shown in figure 4–13.

Finally, he passed out sheets containing eleven more figures (see figure 4–14). He asked each member of the class to make a classification scheme for them and explain that scheme.

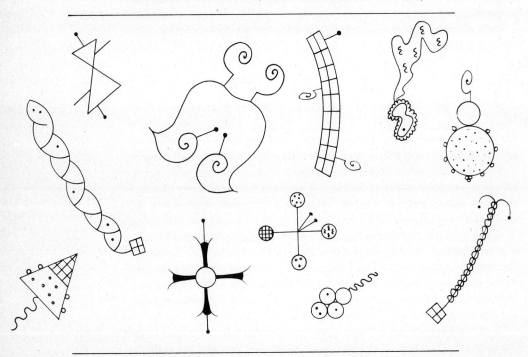

Figure 4–14

1. Analyze Mr. Knox's activity by discussing the extent to which it illustrated the characteristics of an experiential activity.

2. Identify the planning, implementing, and evaluating phases in Mr. Knox's lesson and describe them.

Exercise 4.1
Feedback

The first phase of the experiential model, open exploration, occurred when the students cut out pictures of food, mounted them on paper, and discussed them with their neighbors. During teacher-guided exploration, members of the class came to the front of the room and shared their pictures with the whole class. The teacher augmented these presentations by presenting supplementary questions to the whole class. In the final phase of the model the teacher selected a number of the pictures and asked the class to place them in groups (classification). Notice how the teacher in this activity, like the one involving Ms. Lee, concluded the lesson by measuring students' ability to classify. While this is not a formal component of the model, we recommend that the teachers measure students' acquisition of the skills they are teaching whenever possible.

Exercise 4.2

1. This activity is experiential. The teacher is merely having the children manipulate the objects and mirrors, as opposed to teaching them a particular concept or generalization.

2. This activity is not primarily experiential, but discovery. Radioactive decay is a concept and the teacher is actually using a clever example to help the students form this concept.

3. This activity is primarily experiential. It is designed to help children develop process abilities.

4. Finding causes for the burning rate of a candle is primarily an inquiry activity. For a description of this activity see chapter 9.

5. This example is a conceptually-oriented discovery activity. Note the close relationship between this activity and the one at the beginning of this chapter. The difference between them is that this activity has content acquisition as its primary focus, using processes as means toward that end.

6. This is an experiential activity involving the processes of observation and classification.

7. This is an experiential activity, though there probably would be opportunities to teach content in the form of concepts such as monocotyledon and seed embryo.

Again we want to emphasize that in nearly any activity some features of all three phases of science—experiential, conceptual (discovery), and inquiry—will be present. The phase the lesson is in actually depends on the teacher's emphasis. In the previous example with the lima bean seeds, the teacher was primarily focusing on the experiential phase. She could have planted beans and other plants and shown the children roots, stems, flowers, and leaves. If her goal was to teach the plant parts and have the students form a concept of *plant,* the activity would primarily be conceptual or discovery. While the children would still be acquiring experiences, the teacher's goal and emphasis would be slightly different. If her goal had been to have the students investigate what determines the rate of growth of bean plants, the activity would be an inquiry exercise.

Exercise 4.3

The following is a list of observations of a candle. The list is not exhaustive but serves to represent the process of observing in the activity.

1. White.
2. Flame is hot to the touch.
3. Wick is white (just under the burned part).
4. Wick is woven.
5. Candle has soot running down it.
6. Sooty odor from flame.
7. Black stream coming from flame.
8. The wax is melting.
9. Candle is cold at bottom.
10. The candle is becoming shorter.
11. Just under the flame the wax is wet.
12. Melted wax turning solid at bottom is yellow.
13. Candle is sitting up at an angle.
14. Candle at bottom is yellow.
15. Flame is fluctuating.
16. Wick is crooked.
17. Wick has red color at tip.
18. Wick is black where it has burned.
19. Bottom of flame is blue.
20. Feel heat and moisture coming from flame.
21. Candle is softer at top than bottom.
22. Rings make up candle's body.
23. Hexagon base.
24. Whole candle is cylinder in shape.
25. In melted wax on top, can see flame's reflection.

26. The wax is dripping down the candle.
27. Two little dirt marks at candle's base.
28. Black ring around area of candle's top.
29. Candle is ten inches tall.
30. The flame is yellow at top.
31. The melted wax burns your fingers to the touch.
32. The wax once melted and dried is cold.
33. The candle is smooth.
34. The candle is sticky to the touch.
35. The candle is odorless.
36. The melted, cold wax is very brittle when pressure is applied.
37. Candle has no taste.
38. If the candle is turned upside down, the flame goes out.
39. If the candle is turned upside down, wax drips faster (quickly).
40. When the candle is blown upon hard, the flame goes out.

Exercise 4.4

Two possible classification schemes are shown in figure 4–15. Certainly there are others. The ones you see are merely suggested as representative and not the only correct ones.

Exercise 4.5

1. a. Open exploration occurred when the students cut out the pictures and discussed them among themselves.
   b. Teacher-guided exploration occurred when the teacher called the small groups together and through questioning, encouraged each student to describe his picture to the rest of the group.
   c. Classification occurred when students grouped the pictures on the basis of similarities.
2. a. Exhaustive sorting was required when Ms. Cole asked, "Does anyone see any other pets?" In doing this she was asking students to scan the remaining pictures to see if any of those belonged in the group "pets."
   b. Reclassification occurred when Ms. Cole asked if there were any other way to group the animals. When students encountered difficulties she prompted them by asking if they all ate the same kind of food. When students are first introduced to the idea of reclassification, helps like this may be necessary.
   c. Hierarchical classification occurred when students formed groups and broke them down into subgroups, such as grouping pets into those that can be played with and those that can't.

Figure 4–15
Classification Schemes

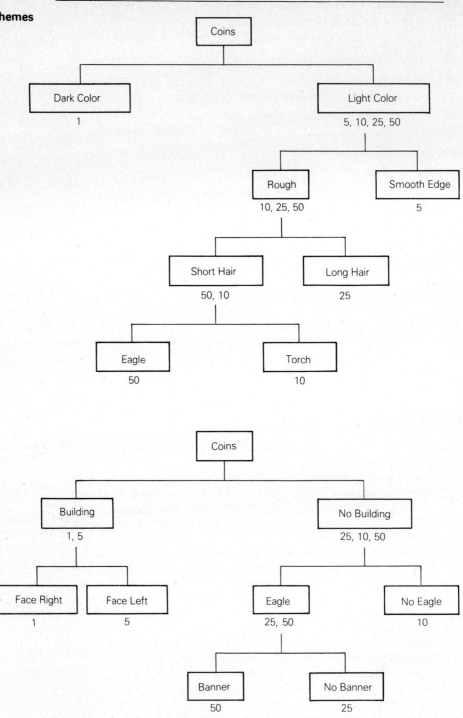

3. Listed below are a number of alternative ways to group the animal pictures. There may be others.

   a. How they move
   b. Kind of covering
   c. Color
   d. Size
   e. How they protect themselves
   f. Where they live
   g. Sounds they make
   h. How they reproduce
   i. Homes they live in

Exercise 4.6

1. Observation

2. Observation

3. Observation

4. Observation

5. Observation

6. Generalizing inference

7. Observation

8. Explanatory inference

9. Predictive inference

10. Predictive inference

11. Generalizing inference

Exercise 4.7

Inference A is probably better. Remember some other, unrelated inference may be better than either. Each of the three plants has four leaves in the same arrangement, suggesting that they are the same flower at different times. Also the structure of the flower on each plant is essentially the same, further suggesting that the pictures represent the same plant.

Exercise 4.8

1. Mr. Knox's activity was primarily experiential for the following reasons. First, the emphasis was on process. The students in his class, through concrete, sensory experiences, made observations and classified objects on the basis of these observations. In addition, there was no specific content goal for the lesson.

   Also, in implementing the activity, he first allowed students to make and share observations. Then the members of the class, through the guidance of the teacher, explored and discussed the drawings students had made. Finally the class classified the figures, both as a group activity and individually.

2. Mr. Knox's *planning* phase was very simple. After deciding upon process development as his goal, and selecting an experiential activity as a vehicle, he prepared the data for the activity by constructing the figures himself. He also planned for additional data by having the students draw their own figures.

In *implementing* the lesson he had students draw figures and share these drawings with each other (phase one). Next the members of the class discussed the drawings as a group activity (phase two) and then classified them (phase three).

Mr. Knox *evaluated* his students by presenting additional cards and having them classify the figures in each case. In this way he measured their ability to demonstrate the process skills of observing and classifying. Because he was measuring a process skill, it was important to present figures the students had not encountered previously.

References

Anderson, R. C. "How to Construct Achievement Tests to Assess Comprehension. *Review of Educational Research* 42 (1972): 145–170.

Blitz, B. *The Open Classroom: Making It Work.* Boston: Allyn & Bacon, 1973.

Bloom, B., ed. *Taxonomy of Educational Objectives. Handbook I: Cognitive Domain.* New York: McKay, 1956.

Dunn, R., and Dunn, K. *Practical Approaches to Individualizing Instruction.* West Nyack, N.Y.: Parke, 1972.

Klausmeier, H., Ghatala, E., and Frayer, D. *Conceptual Learning and Development.* New York: Academic Press, 1974.

Kofsky, E. "A Scalogram Study of Classificatory Development." *Child Development* 37 (March, 1966): 191–204.

Stephens, L. *The Teacher's Guide to Open Education.* New York: Holt, Rinehart and Winston, 1974.

Thomas, J. *Learning Centers.* Boston: Holbrook Press, 1975.

Wilson, O. L. *The Open Access Curriculum.* Boston: Allyn & Bacon, 1971.

This chapter is presented as both a supplement to chapter 4 and a source of ideas for experiential lessons you may wish to teach in your classroom. Each lesson in this chapter has the following organizational structure:

Objective

The objectives focus on the process skills to be developed as well as the major topic of study.

Background Information

This section is designed to provide you with information pertinent to the topic of the lesson.

Chapter 5 Experiential Activities

Materials

The materials section can help you in planning for the lesson as well as providing you with a checklist to scan the day of the lesson.

Procedure

The procedures contain suggestions concerning the sequence of steps to follow in teaching the lesson. This sequence is the same as that described in chapter 4 and includes unguided student exploration, teacher-guided exploration, and classification. These procedures are merely suggestions and should not be interpreted as rigid directions for implementing the lesson. We encourage you to adapt them in any way that makes professional sense to you as a teacher.

Related Activities

The related activities are suggestions for additional lessons, both in science and other subject matter areas. We encourage teachers to use these activities to develop comprehensive units of science instruction as well as to integrate science lessons with other areas of the curriculum.

Objective

Students will develop their observational and inferential skills and learn about insects.

**Activity 5.1
Insects**

Background Information

Insects are the most numerous group of animals and are found virtually everywhere people live. Characteristically the insect has six legs in the adult form (as opposed to arachnids—spiders and ticks—which have eight) and the body is composed of three main sections. Many insects, such as bees and silk worms are valuable to people, while others cause billions of dollars of damage to humans' homes, food, and clothes.

Materials

Jars, pieces of cloth, rubber bands, butterfly nets, magnifying glasses. This activity is best done in the spring or fall.

Procedure

1. Begin the activity by having students construct houses out of jars for the insects. The cloth pieces can be placed over the top with a

rubber band. Small branches and leaves can be placed in the jars to provide a living environment for the insects.

2. Have students take the jars home and collect insects, or take the students on a field trip around the school to gather specimens. Good places to look for insects are under rocks and leaves and near rotting wood.

3. Place the insects in a corner of the room and allow students time in the next few days to observe the insects. Provide magnifying lenses to help them in their observations.

4. Bring the insects to the front of the room and ask the class as a group to discuss the insects. Ask which is biggest, smallest, prettiest, brightest colored, and so on.

5. Ask students which insects go together. Classification can be on the basis of size, color, shape, and kind and number of wings. When you have completed this activity be sure to release the insects outdoors, explaining to students why scientists attempt to preserve life whenever they can.

Related Activities

The activity can be related to activity 9.15, in which meal worms (the immature larval form) develop into beetles. This could serve as a starting point for a discussion of the life cycle of insects.

Students can also use their insects to construct an "insect zoo" by using reference books to find out information about each of their insects. This information can be put on cards which are displayed by the different insect cages. Invite other classes in to see your zoo.

This activity can also be related to art projects in which students draw the insects in their collection or construct models from clay.

Finally, this lesson can be extended into a social studies lesson, in which the economic significance of insects is investigated. Using reference books, students can investigate how insects have both helped and hindered human progress through the years. Students can also read about and discuss the advantages and disadvantages of insecticides.

Activity 5.2
Ecological Study

Objective

Students will develop their process skills and learn about one method of studying the ecology of an area.

Background Information

Ecology is the study of the environment and its effects on living things in an area. Scientists, as well as people in general, are becoming more sensitive to the ways in which physical changes in an environment affect the plants and animals that live in that environment. As rare and potentially extinct species become threatened by changes in their environment, scientists are rushing to understand these changes and to devise ways of minimizing their harmful effects. An important first step in understanding the ecology of an area is through examination and study of that area.

Materials
Popsicle sticks, string, magnifying glasses, spoons, meter sticks, thermometers

Procedure

1. Break the class up into groups of three or four and supply each of the group with the necessary materials. Have each group mark off a meter-square section of ground outside. Encourage students to select a variety of locations.

2. Have students list all the different kinds of plants and animals in their study area. If they wish, they can further subdivide the square into quarters or eighths to make their observations more precise. Have students record the temperature at different locations in the plot. To motivate students, you might make this a contest to see which group can find the most living organisms in its square.

Encourage students to keep accurate records of their observations in a log and explain to them that accurate record keeping is an important tool for scientists.

3. As a large group, discuss the findings. List all the living organisms on the board and try to get class members to explain why certain locations have more organisms than others. Possible explanations include temperature, shade, water, and the influence of humans.

4. Have students classify the organisms into groups. Students can also classify the different locations on the basis of locale, appearance, or kind or quantity of organisms found in the area.

Related Activities
Try this activity at a different time of the day and see what effect this has on the observations. Also try the same activity at a different time of the year. Or, take a representative square and follow it systematically during the school year. Discuss how the same procedures could be done for a classroom and how time of day and time of year would effect the observations.

Investigate areas where population growth has had a definite effect on the environment (such as parking lots or pathways). Discuss whether this effect has been good or bad.

Take two roughly comparable plots and modify one by watering every day. Record the changes that occur. (See activity 7.6 for some data gathering ideas.) Discuss different ways people can change the ecology of an area. Try to identify both good and bad aspects of these changes. This might be an appropriate time to introduce the concept of erosion (activity 9.2).

Introduce the concept of density (number of organisms per area); have students compute the densities of different organisms at various locations. Relate this information to data gathered in discovery activity 7.12, Overcrowding.

Activity 5.3 Seeds

Objective

Students will develop their process skills and learn about characteristics of seeds and plants.

Background Information

Each type of plant has a unique kind of seed that sprouts and grows best under a unique set of conditions. In general, though, seeds sprout best in moist (not wet) soil that is warm.

Seeds (and plants) can be divided into two main types, monocotyledons and dicotyledons. The dicotyledon, like a bean or pea, has two halves and the seed embryo is contained between the two. The monocotyledon, like grass and corn, stores its energy in one section, or cotyledon, as the name implies.

Materials

Bean (lima and other) pea, corn, radish, swiss chard, lettuce and grass seeds, paper towels, magnifying glasses, soil, and milk cartons with holes in the bottom for drainage. If possible, try to get several different varieties of each kind of seed. For example, try to get green bean, lima, and pinto bean seeds, which can be purchased fairly inexpensively in large quantities from seed stores in the spring. Most of the seeds can be saved for the next year and used again, although the germination rate might be slightly lower.

Procedure

1. This activity can be started as a learning center or as a small-group activity. In a learning center, place all the seeds together in a large bowl or glass jar and have students sort them out on the basis of size and appearance. For a small-group activity, give each group a handful of seeds and ask them to describe the seeds.

2. Soak some of the corn and lima bean seeds in moist paper toweling three days, two days, and one day before the activity. Distribute these to students and have them compare the different stages of growth and the differences between the two kinds of seeds. Split the seeds open and look for the plant embryo in the middle of the seed. With the bean seeds, plant each half and observe what happens.

3. Discuss the seeds with students and ask why some of the seeds look alike. Plant the different seeds in different containers and dig them up at two or three-day intervals to check on the growth. Compare the plants that are produced. Ask students why certain plants look alike.

4. Discuss different ways that the seeds and plants could be grouped. Possible classification schemes include size, color, shape, or type of leaves.

Related Activities

Allow some of these plants to grow to maturity and observe the flowers and fruit they develop. This could most easily be done with bean, radish, or grass seeds. Plant the seeds that are produced and ask students to predict what the plant will look like.

Search around outside for other seeds to plant. One way to do this is to put a pair of wool socks on over shoes and walk through a field in the fall. The seeds stick to the socks and can be pulled off and planted back in the classroom.

Bring in seed spices such as sesame seeds, poppy seeds, dill, carroway, and fennel. Often these seeds have been treated to prevent sprouting, but you can try to sprout them anyway. If students are interested in growing them, many of these seeds can be bought at seed stores.

Try sprouting alfalfa, bean, or other edible sprouting seeds, and let students taste them. Sprouting kits or directions can be found at most health food stores.

Discuss other ways that plants reproduce. Bring in philodendron, ivy, and coleus plants, and root cutting slips in water. Also, you can start a sweet potato plant by sticking one end in water. The same can be done with an avocado seed. (Place toothpicks in the avocado seed so that the fat end is submerged in water.)

This lesson can also be related to discovery activities 7.12 and 7.20, which deal with the concepts of overcrowding and plant nutrients and inquiry activities 9.7 and 9.8, which investigate factors that influence germination and plant growth.

Objective

Students will develop their process skills while learning about factors that influence our weather.

**Activity 5.4
Weather**

Background Information

The weather we receive each day is influenced by a number of local factors such as latitude and longitude, time of the year, elevation, and large physical formations such as mountains and lakes.

Each of these factors exerts a characteristic influence on the weather we receive. By studying these factors, meteorologists can predict our weather with a high degree of accuracy.

Materials

Thermometer, barometer, compass, calendar with space for weather symbols

Procedure

1. Introduce the topic of weather by discussing different kinds of weather that your region receives during the year. Decide upon symbols to use to represent the different weather conditions, such as a smiling sun for sunny weather, raining clouds for rain, people in bathing suits for hot weather, and others.

2. Establish a time each day when the class as a whole discusses the weather. Mornings are usually best. During this time, record the following weather conditions: whether it is cloudy or sunny, dry or wet, warm or cold; how much wind there is; and which direction it is blowing from. (A stick with a piece of yarn attached to it works nicely here.)

3. Record each of these conditions on the calendar and compare to the day before. Ask students to predict what the weather for the rest of the day will be like and what kind of weather tomorrow will bring. Write these predictions on the board and discuss their accuracy the next day.

4. Some of the information (for example, temperature and precipitation) can be charted in a daily graph; any trends can be discussed.

Related Activities

Other activities that could be related to this topic include measuring temperature (5.5), phases of the moon (7.5), temperature variations (7.6), shadows (7.24), and storing solar energy (9.14)

For more sophisticated students, the barometer can be used to predict weather conditions more accurately. A barometer measures the atmospheric pressure; a rising barometer typically means stable, clear weather, while a falling barometer usually is associated with changing conditions.

Bring in the weather column from the local newspaper and compare with the students' predictions. Also, call the National Weather Service or a local television weather reporter and tape-record the conversation for the class to hear. Have students make up questions to ask the experts.

This activity could be nicely expanded into an inquiry lesson where the problem would be, "What factors determine the type of weather we have?" Students could then follow television or newspaper weather reports and investigate variables such as temperature, humidity and barometric pressure, and their effect on the weather.

This lesson could be related to a social studies lesson on the effect of weather on our lives. Seasonal changes as well as weather differences in different parts of the country could be compared and their effect on clothing, agriculture, travel, and recreation could be discussed.

Activity 5.5
Thermometers

Objective:

Students will develop their process skills of observation and inference and learn how thermometers can be used to measure temperature.

Background Information

Thermometers are instruments used to measure temperature. The most common kind of thermometer involves a glass tube with mercury inside. As the temperature increases, the mercury expands in the tube and rises. Another type of thermometer uses the expansion of a coiled metal strip. Thermometers are calibrated by placing them in ice water (0°C) Celsius and boiling water (100°C) and marking the level of the mercury each time. The distance between the two marks is then divided up into one hundred marks.

Materials

Thermometers, ice, hotplate

Procedure

1. Introduce students to the topic of heat and how temperature is a measure of heat. Ask them how we measure heat. Compare this process to the measurement of length and weight, and discuss similarities and differences.

2. Break students into groups and distribute thermometers to each student. Check to make sure that students know how to read their thermometers. Slight differences in the readings of different students' thermometers may be due to environmental factors such as being close to a heater or inherent thermometer differences. If the latter, this provides an opportunity to discuss the concept of measurement error.

3. Ask students to find the hottest and coolest place in the classroom. Also ask them to find ways to make the thermometers go up and down.

4. Make a list of places in the room that are warmer and cooler than the room average. Have class members try to explain why these places have the temperatures that they do. Compare ways of making thermometer readings go up and down and ask students to explain these.

5. Keep a record of the temperature changes over several weeks' time and at different times of the day. Ask students to classify these recordings into groups.

Related Activities

Thermometers can be used to measure temperatures in other places outside the classroom. For example, students can measure the temperature in their refrigerators or freezers, in a car parked in the sun, or in a basement and an attic. Using a thermometer in a variety of places helps students understand the utility of an instrument that can be applied virtually everywhere.

The effect of different types of ground covers on soil temperature can also be measured. This can be done by placing the bulb of the thermometer in bare soil, soil that has plants growing in it, and soil that has a leaf covering. Take readings at different heights above these soil areas by pounding a stake in each area and hanging thermometers at intervals of twenty centimeters. The temperature at heights above the ground can also be measured by attaching a thermometer to a kite.

Students can take their own temperatures by placing their thermometers under their arms. These readings can be compared to the readings they get with an oral thermometer borrowed from the school nurse's office. Students can also investigate the effect of exercise on body temperature and the effect of indoor and outdoor temperatures on body temperature.

Students can check the accuracy of their thermometers by placing them in ice slush and boiling water. (Make sure that the thermometers will not melt.)

Activity 5.6
Smell

Objective

Students will develop process skills and increase their understanding of the sense of smell.

Background Information

The sense of smell is probably the poorest developed of our five senses.

Other animals have a much more acute sense of smell and use it to hunt for food and avoid capture.

Our noses smell things when molecules or small particles of the substance are carried through the air to specially adapted nerve endings in the insides of our nose. These nerve endings then carry the message up to our brains where the information is compared to past information and recognized.

Materials

Plastic pill containers, film containers or baby food bottles, gauze, clear plastic wrap, a variety of "smellables": banana chips, cinnamon, cloves, garlic, onion, chocolate, strawberries, and so on

Procedure

1. Place the materials in different containers and cover these with gauze so the students cannot see what is in them. If using the baby food jars, these should be covered with paper so students cannot see inside. With some substances, make two containers, and cover one with clear plastic wrap before covering with gauze. In some containers, mix two substances like chocolate and cinnamon together. Number or letter the containers so you can talk about them later.

2. Pass the containers around to students or place them in a learning center. Have students try to identify the contents of each container.

3. Ask students why different people said different things about containers (the ones that had mixed substances). Also ask why students had difficulty identifying certain containers (the ones that were covered with clear plastic).

4. Ask students to group their observations on the basis of similarities in smells and then reveal what was in each container. Ask students to reexamine their classifications and reclassify with the new knowledge that they have.

Related Activities

Spray an aerosol air freshner in one corner of the room and ask students to raise their hands when they smell it. Clear the air and repeat in another corner. Have students record the time and graph the results, using distance on the horizontal axis and time on the vertical. Repeat the activity with a fan either blowing toward or away from students. Also try spraying the can into a plastic bag and compare this with the other activities.

Encourage students to discuss how we control the spread of smells in our kitchen through the use of different types of containers. Also, discuss how animals use the sense of smell to find food. Experiment with this idea by placing two clear plastic cups with sugar water in them in similar locations outdoors. Cover one with clear plastic wrap and compare what happens to the two.

This lesson could be incorporated in a unit on our bodies that would include lessons on sounds and hearing (5.7), the sense of touch (5.12), and heart rate (9.9).

Activity 5.7 Sounds and Hearing

Objective

Students will develop their process skills and learn about the sense of hearing.

Background Information

The sense of hearing is one of our five senses, and provides us with valuable information about our environment. The process of hearing occurs when sound vibrations in the air strike the ear drum, causing the tympanic membrane in the ear to vibrate. Nerves in our ears then carry the message to our brain where the information is sorted out and understood.

Materials

Tape recorder, string, cans, stethoscope

Procedure

1. Tape-record a number of common sounds around the house. Some possibilities include: a car starting, a doorbell ringing, pans rattling, a door slamming, an alarm clock ringing, a clock ticking, and a saw sawing.

2. Play the tape for students and have them try to identify the sources of the different sounds. Discuss why some sounds are easier to identify than others.

3. Play the tape at different volumes and discuss the effect that this has on being able to identify sounds. If your tape recorder has different speeds, play the tape at a slower and faster rate and discuss what happened. Do the same with a record.

4. List the sounds on the board. Discuss different ways to classify the sounds. Some possible classification schemes include: loud and soft, short and long, high and low, pleasant and unpleasant, metallic and nonmetallic, mechanical and nonmechanical. Encourage students to develop their own classification systems.

Related Activities

Turn the tape recorder on one morning when students are arriving, but do not tell them that it's on. Play it back later and have the students try to identify the different sounds.

Let students construct their own sound tapes. These can be placed in a learning center with response and answer sheets.

Investigate the effect that distance has on sound by placing students at five-meter intervals outdoors. Have them turn away from the sound source (such as a portable radio) so that visual cues cannot be used. Turn the radio on to different volumes and have students raise their hands when they can hear the sound. Ask if they can identify the message. The farther away the student, the harder it will be for them to hear and the longer it will take them to hear. This data can be graphed.

Do the same activity on a windy day and compare the effect of having the sound source upwind and downwind to the listeners. Explain to students that it takes time for sound waves to travel through the atmosphere and that this provides one means of judging the distance of an approaching thunderstorm. The light from lightning reaches us almost immediately (at a rate of about 186,000 miles per second), while sound takes approximately five seconds to travel one mile. So, if students count from the time they see lightning to the time they hear thunder and divide by five, they'll have a crude indication of the distance of the storm.

Sound also travels through solids and liquids, which is why we can hear sound through a wall and under water. This property can be illustrated by constructing a string telephone with cans as speakers/receivers. Have students investigate the effect of string tightness on transmission and see if sound can be transmitted around corners. Sound transmission can also be investigated with conductors (7.8) and insulators (7.21).

Also, if the school nurse has a stethoscope, ask to borrow it and allow students to hear their heart rate and their stomachs gurgling before and after lunch. If a stethoscope is unavailable, an inexpensive one can be made from a funnel and hollow rubber tubing.

The use of the sense of hearing to find direction can be illustrated by having a blindfolded student stand in a circle of students and point to the person who spoke. Our ears can help us locate sounds by registering the time gap between the time that the sound hits either ear; the closer ear to the sound receives the sound earlier. Cover up one ear with an earmuff or plug of cotton and see what effect this has on a person's ability to locate sounds.

Objective

Students will develop their process skills and learn about different properties of rocks.

**Activity 5.8
Rocks**

Background Information

Rocks are composed of different minerals and the composition of these minerals gives rocks their characteristic qualities such as color and hardness. Rocks can be classified into three types on the basis of how they were formed. Igneous rocks, such as granite, basalt, or obsidian, were formed from hot lava or magma that cooled and hardened. Sedimentary rocks, such as sandstone, shale, or limestone, were formed by the accumulation of tiny particles of sediment over the years. These tiny particles can be seen and felt when these rocks are rubbed. Metamorphic rocks, such as slate or marble, were formed when either igneous or sedimentary rocks were exposed to tremendous heat or pressure in the earth.

After rocks are formed, they are exposed to a number of weathering agents, such as water, wind, and changing temperatures. The effect of these weathering agents is to break or wear larger rocks into smaller rocks and to smooth off rough edges. The smooth rocks that you find near water have been smoothed and rounded by the tumbling actions of the water.

Materials

Different kinds of rocks, hand lenses. Students can be encouraged to bring various rocks from their yards, or from their travels. These can be supplemented by going to a garden or construction store. Typically, the people in these places would be glad to give or sell small bags of different kinds of rock. They can also provide information about what kind of rocks they are and where they came from.

Procedure

1. Have students form groups of three or four and provide each group with a set of rocks and at least one hand lens.

2. Ask each group to explore the rocks they have and to make notes to compare with the rest of the class.

3. In a large group, discuss how the different rocks were formed. Distinct layers are clues to sedimentary rocks, and air bubbles are often found in igneous rocks.

4. Discuss different ways to group the rocks. Classifying them as to their origin (igneous, sedimentary or metamorphic) is one way; others include color, shape, smoothness, weight, and hardness. The rocks can be serial ordered in terms of hardness by scratching them against each other. The harder rock of each pair will not be scratched.

Related Activities

Locate a sister classroom in another part of the country and arrange to exchange rock samples with them. Prepare reports on the rocks found in your area and ask the other class to do the same.

In a social studies lesson, investigate the economic uses of rocks in your area. Find out if there are any quarries in the area and invite the manager of the quarry to come speak to the class. Find out where construction firms get their sand and gravel; contact these sources for information.

If there is a rock shop in the area, invite the owner to come speak to the class. Ask if any of the students owns a rock tumbler. If so, bring it to class and put in some of the rocks you have been studying. Tumble them for several days. Also, check to see if there is an active rock and gem club in the area. Members are usually enthusiastic about coming to speak to classes.

The process of sedimentation can be illustrated in several ways. One is to place a mixture of different-sized rocks, dirt, and sand in a larger jar with water. Swirl the contents around and leave it alone until the next day. Notice how the different materials settle out in layers. Relate the process of sedimentation to the phenomenon of erosion (activity 9.2).

To show students how scientists can use the layers of rock to infer things about the rock, examine your wastebasket at the end of the day. Ask students what the different layers of paper tell about the activities of the day (the sequence of activities and perhaps even the duration of some activities). Discuss the problems that scientists have in trying to reconstruct events from layers of sedimentation, and the problems that scientists have in general in trying to form patterns from indirect evidence (activity 5.13). You may also want to share the story found in chapter 2 about scientists trying to explain the existence of dinosaur bones at Dinosaur National Monument.

The activity could also be nicely expanded into discovery and inquiry activities. Different types of rocks, e.g., igneous and sedimentary could be displayed and compared according to texture, hardness, etc., and the concepts could be developed from there.

Activity 5.9
Lenses

Objective

Students will develop their process skills and learn about different properties of lenses.

Background Information

Lenses work by bending the light rays that pass through them. A convex lens bends light rays outward and the image looks bigger (figure 5-1). Most lenses in binoculars and microscopes are convex.

Figure 5-1
A Convex Lens

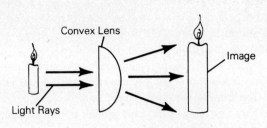

A concave lens, on the other hand, bends light rays inward to make things look smaller (figure 5-2). Double concave or double convex lenses, which have this shape on both sides, increase this effect.

Materials

Hand lenses, old glasses, old camera, microscope, newspapers (including picture sections and comics) magazines, different scraps of fabric, salt, sugar, seeds, and leaves; round jars, some with concave bottoms

Procedure

1. Assemble the materials for work in small groups. Each group should have at least one hand lens and a collection of different objects to look at.

2. Ask each group to look at the different objects and to take notes and draw pictures of what they see.

3. Pass around the different lenses (use old eyeglasses, cameras, and so on). Ask students to try to figure out how they work. If a microscope is available, set it up to look at the salt and sugar crystals and other materials.

4. Discuss the different lenses and ask the class to categorize them as to whether they magnify objects or make them look smaller.

Related Activities

Experiment with the overhead projector in your room and ask students to explain how lenses are used in it. Do the same for slide and movie projectors. Examine bifocal and trifocal eyeglasses if they are available and try to figure out how they work.

Have the school nurse come in and give eye examinations to students.

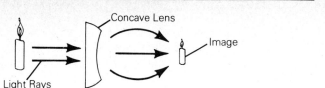

Figure 5-2
A Concave Lens

Explain to students how glass lenses can be used to correct near and farsightedness.

A simple magnifying glass can be made with a piece of wire and a drop of water. Bend a ten-centimeter piece of wire so that there is a small loop at one end. Place a drop of water in the loop and observe what happens. Some of the earliest magnifying glasses were made in this fashion.

Experiment with different-sized jars to see how they can act as lenses. Try looking through them with and without water. Also try looking down into different depths of water.

If the school has a prism, bring it to class and hold it up to sunlight. If a prism is unavailable, the same effect can be obtained with a piece of cut glass, like the pieces found in chandeliers. Or make a prism by placing three glass microscope slides upright in clay to form a triangle. Tape the edges together with thin strips of transparent plastic tape and fill with water. Try the prism out on different sources of light, such as sunlight, candle flame, and a flashlight.

This activity can also be related to discovery activity 5.17, where the effects of lenses and mirrors could be compared to their effect on images.

Objective

Students will develop their process skills and learn about properties of liquids.

**Activity 5.10
Liquids**

Background Information

Liquids are one of the three states of matter (the other two are solids and gases). Liquids have weight and volume but take the shape of the container in which they are placed.

The molecules of a liquid have a certain amount of attraction for each other, which varies with different liquids. This attraction is manifested in surface tension, that causes round drops of water to form on a waxed car, (waxing reduces the attraction between the paint and the water).

Surface tension also allows a glass of water to be filled over the top without spilling.

Materials

Different-sized water containers, plastic bags, graduated cylinders, eye droppers, wax paper, aluminum foil, plastic wrap, liquid detergent, white vinegar, alcohol, oil, sugar, salt, syrup

Procedure

1. This activity is probably best done at a learning center where a faucet and sink are available, as students will be pouring water into containers and some spilling is to be expected.

2. Place equal amounts of water in different-sized containers, including a plastic bag, and ask students to guess which container has more.

3. Have students pour the water into graduated cylinders to measure the volume and then weigh the liquids on a scale. After they've done that, encourage students to pour the liquid back into the original containers.

4. Discuss what happened. Encourage students to try to explain why some containers look like they hold more or less of a liquid.

Related Activities

Place drops of different liquids on waxed paper and view from the side to get a view of the drop shape. Try mixing liquids and see what effect this has on the shape and size of the drop. Place the drops on different kinds of surfaces (aluminum foil, waxed paper) and see what effect this has.

Fill glasses with water until the liquid is flush with the top. Have a contest to see who can add the most drops before the liquid spills over. Add a drop of soap or alcohol to the bulging water and see what happens.

Float a razor blade on the water, or punch small holes in the top of a jar lid and place on top of the water. If the holes are small enough, surface tension will prevent the water from flowing in the holes. Then add a drop of detergent to the water and see what happens.

Punch a small hole in the bottom of a can and put water in it. Measure the length of the column before it breaks into drops. Try this with different liquids and compare these results with the shape of the drops formed earlier. This lesson can also be related to discovery activities 7.3 and 7.4, which deal with the distillation and buoyancy, and with inquiry activity 9.12, which deals with viscosity.

Objective
Students will develop their process skills and learn about birds.

Background Information
Birds are one of two warm-blooded species of animals, the other being mammals. Descended from reptiles, birds have a number of structural modifications that allow them to fly. These include hollow bones for lightness, special bone growths to attach the muscles for flying, and feathers.

Birds reproduce by laying eggs. This typically occurs in the spring. Each species lays a characteristic number of eggs. The male of each species is typically larger, and is more brightly colored to attract the female during mating season.

Birds are a broadly diversified species, found in virtually every place people live. Birds have developed a number of adaptations to accommodate to these different environments. Adaptations include modified bills and feet as well as specialized body structures (as in flamingos).

Materials
Bird feeder, bird feed, bird identification book, binoculars

Procedure

1. Set up one or more bird feeding stations outside a class window and stock with bird feed. If possible to set up two, stock them with different kinds of food, such as birdseed in one and bread in the other. If space is available, put a pan of water out for birds to drink and wash in. If birds become distractive during other class activities, the shade at that window can be drawn.

2. After about a week or so, start to record the feeding patterns of birds at different times of day and at different seasons.

3. As different birds appear, try to identify the species and whether male or female. The bird identification book will probably be essential here.

4. Discuss the different types of birds and their feeding patterns. Daily or weekly graphs can be constructed to chart their appearance. Ask students to group the birds. Possible classification schemes include size, color, what they eat, and when they come to the feeder.

Related Activities
Take a walk in a wooded area around the school and try to find as many different kinds of birds as possible. Compare your sightings with the

number and kinds of birds that appeared at your feeder and ask students to explain differences. Possible explanations include differences in diet and proximity of the school to their natural habitat. Discuss similarities and differences between bird behavior and that of fish (9.14) and insects (9.5).

Find out if there is a local chapter of the Audubon Society and ask members to come to the class to speak. People in this organization are usually very knowledgeable about the bird life in an area.

Discuss the different kinds of bill and feet structures of different birds. Have students explain the functions of these different modifications.

Investigate the process of bird migration. Find out from reference books which of the birds in your locality migrate and when to look for them. If you are near a major migratory flyway, make a field trip to a marsh area in spring or fall.

Bring the bones from a roast chicken to class. Have students identify similar bone structures in other animals, including humans. Point out structural characteristics in birds that help them fly. These include light, hollow bones and an enlarged sternum (breast bone) for the attachment of the chest muscles used for flight.

Activity 5.12
The Sense of
Touch

Objective
Students will develop their process skills and learn about the sense of touch.

Background Information
Touch is one of our five senses. It provides us with valuable information about the world around us. Nerve endings in our skin relay information about the weight, hardness, temperature, and texture of objects. This information is relayed to the brain, where it is coordinated with information from our other senses and with our past experiences.

Several factors can dull the sense of touch. Drugs, administered either locally to the nerve endings or to the brain, prevent us from feeling pain during dental work or surgery. Our sense of touch can also be dulled by habituation. For example, before we called your attention to it, were you aware of the pressure from the clothes you are wearing?

Materials
Cardboard box with two armholes cut in the sides and a variety of different-sized, -textured, and -shaped objects such as smooth and rough wood blocks, a plastic toy, rock, tissue, a stuffed toy, eraser, spoon, clothespin

Procedure

1. Arrange the box so that the students can put their hands in the box but not see inside it.

2. Have students take turns coming up in front of the class and trying to identify the object that you place in the box. If you wish, the back of the box can be left open so the class members can see.

3. Discuss the different kinds of clues that students used to identify objects. Discuss why some objects are harder to identify than others.

4. Ask students to classify the objects on the basis of touch only. Some possible classification schemes include shape, size, weight, and texture. Then include other senses and encourage them to develop other classification schemes.

Related Activities

Discuss the problems that blind people have in trying to lead their lives. Discuss how other senses are used to compensate for this problem and how the blind use indirect evidence (activity 5–13) to deal with the world. If braille books are available, share these with the class. Make letters out of sand paper and see if students can guess the letters without seeing. If they can, expand the activity to words.

Have students take turns writing letters on the backs of other students. As students get better at this, they can write their names on a person's back, one letter at a time, and the person has to guess who is doing the writing.

Using the same box apparatus, weigh different objects and place these objects of different weights in students' hands and have them order them by weight. Do the same with different-sized objects. To make the weight problem more difficult, tie the weights to strings so size is not a clue. If students are having trouble with the activity, limit the number of objects to two or three initially, slowly working up to more objects.

The same type of activity can be done with containers of water at different temperatures. Also, have the left hand in warm water and the right hand in cold water for a minute. Then ask the student to put his or her hands in two containers with water at the same temperature. The hand in the warm water will report that the water is colder than the hand that was in the cold water.

Objective

Students will develop their process skills and learn about the process of model building.

Activity 5.13
Indirect Evidence

Background Information

This activity introduces students to two important scientific activities; inferring on the basis of partial evidence and model building. Often scientists have to construct images of objects on the basis of partial evidence. For example, the scientists at Dinosaur National Monument reconstructed the sequence of events that produced the large concentration of dinosaur bones at that site from partial clues found at the site. In addition, astronomers attempt to describe the characteristics of stars that are millions of light years away by partial evidence such as their brightness, color, and movement in the skies. (A light year is the distance that a beam of light would travel through space at the rate of 186,000 miles per *second.*)

As scientists gather this partial evidence they attempt to make sense out of it by building a model or some type of representation of the thing being studied. For example, one model of learning involves a stimulus and a response and the strengthening of the bond between them. Scientists build models to help them understand and explain the phenomena they are working with.

Materials

Shoe boxes; clothes hangers; and diverse objects such as tennis shoes, balls, and wooden blocks, some of which are irregularly shaped. Put one or more objects in the shoe boxes and tape the boxes closed. Punch several small holes in one side of the box. Number the boxes for later reference. Break the coat hangers into pieces and use a piece of the straight wire to poke in the holes as a probe. (Children are less apt to cut themselves on thin wooden dowels, if available. Any long thin object will function as a probe.)

Procedure

1. Have the children work in pairs. Tell them they should try and determine the contents of the box without removing the cover. Tell them they may lift, shake, and poke into the box and do anything else that will give them information.

2. Have them record observations and inferences about the boxes' contents: whether it is hard or soft, shape, size, weight, and so on.

3. Pass the boxes around among the groups.

4. In a large-group discussion, compare the findings of the different groups. See which group made the most observations. Ask students to differentiate between their observations and inferences. Discuss which objects were hardest to identify and ask students to explain why.

Related Activities

Discuss how the five senses, used together, provide more information than just one alone. In this activity, discuss which of the five senses is used the most; which the least. Talk about ways that our senses are amplified, such as through eyeglasses, stethescope or even through the use of a wooden dowel or coat hanger as a probe.

Record the time it takes different groups to identify different objects. Do the activity again and compare the results. Discuss these results in terms of learning curves. Try the same activity with two objects in the box and compare the identification time with just one.

With older children, a discussion of *model building* and how it is used in science would be valuable. For example, the little solar system we visualize as the atom is a model that does not necessarily accurately represent reality. It is a device to help us visualize something we cannot otherwise see. The atom is "poked at" with electron beams, lasers, particles and so on. These probes allow us to infer things about the atoms we are investigating. In this sense, the atoms are investigated with a process identical to the procedure outlined in this activity.

Objective

Students will develop their process skills and learn about the process of measuring.

Activity 5.14 Weighing and Measuring

Background Information

The process of measurement is an important process for scientists because it allows them to quantify and consequently make more accurate observations. Measurements using number are not only more descriptive, they also allow accurate communication between scientists.

One of the most common scientific problems in making measurements is measurement error. The two major sources of measurement error are inaccurate or faulty instruments and human mistakes. Measurement error can be seen quite clearly when different individuals measure the same substance and get different readings.

Materials

Centimeter rulers, equal arm balance (perhaps homemade, as shown in figure 5–4), weights or paper clips (weighing about one gram), and wooden blocks

Procedure

1. The purpose of this activity is to introduce young children to the process of measuring and what a measurement unit means. As a large-group activity, begin helping them read common measuring devices, such as a meter stick or a scale. A large model of a ruler or scale for all to see would be an excellent aid.

2. Pass around standard-sized objects, such as a piece of paper, a book, a new pencil, and have students measure them and compare their results.

3. After the children seem to have grasped the process, assign them in groups to a variety of stations to record the dimensions and weights of various objects such as the wooden blocks or coins. They can also measure things like desktops and the height of tables.

4. Have each group record their measurements on the board to see how consistently each group measured.

5. Discuss the results of the different groups. Particular measurements can be graphed with the measurements on the vertical axis and number of people or groups on the horizontal axis. The shape of the curve should approximate what is called a normal or regular curve, as follows:

Figure 5–3
A Normal Curve

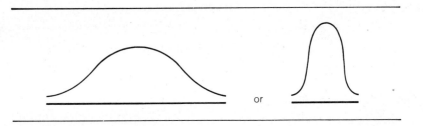

or

The narrower the curve, the less measurement error.

Related Activities

This activity is totally process oriented and designed to help children develop skills in measurement. A related measurement lesson on temperatures is found in activity 5.5. These measurement skills are prerequisite to success in a variety of other activities such as discovery activity 8–16 in which density is calculated and activity 7–4 where bouyancy is discussed. The lesson also is an excellent vehicle for developing children's skills with metric measurements.

Have students do some of the same measurements in a timed situation in which they are fairly rushed. Compare the graph of this activity with previous ones and discuss why they are different. Also talk about different ways to minimize measurement error, such as everyone using the same instrument, or everyone using more precise instruments. Also, have the class make a number of measurements over time and discuss what happens to the measurement error.

An alternative way of beginning this activity is to ask students to measure objects without providing them with the necessary measurement tools. Encourage them to improvise their own instruments, such as foot length or hand span. Compare the results of these measurements in a large-group discussion and discuss problems with this approach.

With older students, you may wish to introduce the topic of measuring for volume. This can be done with liquids, if the container is empty or by multiplying the height times the length times the width. Distribute containers to the groups and compare the results using linear and wet measures. You can also discuss the problems involved in measuring the volumes of irregularly-shaped objects. If they do not float, their volumes can be measured by placing them in water and measuring the amount of water that was displaced. The measurement of volume can also be extended to include the topic of density.

The diagram in figure 5–4 shows how a simple balance can be built for weighing light objects, such as coins and pencils. You may also consider modifications to make the balance more sturdy.

Activity 5.15
Animals

Objective
Students will develop their process skills and learn about the animal kingdom.

Background Information
Scientists have been attempting to categorize and describe members of the animal kingdom for centuries. Initial attempts, using observable characteristics as the major criteria, grouped together such diverse animals as birds, bats, and flying squirrels or fish, seals, and whales.

Later, scientists noted physiological structures and began to classify animals on the basis of similarities in bones, and internal and external organs. This process became further refined when cell and tissue similarities were noted and similar patterns of development were found.

Materials
Colored pictures or slides of a variety of familiar and unfamiliar animals

Procedure
This activity probably is most appropriately done in a large group where the teacher can use questions to help students practice making observations and inferences.

Figure 5–4
Some Sample Balance
Scales

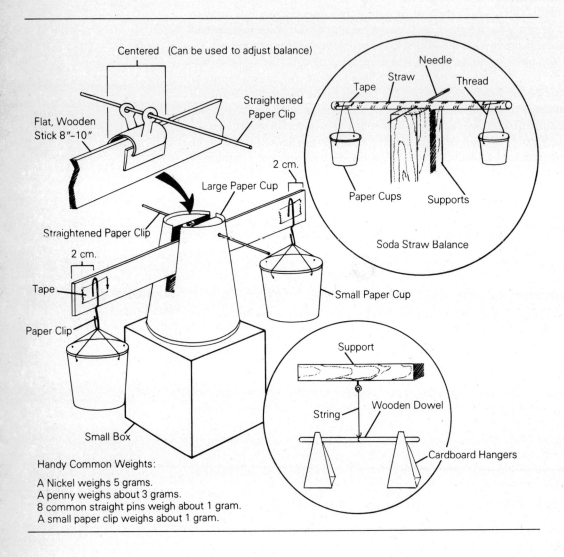

Centered   (Can be used to adjust balance)

Straightened Paper Clip

Flat, Wooden Stick 8″–10″

Needle

Straw

Tape

Thread

Paper Cups

Supports

Soda Straw Balance

2 cm.

Large Paper Cup

Straightened Paper Clip

2 cm.

Tape

Paper Clip

Small Paper Cup

Support

String

Wooden Dowel

Cardboard Hangers

Small Box

Handy Common Weights:

A Nickel weighs 5 grams.
A penny weighs about 3 grams.
8 common straight pins weigh about 1 gram.
A small paper clip weighs about 1 gram.

1. Show students a picture or slide of an animal and have them describe the picture in detail. Try to get each student in the class to make at least one observation.

2. Suppose the animal is a musk ox (a shaggy member of the cattle family that lives in the arctic). Ask questions such as:

> Where do you suppose it lives? Why? (Shaggy coat suggests cold weather.)

> What does it eat? Is it a carnivore or herbivore? Is there anything in the picture that tells us that?

> Who do you suppose its enemies are? How might it protect itself?

3. Show another animal and repeat the procedure. Suppose this time the animal is a water buffalo. The teacher could ask the students to compare the two animals by asking the following types of questions:

> Which lives in the warmer climate? How do you know?

> How are the animals similar? (Both are plant eaters, both belong to the cattle family, both have rounded snouts suggesting grass eating, neither has canine teeth.)

4. Continue showing animals one at a time and continue asking the children to compare and contrast what they have seen. You could show a variety of animals, such as snakes, mammals, birds, and even fish. Continue the procedure until you feel the children are tiring or their interest is beginning to wane. With young children this may be only fifteen to twenty minutes.

5. With all the animal pictures displayed or with the names of all the animals on the board, ask students to classify the animals into groups. Some possible classification schemes include: color, size, locomotion, where they live, kind of covering, and so on. Encourage reclassification.

Related Activities

This activity could serve as a prelude to a trip to the zoo. At the zoo, students could be asked to observe carefully and take notes on specific animals. These notes could then be used as the basis for a later classroom discussion.

A similar activity can be done with dinosaurs, using either pictures or plastic toy models. For some reason, young children have a fascination for dinosaurs, and a classification exercise like this encourages students to examine these animals more thoroughly, and in doing so, develop their process skills.

As a follow-up activity, children could be introduced to existing classification systems for plants, animals, and dinosaurs to show how the process is employed by other people. These systems are described in science books, encyclopedias, and even some picture books of animals. In doing so, children should be encouraged to understand that the classifications are devices people have contrived and used to describe the world, rather than forms of reality that exist and are waiting to be discovered. For a detailed discussion of this topic see chapter 4.

This activity can also lead directly to a number of concepts and generalizations. For example, pictures of animals eating grass could lead to the concept *herbivore* (assuming they do not already know the concept), animals eating other animals could lead to the concept *carnivore.* Other examples could also lead to concepts such as reptile, amphibian, and so on.

Each of the concepts mentioned above could also be the topic for a discovery activity such as *camouflage,* which is the focus for activity 7.4. As further extensions of the activity, inquiry activities 9.4 and 9.5, which deal with fish and insect behavior, could also be related to this exercise.

Activity 5.16
Vegetables

Objective

Students will develop their process skills and learn about vegetables.

Background Information

Vegetables can be classified in a number of ways on the basis of how they grow, what part of the plant we eat, and the large family to which they belong. For example, onions and garlic, swiss chard and spinach, and squash and pumpkins all belong to distinctive families. Family membership can often be inferred by structural characteristics and by similarities in smell and taste.

Materials

A wide assortment of vegetables. You can bring these in, or assign individual students to bring in different vegetables.

Procedure

This activity is probably most appropriate as a large-group lesson.

1. Display the vegetables in front of the children and have them taste the vegetables, smell them, and feel them. Cut small pieces out of each vegetable so that they can smell them and taste them more easily and see what the insides look like. Continue the process of open exploration until you feel the children have had ample opportunity to familiarize themselves with the vegetables.

2. As a large group, discuss the vegetables one at a time, noting characteristics such as size, color, texture, and smell.

3. Have students group the vegetables on some basis. This grouping

can be done physically by placing similar vegetables together. Continue the process until all the vegetables are in a group. Discuss the common characteristics of the group.

4. Regroup the vegetables on a different basis. Again discuss the common characteristics of the groups.

Each time the vegetables are grouped and the common characteristics are described, label the group. Some possible labels include: thick-skinned, bitter, mushy, juicy, and so on.

Related Activities

Wash and cut up the vegetables and eat them as a snack, or cook them and compare their color, texture, and hardness before and after. Talk about different ways of preserving vegetables for eating, and bring in some frozen, canned, pickled, and dried vegetables for students to see.

This activity can be related to a unit on nutrition in which the nutritional contents of each vegetable are discussed.

Cut up some of the vegetables into thin narrow slices and weigh them. Then place them on racks in a warm, sunlit, well-ventilated place to dry. Continue weighing over a week or two and graph the results. Ask students what implications these results have for the growing of vegetables.

This lesson could also be extended to discovery lessons such as teaching the generalization, "Sometimes we eat the root, sometimes the stalk, and sometimes the leaf in vegetables," or to lessons teaching the difference between fruits and vegetables.

Objective

Students will develop their process skills while learning about mirrors.

Activity 5.17
Mirror Images

Background Information

Any object that has a smooth, shiny surface can act as a mirror. Light rays strike mirrors and are reflected at the same angle that they struck the mirror. For example, if the light source is at a 90-degree angle to the mirror, the light rays will reflect back at this angle. If the light source is at a 45-degree angle to the mirror, the reflected rays will leave the mirror at a 45-degree angle (figure 5–5).

Materials

Small hand mirrors, pictures from magazines, outline drawings of simple geometric shapes, headlines or captions from newspapers, compasses, string, and pins

Figure 5-5
A mirror Image

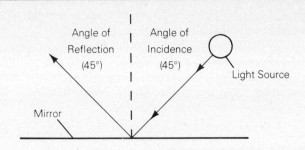

Procedure

This lesson is most effectively done in small groups and would be an excellent learning center activity.

1. Pass the mirrors out to groups of students along with the pictures and outline drawings and allow students to experiment with the mirrors and objects.

2. Discuss the results of their experimentation. Ask what happens to the shape and size of things when they are reflected. Also ask about right and left and up and down.

3. Pass out exercise sheets like those shown in figures 5-6, 5-7, and 5-8 and ask the students to use their mirrors to make the prescribed shapes.

With this butterfly, plus a mirror, make this:

Figure 5-6

With this shape, plus a mirror, make this:

Figure 5–7

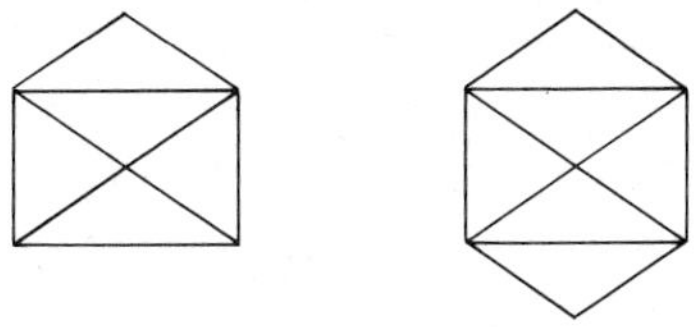

With this shape, plus a mirror, make this:

Figure 5–8

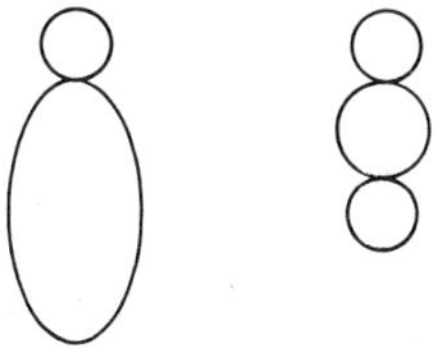

Related Activities

Have the children select some common objects, create unique figures with the mirror, and draw what they have created. These creations can then be displayed as artwork.

As an outdoor activity, have children reflect the sunlight to each other to send messages. Explain to children that this was a common communication tool before the invention of telephones and radios. Students could develop their own code system or could look up and try to use the Morse code. Also, ask students what they learned about holding the mirrors at different angles.

Place a mirror on the edge of a piece of paper and have students measure the angle of incidence (from the object to the mirror) and the angle of reflection. Do this with several angles and discuss the results. Also, hold a large mirror up in front of the class and ask class members in different parts of the class to tell who and what they see. Relate this activity to the previous one.

Experiment with different kinds of materials to make mirrors. Place a pan of water in a sunny window and look for the reflection. Note how it changes during the day as the sun moves. Hit the pan of water to make waves and see what this does to the reflection.

Place a clean pane of glass over white and black construction paper and use as mirrors. Which works better? Ask students to try to explain why. Experiment with aluminum foil mirrors. Which side is better? What happens when the foil is crinkled up and folded out again? Try dusting a mirror with chalk dust. What does this do to its reflecting ability?

Discuss with students why mirror images are backwards and upside down. Experiment with mirror messages, in which students write the messages with mirrors and need to use them to read them again. Experiment with different letters of the alphabet and decide which have bilateral symmetry (see activity 7.22).

Mirrors can also be curved to allow us to look around corners and to magnify objects. Borrow a magnifying mirror from a dentist's office and discuss with students similarities between it and magnifying lenses.

**Activity 5.18
Foods**

Objective
Students will develop their process skills while learning about foods and nutrition.

Background Information
The food that we eat provides the fuel or energy for our bodies, in addition to the necessary nutrients needed by our body to maintain and repair tissues. Ample evidence exists that how and what we eat influences our health.

There are three main categories of food: protein, carbohydrates, and fats and oils. Proteins, primarily found in meats, fish, dairy products, and legumes (peas and beans) are used to repair and replace body tissues and for energy. Carbohydrates, consisting of sugars and starches, are a primary energy source for the body, as are fats and oils.

Materials
Pictures of different kinds of food mounted on construction paper and snack foods like apples, carrots, celery, peanut butter, raisins, and so on

Procedure
This activity can be done with pictures or real foods. One advantage of working with real foods is that they can be eaten afterward as a snack.

1. Pass out pictures of the different foods to small groups of students and ask them to make as many observations as they can about the picture and to be ready to share these with the class as a whole.

2. As a large group, discuss the different foods one at a time, calling on different students to make at least one observation about the different foods.

3. Using masking tape on the back of the pictures, mount these on the wall in groups according to the classification systems that students suggest. Some possible classifications schemes include: color, whether eaten hot or cold, source (animal or plant), time eaten (breakfast or dinner), texture, smell.

Related Activities

Involve students in cooking projects in which they help to plan for, buy, and prepare foods. Some interesting and easy foods to make include oatmeal cookies, pizza, pumpkin pies (from a real pumpkin), and sugar cookies in which students make faces or write their names in icing on their own cookies.

Visit the school cafeteria and have the school dietitian talk about how he or she plans the school lunch program. Introduce the term minimum daily requirements and calories. (A calorie is the amount of heat needed to raise the temperature of one liter of water one degree celsius.) Bring in a number of empty food containers and read the nutrition information on the containers.

Have students keep a log of the food they eat over a week period. Discuss these logs in terms of nutritional and caloric content. Have students design a meal in cooperation with the school dietitian.

Take one school lunch and thoroughly investigate the foods in it. How much did the lunch cost? How was the food cooked? Where did the food come from? This last question can be answered at several levels, even looking at how different foods, such as spaghetti or cheese, are made. Students can also investigate how different parts of our country produce different products.

Take a field trip to a grocery store and have the store manager explain how the store operates. Discuss the classification systems used by the store and compare them to those of students. Talk about different ways foods are stored in the store—such as canning, drying, freezing, and refrigeration. Discuss the use of freshness dates and stock rotation as means of ensuring the quality of food. Check the prices of different quantities of foods and ask students to compute cost per unit.

This lesson can also be integrated into a social studies lesson, in which the foods of different regions of our country and other countries are investigated. Encourage students and parents of different ethnic backgrounds to come to class and share some representative foods from their different cultures. Ask students to prepare reports on different countries and to bring in one product from that country to taste. If possible, visit different ethnic grocery stores and ask the owner to talk about different foods and how they are eaten.

Activity 5.19
Cloth

Objective

Students will develop their process skills and learn about different kinds of cloth.

Background Information

Most of the cloth we use can be divided into two categories, natural and synthetic. Up until twenty or thirty years ago, virtually all the cloth that we used came from natural sources. The most common sources were cotton and wool, with some cloth being made of linen (from flax plants).

Recently, more and more of our clothing is made from synthetic sources. These synthetic fabrics are made by combining different chemicals at different temperatures and by drawing these chemical mixtures out into thin threads. These threads are then woven into a fabric in much the same way as natural fibers.

Materials

Pieces of cloth, different detergents, hand lenses, and graduated cylinders. The pieces of cloth can be obtained quite inexpensively as remnants from a fabric store.

Procedure

1. Pass out scraps of cloth to the different groups and ask them to make as many observations as they can. Encourage students not only to look at the different fabrics but also to feel their textures. Also, have them use their hand lenses to inspect the individual threads.

2. In a large group, discuss these observations, making comparisons between different cloths.

3. Throw all the pieces of cloth in a pile and have students sort them into classes. Some possible classification schemes include color, pattern, texture, and weight.

Related Activities

Discuss the advantages and disadvantages of different kinds of cloth for different kinds of clothes. Cost, warmth, and durability are all factors that enter into cloth selection. Discuss the different kinds of clothes we wear at different times of the year. Compare the clothes we wear with those worn by other cultures.

Test the different kinds of cloth for shrinkage. Do this by cutting out equal-sized pieces of cloth and soak in hot water for a half hour. Hang on a line to dry; when dry, measure these pieces again. Do the same activity again with the same pieces of cloth and see if they will shrink the same amount the second or third time.

Compare different kinds of cloth for their ability to absorb water. Do this by placing equal-sized samples of cloth in a graduated cylinder filled with water. Pull out and let each piece of cloth drip for a minute and then measure the amount of water that is missing. Hang the pieces up to dry and compare their drying rates to their absorption capacities.

Check for durability by tacking strips of cloth on a piece of plywood and placing the piece of plywood in a doorway where people will walk on the samples. Watch them over a period of days and observe which ones wear out first.

Compare the cleanability of different types of cloth by staining cloth samples with the same substance (dirt, grease, or ink). Wash and dry under similar circumstances and check for stains afterwards. Try a similar activity with the same cloth and stains and with different detergents or with different washing conditions (hot versus cold water).

Activity 5.20
Wood

Objective
Students will increase their process skills and learn more about different kinds of wood.

Background Information
Wood is one of our most valuable renewable resources and is a major building product in most homes. Factors such as cost, strength, weight, durability, and ease of handling all affect the type of wood used in a particular situation.

Woods can be grouped into hardwoods and softwoods. The hardwoods typically come from deciduous trees, which grow more slowly than coniferous trees, and are generally more expensive. Softwoods typically come from coniferous trees and are cheaper and easier to work with.

Trees typically show rings of growth, which mark the amount that they grow in a year. The wider an annual ring, the more favorable the growing conditions. Water, minerals and food products are distributed through the tree by vascular bundles called the xylem and phloem. The xylem is responsible for carrying water and dissolved minerals up from the roots while the phloem carries nutrients manufactured in the leaves down to the other parts of the tree.

Materials
Scraps of wood, nails, hammer, saw, hand drill. Wood scraps can be obtained free or at little cost from lumber yards or mills or from a

building materials store. Other kinds of wood can be obtained from junk furniture that people have thrown away.

Procedure

1. Pass out scraps of different kinds of wood to small groups of students and ask them to examine them and find out as much as they can about them. Give each group a nail and have them test the woods for hardness by scratching.

2. Discuss the results in a large group. Compare findings and try to determine if different pieces of wood are the same kind. Do this by matching color, weight, texture, and smell.

3. Group the pieces of wood into classes. Some possible classifications schemes are: color, texture, grain, size, weight, and hardness.

Related Activities

Test the different kinds of woods for hardness by measuring the amount of time it takes to drill through a standard-sized piece of wood, or by counting the number of times it takes to hammer a nail a standard distance into different pieces of wood. Compare these results with the density of the wood. Density can be determined by weighing standard-sized pieces of wood (for example, 2-cm. cubes). (Also see discovery activity 7.16, Density.) Place these standard-sized pieces of wood in water, noting how high they float, and relate this characteristic to hardness and density.

Test the strength of different kinds of wood by cutting standard-sized thin strips of wood that are approximately 20 cm. long and .5 cm. high and wide. Fasten these to the edge of a table so that they all hang over the edge by the same amount. Tie a string to the end that is out from the table and attach a container like a yogurt cup to the string. Gently place weights in the container until the wood snaps. Compare these results with the hardness, density, and floating data.

Compare the burning rate for the different kinds of wood by holding similar-sized pieces of wood over a candle flame. Measure the time it takes for the different pieces to ignite. Determine if ignition times are the same for different pieces of the same kind of wood.

Bring in branches from trees around the community and cut these so the wood can be viewed. How are the seasoned and unseasoned woods similar and different? See if you can find the growth rings in the branches, or locate a stump and count the rings there.

Have students read about and investigate the lumbering industry. Find out if any lumbering is going on in your area; if there is, visit a lumber mill.

In the previous chapters we discussed the experiential model, a teaching strategy designed to provide young students with the opportunity to work with data and develop their process skills. The discovery model is another process-oriented teaching strategy that teaches science content through induction. Process oriented means that observation and inference are emphasized in the procedure as concepts and generalizations are being taught. Inductive activities provide students with data and ask them to form patterns and regularities out of this data. Many of the regularities that scientists find are formed in this way. To illustrate what we mean by *process oriented, inductive,* and *discovery model* we will see how a science teacher uses this strategy to teach a science lesson.

Chapter 6 The Discovery Model: A Process Approach to Teaching Science Content

The Source of Sound: A Discovery Lesson

Mr. Kane wanted to teach his fourth-grade class about factors that affect sound. He began the class by dividing students into groups of three or four and passing out empty soda bottles, which he had borrowed from the rack by the pop machine in the teachers' lounge. When all the groups were settled he said:

"How many of you know how to use pop bottles as a whistle? Joey, do you know how? Why don't you show the class?" Joey then showed the class how to blow in the top of the bottle to make a fog-horn sound. The rest of the class soon caught on and in no time, thirty hooting pop bottles could be heard. After everyone had had a chance to try a bottle, Mr. Kane continued.

"Okay, now I'd like to see if any of you know how to make different sounds with your pop bottle. If we're successful in making different sounds, maybe we can form a band and play at the next school assembly. Go ahead and try it."

After the class had had a few minutes to try out their bottles, Mr. Kane asked, "Who was able to make different sounds with their bottle? Sally? Come up to the front of the room and show us how."

Sally went to the front of the room and produced a number of different-sounding toots on her bottle. "Excellent," praised Mr. Kane. "Now who can tell us what happened? Mary?"

"Well, when Sally blew soft, the noise wasn't as loud and when she blew harder the noise got louder."

"Good, and who can tell us what the name for that is? Karla?"

"Volume."

"Fine, so now we know how to vary the volumes of our instruments. How else can we make them sound different? Anyone? Well, why don't we try this. There are some water containers and funnels over on the counter. Each group take a container and funnel to their tables and fill the bottles to different levels. Leave one empty and fill one almost full and fill the rest somewhere in the middle. Then blow in them and see what happens."

After students had a chance to do this, Mr. Kane asked,

"What happened? Did the water change the sound? Angie?"

"Yes, the bottles got higher or squeakier."

"Okay, I'm going to draw four bottles on the board and you tell me how they sound." He drew figures on the board (figure 6–1).

"Now who can tell me which bottle makes the lowest and highest sounds, Gerry?"

"D makes the highest, C makes the next highest, then B, and then A makes the lowest."

"Does everybody agree with Gerry? Okay then let me label them. Then let's put these aside and look at another instrument for our orchestra."

After passing out plastic drinking straws to each person in the class he

Figure 6-1
Bottles

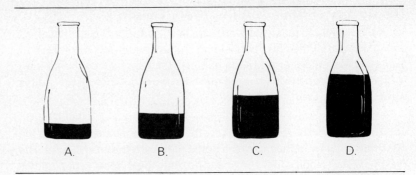

A. B. C. D.

said, "Watch carefully and I'll show you how we can make instruments out of these. First you have to flatten one end and then take your scissors and cut the edges off of that end like this."

Figure 6-2
Straw Instruments

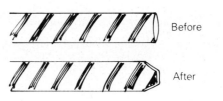

Before

After

After he had drawn this figure on the board and had given all the students a chance to cut theirs, he proceeded.

"Now if you want to make your instrument work you put the cut end against your lips and blow on it so the ends vibrate against your lips."

After he had given the class a chance to practice blowing on their straws he asked one of the class members to come to the front of the room. As she did, Mr. Kane continued.

"Now I'd like the rest of you to watch and listen very carefully while Sheila plays her instrument."

He then positioned Sheila so that she was standing sideways to the class. As she blew on the straw he took a pair of scissors and quickly cut inch-long pieces from the end of the straw. Then he asked, "What happened? Can anyone tell the rest of the class? Jim?"

"Well, when you cut the straw the sound changed."

"And how did it change?"

"I think it got higher."

"Why don't we check that out more thoroughly. I'd like each of the groups to take a pair of scissors and cut their straws so that one is real long and one is real short and the rest are in the middle. Then listen very carefully and see what happens."

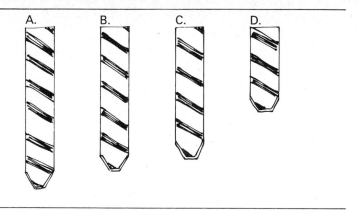

Figure 6-3
Lengths of Straws

After the class had time to try their new instruments out, Mr. Kane called the class back together again.

"Now let's see if we can draw on the board what happened. Look at these four lengths of straws on the board." (Mr. Kane drew the shapes in figure 6–3). "Which one makes the highest noise? Tanya? A, B, C, or D?"

"D makes the highest sound and A makes the lowest sound."

"Do the rest of you agree? That's very good, Tanya. Now I'd like to ask the whole class to look at all the data we've collected on the board. Can anybody see anything similar about the two activities that we did? Sharon?"

"Well, in both we made sounds."

"Good, Ken?"

"And in both we blew into something?"

"Okay, anything else? Well how about the size of the instruments? Did that make any difference, Jenny?"

"Oh, I know. The bigger the instrument the lower the sound."

"Does everybody agree with that? Is that what the diagrams on the board tell us? Okay then let me put that on the board. What else can we say about the data, Tom?"

"Well, this is kind of like what Jenny said, but the smaller the instrument the higher the sound."

"Does everybody agree with that? If you do I'll put that on the board, too. What's the matter, Joey?"

"Well, that isn't quite right for both of the things, because the size of the pop bottles didn't change."

The lesson continued with Mr. Kane introducing the idea of a vibrating column. He explained that when their instruments got "bigger" and "smaller" what was really changing was the length of the vibrating column. Then he brought out a bamboo flute and played it for the class with all the finger holes covered. He asked them to predict what would happen if he took his fingers off the farthest hole. After the class had a chance to experiment with the flute and see if it followed the generalization they had formed, Mr. Kane brought out a guitar and asked the class how what they had learned related to playing the guitar. This completed the lesson.

Discovering Regularities

Now let us briefly analyze Mr. Kane's activity, an example of the discovery model being used to teach a generalization. It is called the discovery model because students "discover" the generalization by analyzing data and identifying regularities or patterns. The teacher facilitates this process by providing students with examples and by asking questions that help them focus on important aspects of the data. Although the teacher helps students in these ways, the primary focus of a discovery lesson is on the active exchange between the students in the class and the environment in the form of concrete examples.

Let us contrast these discovery lessons with more traditional lecture techniques. For one thing, in a lecture the teacher does most of the talking and does not ask as many questions. In addition, when concepts or generalizations are taught, they are typically defined at the beginning of the lesson and *then* illustrated with examples. Discovery lessons, by contrast, start with examples and then proceed to a concept definition or generalization that described the data. The students, not the teacher, define or describe the concept or generalization. These differences are summarized in table 6-1.

Table 6-1 **Differences Between Lecture and Discovery Techniques**

Lecture	Discovery
Teacher does most of the talking. Typically, there are few questions.	Teacher talk is mainly questions. Students are actively involved in lesson.
Concept or generalization defined first, then illustrated with examples.	Examples are presented first. Students analyze these to determine concept or generalization.
Teacher defines abstraction.	Student defines abstraction.

Discovery lessons are also characterized by the sequence of steps the teacher takes in teaching the lesson. The lesson begins with the presentation of data. Mr. Kane's students did this by providing their own data with the bottles and straws they adapted. At other times the teacher can provide all of the data needed for analysis. However this is done, the data should be presented sequentially in small increments to allow students to process each bit of information thoroughly. After the data is presented, the teacher asks the students to make observations. When students have had an opportunity to make a number of observations, and are familiar with the data, the teacher asks students to put the observations together into patterns or regularities. These are typically written on a board or projected overhead for the whole class to see. A discovery lesson concludes with an extension phase in which students are helped to see the application of what they have learned to situations in their everyday world. These seven steps of the discovery model are:

- Data presentation
- Observations
- Additional data
- Additional observations
- Generalizing inferences
- Closure
- Extension

The planning phase of discovery lessons is crucial; the success of discovery activities depends in large part on the actions of the teacher prior to the activity itself. The teacher must consider the goals of the lesson, be able to select content that is appropriate for a discovery lesson, and must be able to select data to illustrate this content. Selecting appropriate data is especially important; the data are the primary tools that students have to form the abstraction being taught.

Planning Discovery Activities

The Goals of Discovery Activities

After completing this section of the chapter you should be able to meet the following objectives:

- You will understand the goals of discovery lessons so that, given a series of goals, you will identify those appropriate for the discovery model.

- You will understand how to select data for discovery lessons so that, given a list of abstractions, you will describe the best kind of data to illustrate each.

Planning any lesson must begin with a consideration of goals, and the goals of discovery lessons are threefold. One is to teach concepts and generalizations, the content goals. A second, interrelated, goal is to teach process skills, which students learn by practicing observation and inference in the course of the lesson. A third goal of discovery lessons is to give students a feel for the nature of science. By working with data, analyzing it for patterns, and forming usable concepts and generalizations, students directly experience the activities of scientists.

Experiential activities also emphasize process, so we can make a brief comparison of the experiential and discovery models by looking at two lessons: Ms. Lee's lesson on leaves in the last chapter and Mr. Kane's lesson on sound in this chapter. Ms. Lee wanted her students to develop their ability to observe and classify, an experiential goal. Her emphasis was on process, not on any particular content. By contrast, Mr. Kane wanted his students to learn about sound and to understand the effect that the vibrating column had on the pitch of the sound. In identifying this pattern, the content goal, students were strongly involved in process. What differentiates experiential lessons from discovery lessons, then, is relative emphasis. Experiential lessons are designed to stress process development while discovery lessons are more content-oriented.

To reinforce these ideas consider the following goals and determine their appropriateness for a discovery activity.

Exercise 6.1

Directions: From the following list, identify the goals appropriate for a discovery lesson.

1. A fifth-grade teacher wants her students to understand Archimedes's principle (a floating object displaces its own weight of water).

2. A kindergarten teacher wants students to sort a variety of shells into several groups.

3. A sixth-grade teacher wants students to determine what factors influence how strong an electromagnet will be.

4. A first-grade teacher wants her children to know what camouflage is.

5. A third-grade teacher wants students to identify factors that influence how fast a liquid will evaporate.

6. A second-grade teacher wants students to taste a large number of vegetables and compare their different characteristics.

7. A fifth-grade teacher wants his children to know how a lever works.

Turn to the feedback at the end of the chapter to check your responses, then continue to the next section.

Preparation of Data

Once the teacher has identified a goal and determined that it can be appropriately taught with the discovery model, he or she is prepared to move to the next planning step, *preparation of data.* The teacher selects examples that will illustrate the concept or generalization that is the goal of the lesson. Mr. Kane prepared his data by gathering pop bottles, straws, and musical instruments. A teacher wanting small children to acquire a concept of *vegetable* would bring actual vegetables to class and have the children feel, smell, and taste the vegetables. A teacher wanting the children to form the generalization, "Current flows between positive and negative poles," would bring batteries, wire, and flashlight bulbs to class. Table 6–2 shows other examples of content goals (concepts or generalizations) and the data the teacher would use in teaching them. Notice that in each of these examples the data are in the form of real, concrete examples. Actual vegetables are preferable to pictures of vegetables, and actual rocks are preferable to pictures of rocks.

Table 6–2 **Content Goals and Data Needed**

Content Goals	Type of Data
Sedimentary rocks	Different rocks brought in from the surrounding area
Days get shorter in the fall and longer in the spring.	Students' recordings of sunrise and sunset data
Insects	An insect zoo students built and provide with insects found in the neighborhood
Lack of sunlight causes plants to grow tall and spindly.	Plants grown by students in the dark and in sunlight
Tendons	Tendons on chickens and beef bones obtained from the butcher
Cumulus clouds	Actual clouds in the sky

Allowing students to work with concrete objects provides a welcome change of pace from other, more abstract activities. In addition, real objects help students understand that the science activities done in the classroom relate to the world and consequently that the knowledge and skills gained in the classroom are applicable to the world at large. In a sense the data represent a subset of reality; the more concrete the data the more accurately reality is represented.

Motivation and Learning

Another reason for allowing students to manipulate the examples in a discovery lesson relates to motivation. Tinkering with levers, messing around with batteries, and collecting insects is fun. Science, when taught in this manner, can be a welcome break from the abstract world of math symbols and words.

Whenever possible, the teacher should provide students with the opportunity to interact with and explore the data. If rocks are the data for the lesson, the teacher should pass them around so students can lift them, feel them, observe them closely, and in general familiarize themselves with the data. The developmental reasons for this have already been discussed in chapter 3. To internalize ideas about the world, students need to be actually involved in manipulating and interacting with that world. The child's world is a world of activity and exploration. By providing data to work with, the teacher is helping to ensure that the abstractions taught will be internalized and meaningful.

The Methods of Science

A third reason for providing opportunities to interact with the data relates to the nature of science. Anyone who has observed a chemist or

Figure 6–4
**A Concrete-Abstract
Continuum**

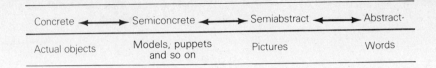

biologist working in the laboratory will attest to the idea that "science is doing." Allowing students to manipulate objects provides them with an insight into the activities of scientists and the nature of science. Of course it is impossible to bring zoo animals into the classroom and it is not always possible to go to the zoo; in this case, pictures will have to be used, and the children will learn much from the pictures. Our point is that the more realistic the data the more complete the students' understanding will be. It is relevant here to repeat our earlier diagram of a concrete-to-abstract continuum (see figure 6–4). Our primary concern is that you avoid teaching concepts and generalizations *solely* with words. When words *alone* are used the students tend to memorize them and their understanding is limited to recall. When concepts and generalizations are reduced to the level of facts, they lose their ability to summarize data and simplify the world.

Some Limitations of Concrete Data

Two other factors in data preparation and selection are cost and safety. Sometimes the cost of purchasing items for everyone is prohibitive. Prisms, expensive lenses, and other types of data-collecting devices are expensive and easily broken; they might be better used in teacher demonstrations or possibly in a science corner. In addition, some activities involve fire or chemicals the teacher might want to handle personally. Activities like this involve student *watching* rather than student *doing,* and so should be held to a minimum if possible.

Selecting Relevant Data

In planning to teach a content goal, it is helpful to analyze the concepts by considering characteristics and related concepts. Remember that concepts are categories or sets; membership in these categories is determined by the defining characteristics. For example, the concept *insect* has the following characteristics: body in three parts, an exoskeleton or outer protective covering rather than a spinal column, three pairs of legs, and (often) wings. Using these characteristics students would determine whether a particular animal was an insect. Teachers would select examples that clearly show these characteristics. Some examples of insects would have wings and some would not, so that students could see that wings are not essential characteristics.

The teacher should try to provide as many and diverse examples as possible. As mentioned earlier, young children sometimes have difficulty understanding that concepts refer to *classes* of objects rather than specific objects themselves. A variety of examples helps students to understand that the concepts they learn are really categories and not specific objects.

It is also helpful to provide students with negative examples, so they can understand what the concept is not. For example, in teaching *insects,* it is helpful to contrast the positive examples with negative ones like spiders and ticks (spiders and ticks are arachnids and have eight legs). Similarly, when teaching students to recognize *cumulus clouds* (a concept) it would be helpful to provide students with some negative examples like nimbus and cirrus clouds. These examples help students understand what the concept does not include; consequently, students form a clearer and more accurate concept.

Selection of data to teach generalizations in a discovery format is a complex process because generalizations involve the interaction between two or more concepts. Data must show this interaction. To teach the generalization, "Lack of sunlight causes plants to grow tall and spindly," the teacher should provide examples that show the interaction between *lack of sunlight* and *tall and spindly growth.* Students could grow bean seeds in a dark cupboard in the classroom. Negative examples would be plants grown in sunlight that are not tall and spindly. The generalization, "Days get shorter in the fall and longer in the spring," could be illustrated by having students record relevant data during the fall and spring. The procedure not only allows students to see the interactions contained in the generalization, but also reinforces the idea that science deals with the real world and not a world of books and symbols.

Organization of Data

You have now nearly completed the planning phase of the discovery model. You have identified your goal and prepared the data. The final consideration is how to organize the data for presentation to the students.

The problem of how much to organize data before presenting it to students does not have any clear-cut, definitive answers. With each lesson the teacher must weigh several factors: the amount of time available for a lesson, the ability level of students, the relative importance of content and process goals, and the importance of communicating an accurate view of science. As these goals are given different priorities, the amount of structure the teacher imposes upon the data will vary.

Mr. Kane had his data quite structured, and gave explicit directions to students about how to interact with the data. An alternative procedure would have been to give the students the bottles and the water and to allow them to figure out what to do with them to create different sounds.

Data that is more organized than necessary gives students an inaccurate view of what science is all about. We have seen that scientists usually work with unprocessed and unorganized data. One of the first tasks for a scientist is to try and find some pattern or trend so that the formulation of concepts and generalizations can proceed. When this is all done for students, they are given a false view of science and the activities of scientists.

Overorganized data does not allow students to wrestle with the data to make sense out of it.. It deprives students of the opportunity to practice their skills of working data into some comprehensive pattern. In summary, the degree of organization of data prior to the lesson depends on your judgment, as do many decisions in teaching. Judgment is what separates a professional teacher from a technician.

Take a moment now to answer the questions that follow before continuing to the implementation section of the chapter.

Exercise 6.2

Directions: Examine the following concepts and generalizations and try to determine the optimal kind of data to use in illustrating these abstractions.

1. Fires need the oxygen in air to burn.

2. Bilateral symmetry is a form of organization in which a longitudinal axis divides an organism in half.

3. Mammals are warm-blooded animals that have fur, give live birth to young, and nurse their young.

4. The coldest season is winter.

5. The greater the density of a liquid the greater its buoyancy.

Implementing Discovery Activities

After completing this section you should be able to meet the following objective:

■ You will understand the steps in implementing a discovery activity so that, given a description of an activity using the model, you will identify each step.

We have already established that a discovery lesson is one in which students are presented with a subsection of the environment and asked to form patterns or regularities about that environment. The environment is represented in the data or examples provided and the regularities are the concepts or generalizations that students form. The role of the teacher is to provide students with data and help them analyze the

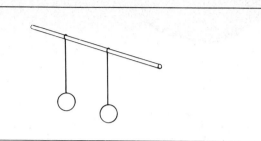

Figure 6–5
Ping-Pong Balls Tied to a Dowel

data. The student's primary role is as an active investigator as he or she makes observations and forms generalizing inferences.

The three goals of discovery lessons, to teach science content, to teach process skills, and to give students a feel for the nature of science, have already been discussed. By working with data, analyzing it for patterns, and forming usable concepts and generalizations, students directly experience the activities of scientists. These interrelated goals directly and indirectly influence the actions of the teacher during the discovery lesson.

Discovery lessons begin with the presentation of data, from which students are called upon to make observations and then inferences. Additional data are provided if necessary. Once students have formed the concept or generalization, the teacher helps them clarify this concept and test its relevance in other situations. These steps, which we listed at the end of the introductory section of this chapter, are illustrated in the lesson that follows.

The Discovery Model: An Additional Illustration

Ms. Sims was trying to teach her sixth-graders some characteristics of air and to show how these characteristics related to the flight of airplanes. She began her lesson by saying, "Today, we're going to continue our discussion of air and I'm going to show you some things and ask you to make some observations."

Ms. Sims brought out two ping-pong balls that were glued to pieces of string and tied to a wooden dowel. The apparatus is shown in figure 6–5. She showed the device to the class and asked them what would happen if she blew between the two balls. The class agreed that the two balls would fly apart, but when Ms. Sims blew between them, they came together. The class looked at her somewhat suspiciously, so she had several class members do the same with similar results. Then she asked the class to tell her what they saw.

"What happened? Anyone? Joe?"

"Well, at first the balls kinds of vibrated a little. Then they went together instead of going apart."

"And what did we do to make them do that, Kay?"

Figure 6–6

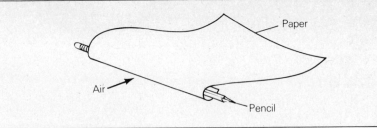

"We blew between them and they came together."

"Good. Can anyone figure out why that happened? No one? Okay, let's look at some more data to see if we can figure this out."

She then had each of the class members take out a pencil and a piece of paper. She showed them how to place the paper on the pencil so that only the edge of the paper was connected to the pencil. Then she asked the class what would happen if she blew on the pencil and paper, as shown in figure 6–6.

"It'll just stay where it is," replied Sherry.

"No, I think it'll go down, because the paper is heavy," added Mike.

"Any other ideas? Well, let's see what happens. Why don't all of you try this one out."

The members of the class then blew on their pencil-and-paper devices. To their surprise the paper rose until it was horizontal with the floor. As long as they kept blowing on it, the paper would stay up, a result that was contrary to their expectation. Then Ms. Sims continued, "Let's look at what we've just done and try to figure out what happened. First we put the paper and pencil together like this and blew on it like this. Where did the air from our mouths go?"

She then drew a diagram on the board (see figure 6-7).

Figure 6-7
Initial Diagram of Air Hitting Pencil and Paper

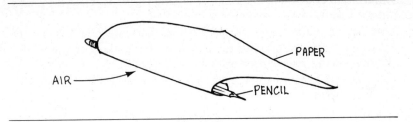

"It hit the pencil and went around it," answered Jake.

"And how did it go around? Who can come up to the board and draw a picture of how the air went and then what happened to the paper, Sarah? Good."

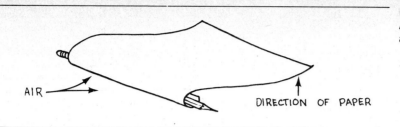

Figure 6-8
**Air flowing over pencil
and paper**

Sarah went to the board and added some information to the drawing (see figure 6-8).

Then Ms. Sims drew another diagram on the board (see figure 6-9).

She said, "Now look at this diagram on the board. Who can draw a picture of where the air went and how the balls moved? Kerry?"

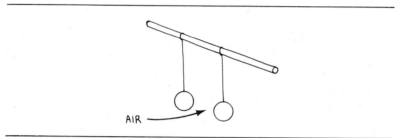

Figure 6-9

Kerry then added this additional information so the drawing looked like figure 6-10.

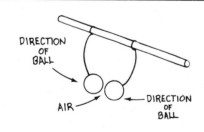

Figure 6-10

Ms. Sims continued, "What do you notice about both of the drawings? How are they similar, Marty?"

"Well, in both we blew on something and it didn't act like it was supposed to."

"How do you mean?" asked Ms. Sims.

"Well, when we blew between the balls, the balls came together, and when we blew on the pencil and paper, the paper went up."

Figure 6–11
**Spool with
Cardboard Attached**

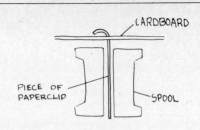

,"Okay, in both we blew on something, and how did the objects move in relation to the moving air, Fran?"

"They moved toward the moving air."

"Good; now let's look at some more data. I have an empty thread spool here and a piece of cardboard with a piece of paper clip through it. The long end of the paper clip goes down into the hole in the spool and the whole device looks like this."

She held up the spool and cardboard for the class to see and also drew a diagram on the board (see figure 6–11).

"What do you think will happen if I blow through the open end of the spool? Anyone?"

Some of the class members immediately answered that the cardboard would fly off, but others, remembering their observations with the previous activities, weren't so sure. So several members of the class came to the front of the room to try it out. Surprisingly, the cardboard did not fly off, but stayed spinning on the spool. This happened no matter how the students held the spool, even upside down.

Ms. Sims continued, "Let's look at the spool and see if we can see if anything here is similar to our other observations. Who can draw a picture of how the air went, Lucie?" (See figure 6–12.)

Figure 6–12
**Air Flowing Through
Spool**

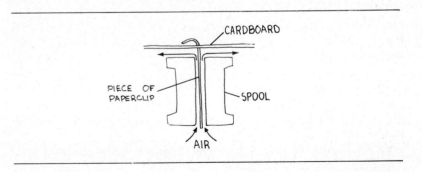

"Now look at this diagram and compare it to the other two. How are they similar? How are they different? Daryl?"

"They're different because they all used different materials like spools and pencils and balls." answered Daryl.

"They're similar, though, because in each one we blew on the objects." Theresa added.

"Fine, and what happens to the air molecules when we blow, in terms of speed? Do they move slower or faster? Jerry?"

"They move faster."

"Okay, now who can tell me how the speed of the air affects the air pressure? Can anyone? No one? Well let's look at the diagram with the balls again. Why do the balls just hang there? Walt?"

"Because of gravity. Gravity pulls them down."

"But why don't they dance around and move back and forth? Vernie?"

"Because the air pressure all around them is the same. If it's the same then they won't move."

"And so what happened to the air when we blew between them? Did the air move slower or faster and how did that affect the air pressure? Ken?"

"When we blew between them, the air moved faster. I thought that would make more air pressure but I guess it doesn't because the balls came together. That means that the air pressure must be less there. That's why the balls came together."

"Hmm, does what you said apply to all the data or just some of it? How does it apply to the spool and cardboard? Sharon?" Ms. Sims continued.

"Yes, because the air was moving fastest in the space between the cardboard and the spool. So the air pressure was less there than on the outer side of the cardboard so it stayed on the spool."

"Hmm. How does all this relate to the pencil and paper? Can anyone explain that? Abe?"

"I think so. When we blew on the pencil and paper, the air had to go around the pencil to go over the top. This air had to travel faster. When it did that, there was less pressure on the top and so the greater pressure underneath pushed the paper up."

"Okay, let's see how your idea works with what I have here. I have a funnel that you can blow through and a ping-pong ball that fits in the funnel. If you didn't think too long about it, what would you guess would happen if I put the ball in the funnel and blew in the narrow end? Greg?"

"It would fly out."

"That seems reasonable, doesn't it, class? But let's look at this again in terms of what we've just been talking about. To do that, let's draw a diagram of the funnel and ball and try to figure out where the air is moving and where the air pressure is greatest and least."

The diagram in figure 6–13 was then drawn on the board.

"Where does the air travel when you blow through the funnel? Kerry, can you draw arrows to show the class?"

After Kerry had done that, Ms. Sims continued. "And so where would the air pressure be the greatest and least and why? Tim?"

Figure 6-13
Ball in Funnel

"I think the air pressure would be least on the bottom and sides because the air is moving fastest there and that it would be more on the top because the air can't move there."

"And what would you predict would happen if we blew through the funnel, Tim?"

Tim paused for a second and thought about the question and then with a frown said, "I guess it would stay in the funnel, but I'm not sure."

The class then proceeded to try this out and to their amazement the ping-pong ball did stay in the funnel. Ms. Sims then asked the class,

"Now who can summarize what we've discovered so far? Who can put in a sentence what we've found out about air movement and air pressure? Julie?"

"I'll try. When air moves fast it exerts less pressure."

"Okay, and what's the opposite of that, Julie?"

"Oh, okay. When it moves slower it exerts more pressure."

"Does everyone agree? If you do, I'll write what Julie said on the board. Now I'd like to give you a problem. Pretend you're trying to design an airplane and have to make the wings. You have a choice of two designs that I'll draw on the board (see figure 6-14). Which do you think would be better, A or B? Remember, we're trying to get the wings to lift the airplane up so it can fly."

"How about you, Max? How would you build your airplane and why?"

"I think B would be better because when it was flying, the air would go past the top and bottom, but to go over the bottom it would just go straight back and to go over the top it would have to climb over the curve. So the air would be moving faster on the top and there would be less pressure there. So the greater pressure on the bottom that has slower moving air would push the wing and the airplane up."

The class continued to talk about Max's idea, discussing whether it applied to the generalization they had formed. Once the members of the class understood the difference between A and B and how B was a better design, Ms. Sims asked the class to explain why shower curtains always bend inwards when the shower is on, and smoke always goes out of an open car window.

Figure 6–14
**Two Airplane Wing
Designs**

Seven Steps to a Discovery Lesson

How does this lesson rate as an example of a discovery activity? To find out, we will be using the seven steps presented earlier. You may wish to take a moment to review those steps before reading on.

Step One: Data Presentation

The lesson began with Ms. Sims showing the class the ping-pong balls and blowing between them. This represented the first step, data presentation. Presentation of data served several functions. First, it provided students with a subset of reality. By using actual objects with which students were familiar, the teacher was able to bring a small part of the real world into the classroom. The use of real objects relates the science activities done in the classroom to the world. Consequently, the knowledge and skills gained in the classroom are applicable to the world at large.

Another function of data presentation is to provide practice for developing students' process skills by observing real and concrete examples. Students not only become better observers and inference makers, they also come to see the role of these skills in the total process of science.

In a lesson on sedimentary rocks, the students might be shown a piece of sandstone, limestone, or other sedimentary rock. In a lesson relating size and camouflage, the teacher would initially show a picture of either a large, uncamouflaged animal or a small, camouflaged animal. All data the students encounter will, when processed, help them form the concept or generalization that is the content goal of the lesson.

Step Two: Observation of Data

Next the students are called upon to make observations, the second step. In asking for observations, the teacher should be receptive to any and all observations and should regard all with equal weight. This procedure is recommended because it more closely approximates the process of science and the activities of scientists. When scientists first start to investigate an area, they are not sure which observations are important and which are not. Consequently, they make a number of observations, often recording these in some sort of log to examine later. The teacher, by accepting all the observations that students make, is able to communicate to students that science is often a trial-and-error, hit-and-miss proposition, rather than a smooth operation in which all the answers are predetermined.

For example, suppose the teacher in the lesson relating camouflage to size showed a picture of a zebra on an open sunlit plain. The children might make several observations: grass, clouds in the sky, six zebras in the picture, and hills in the background, none of which point to the generalization. All observations are accepted as of equal value. As additional examples are presented, students will gradually narrow their observations in the direction of the generalization.

Being nonselective about initial observations also minimizes the students' risk of "failure" in making an "incorrect" observation. Consequently it encourages even the reluctant students to participate. All too often the questions teachers ask have one answer, and the same group of students typically are quickest to answer these questions. It doesn't take other students long to learn that they cannot compete in a lesson or discussion. By beginning the lesson with an activity in which all students can participate, students are encouraged to participate. It offers the opportunity for all students to become involved.

Consider for a moment the accuracy of observations. There are several things the teacher can do to help students make accurate observations. One is to *provide all students with their own materials,* as Ms. Sims did with paper and pencils. When this is not possible, the demonstration can be repeated a number of times. This provides students with multiple opportunities to make observations and again is congruent with the activities of scientists. Scientists typically make a number of observations of the objects they are studying to make sure that their observations are accurate and reliable.

Another way that teachers can help students make accurate observations is to *draw simple illustrations* on the board. This allows the whole class to see clearly what is happening and allows the teacher to clarify points and emphasize essential aspects of the data. Ms. Sims diagrammed the relationship between air speed and the motion of objects. Mr. Kane sketched the pictures of the bottles and the straws on the board. Illustrations allow the teacher to simplify the data, emphasizing important aspects such as the direction of wind flow or the size of a vibrating column. Another way to ensure that students' observations lead to productive concepts and generalizations is to channel these observations through the use of tables and charts.

After students have had an opportunity to make observations, a number of things can occur. Students may be able to form inferences on their own, spontaneously. If not, the teacher may use prompting and probing questions to encourage students to make inferences on the basis of a single example. This would have been the case if Ms. Sims's class had arrived at the generalization on the basis of viewing the ping-pong balls alone. This doesn't happen very often and generally is not a good goal to aim for, since most students do not understand an abstraction with just a single example.

Step Three: Additional Data

To help students form and understand the abstraction, the teacher then proceeds to step three and presents additional data. This option provides students with additional opportunities to make observations and to form concepts and generalizations on their own. The more such opportunities students are given, the more autonomous they will become. Supplementary data also ensures that the abstractions the students form are based upon patterns in the real world and are not just empty verbalizations.

Ms. Sims provided additional data when she showed students the spool and the card. In the camouflage example, the teacher who showed the zebra picture would perhaps next show an insect camouflaged on a flower or a snake blending in with some leaves.

A great deal of flexibility exists in a discovery lesson, and the additional data may sometimes be presented in the form of a negative example. For instance, it would be equally appropriate for the teacher in the camouflage lesson to show another large animal, such as a large brown seal on a white ice flow or an elephant in an open field. This choice would extend the lesson; students would not arrive at the generalization as quickly as if they were shown a small camouflaged animal. The choice depends on the teacher's judgment according to the goals, and these considerations would be made in the planning phase. Showing a second large animal would suggest added process emphasis. Showing a small camouflaged animal would mean the teacher is more concerned with the content goal. In either case, both process and content are involved, but emphasis is slightly different.

Step Four: Additional Observations

After presenting additional data the teacher should again ask the students to make observations. At this point he or she can encourage students to be more selective in their observations, calling for similarities and differences between these observations and previous ones. Mr. Kane called students' attention to the relationship between the water in the bottles, and the size of the straws and the sound they made. Ms. Sims purposely focused students' observations on the air speed and the motion of the objects. The task for students during this phase of the activity is not only to make observations, but to make observations that relate directly to identifying trends or patterns. The focus of the lesson narrows from making a variety of observations to identifying those that are similar in all the examples. The teacher can speed this process by asking appropriate questions that focus students' attention on relevant aspects of the data.

Step Five: Inferences

After students have had an opportunity to make a number of observations, the teacher should ask students if they see any pattern in these observations. Essentially the teacher is now asking students to make generalizing inferences. These inferences may occur spontaneously or may have to be prompted. If necessary, the teacher may have to provide additional data or refocus students' attention on earlier data. Here, the teacher's questioning skills are vital.

When students are able to link the different pieces of data to form a concept or generalization, the teacher should maintain a supportive but questioning posture, refraining from comments like "You've got it" or "That's right!" A questioning posture places the major focus of the lesson on students and their interaction with the data. Discovery lessons should not be viewed as guessing games between students and the teacher, but as active attempts by students to find regularities in a small part of their environment. Teachers can encourage this position by remaining supportive, but responding to suggestions with questions such as, "Does all the data support or agree with what you say?" Mr. Kane responded to his students by asking if the class agreed with the generalizations raised by individual students. Ms. Sims responded by asking the students if the generalization they were forming related to and accounted for all the data. Statements like this remind students that the goal of discovery lessons, like that of science in general, is to formulate descriptions of the natural world that accurately describe reality.

Step Six: Closure

After students have arrived at the concept or generalization, the teacher should help move the lesson to closure by helping students accurately verbalize the abstraction. This can be done by asking students to define the concept or describe the generalization in words that not only describe the data at hand, but also extend to other instances not yet encountered. The abstraction should be stated in general rather than specific terms. If the statement is written on the board or overhead transparency, members of the class have a semipermanent record to see and encode.

When writing the abstraction on the board the teacher should encourage the class to examine it critically to ensure that the statement is complete and accurate and understood by students. In the case of a generalization, the teacher can do this by asking the class whether the generalization as stated accurately describes each of the examples provided. It also provides an excellent opportunity to check whether individual students understand the abstraction. A teacher can help the class examine the adequacy of a concept definition by checking the characteristics in the definition against the examples provided. In a lesson on insects, the teacher would want the class to see whether the characteristics of six legs applies to all insects and whether all insects have wings. Students not only get practice in applying these characteristics to the examples but also further refine the definition and consequently produce a more complete and accurate concept.

Writing down the abstraction also serves as reinforcement. Discovery lessons contain a measure of uncertainty; not all students will arrive at the concept or generalization simultaneously. Further, as we all know, some students periodically "drift off" in even the most interesting lesson. If the abstraction is not written down, some students may leave the class uncertain about what they have learned. Remember that the discovery model is designed to have students form abstractions on their own. It certainly is *not* designed to confuse children, to keep information from them, or to leave them uncertain.

Step Seven: Extension

The final implementing step involves extending or applying the abstraction learned. This step also helps students resolve any uncertainties that might exist. By now the students should be familiar with the concept or generalization reached, since they were responsible for forming it, but this is not always true. The extension phase provides the teacher with an opportunity to see how well the students have understood the information taught. This phase also gives students additional data for self-evaluation. Ms. Sims provided extension of the concept when she asked the class to decide which wing was the better design and why shower curtains bend inwards when the water is on. Mr. Kane extended his students' knowledge of pitch by showing how the same principles applied to a flute and a guitar. Both of these examples helped students see how the knowledge they acquired in the classroom related to the world at large.

Complete the exercises on the following page before turning to the next section.

Directions: Read the anecdote below and answer the questions that follow.

Exercise 6.3

Mr. Kirk wanted to teach his third-grade students about biodegradable objects. He felt that this was an important idea in the elementary science curriculum because if students knew about biodegradable and non-biodegradable objects, they would be more selective about the kinds of things they threw away and would be less likely to litter. He prepared for this lesson several weeks in advance by selecting a number of objects that were biodegradable and nonbiodegradable. He began the lesson by saying, "Today I've got some objects that I'd like you to look at and see if you can figure out what they have in common. Look at these and tell me what you see."

Bringing out an apple core and some orange peels, and placing them on a table in front of the class, he asked, "What do you see, Kim?"

"There's an apple core and you can see the seeds in it and some orange peels. You can even smell them."

"Okay. Anything else? Jamie?"

"Yes, the apple used to be red. You can see what's left of its skin."

The students continued making observations until Mr. Kirk finally said, "All right, and who can tell me how these objects are similar, Ted?"

"Well, they're both things that we eat."

"Mary?"

"They're also both plant products."

"Jim?"

"And they're also both things that people throw away."

"Fine, now let me introduce a few more objects, and I want you to tell me what they are and how they're similar and how they're different."

With that he brought out a crumpled piece of paper and a nonfilter cigarette butt and placed them with the other objects. In another pile, he placed a piece of aluminum foil and a tin can. The lesson continued with Mr. Kirk asking, "What do you see? Vinnie?"

"Well, you put an old cigarette butt in the one group along with a piece of paper."

"Anything else, Jerry?"

"Yes, you also put a can and piece of aluminum foil together in another group."

"Why do you think we have two groups? How are they different?" Mr. Kirk continued.

"Well, all the ones in the second group are metal and all the ones in the first group are plant products."

"Does everyone agree? Shawn?"

"I think he's right about the metal but I'm not so sure about the plant idea. Both the cigarette butt and the piece of paper are made from paper. Is paper a plant product?"

"Class, can anyone help Shawn out with the answer to that question? Carey?"

"I think so. At least some paper is made from wood and that's a plant product."

"Can anyone think of a name for the group we have here, Jane?"

"How about nonmetallic plant products?"

"Okay, that's an idea. Let's check it out by looking at some more data and seeing how it's related to the data we already have in front of us," Mr. Kirk went on.

He then brought out a piece of cloth and a chicken bone. He placed these in the first pile and brought out a glass bottle and plastic toy and placed these in the second pile.

"Now let's look at the two categories that we have. Let's see if we can figure out how they're similar and different and maybe we can come up with a name for each group. . . . How about you, Jodie? What can you tell us about the groups that we have?"

"Well, the one group can't be plant products because there's a chicken bone in one."

"And the other one can't be metal objects because the bottle is glass and the toy is plastic," added Bret.

"Hmm? So what do we have left? Any ideas? Janet?"

"Well, it might be nonmanufactured products. Aluminum foil, tin cans, plastic toys, and glass bottles are all manufactured."

"No, that can't be right," replied John, "because paper and cloth are in the other group and they're manufactured."

"Any other ideas?" Mr. Kirk asked. "If not, let me show you some more data."

With that he brought out a bucket of soil that had a number of objects embedded in it. He placed the bucket on some newspapers on the table in front of the class and started digging through the dirt. As he did, he brought out a partially decomposed banana peel and put it in the first pile and a metal tab from a soft drink can and styrofoam cup and put these in the second pile. Then he said, "Does this help you any? Why did I put these objects where I did? Can anyone tell? Merv?"

"Well, just look at the banana peel. It's already starting to fall apart. And then look at the other things that were in the bucket. They're almost like new. I think the category is things that fall apart."

"How about the rest of you? Does Merv's idea fit the data? Would all the objects in this group fall apart if we buried them in the dirt? Kyle?"

"I think so, and the reverse is true for the other group. It would take a real long time for them to fall apart if they were buried in dirt."

"Okay, the term that we use to refer to things that 'fall apart' is biodegradable. Look at the objects that we have here and see if we can list some characteristics of biodegradable objects on the board, Tina?"

"Well, they're usually made from plant products," replied Tina.

"Another way of saying that is that they're nonsynthetic," added Barry.

"Usually they're soft, but don't have to be," Jerry contributed, "and they all would decompose pretty quickly if thrown away."

As the class mentioned each of these, Mr. Kirk added these to a list on the board underneath the word *biodegradable.* When the class had completed their list Mr. Kirk continued:

"Fine, now let's look at the rest of the things that are in the bucket and see if the definition we've formed is complete and accurate."

The class did so, and they tested their idea further by taking objects from around the room and placing them in the bucket of soil to be examined at a later time.

Identify where in the anecdote the following phases of the discovery lesson occurred.

1. Initial presentation of data. _____

2. Observations. _____

3. Additional data. _____

4. Additional observations. _____

5. Inferences. _____

6. Closure. _____

7. Extension. _____

Evaluating Discovery Activities

As we discussed in earlier sections, the discovery model is designed to teach three interrelated goals with the primary emphasis on the learning of concepts and generalizations. Discovery lessons also provide students with opportunities to practice their process skills, and students develop a greater understanding of how science operates and how scientists work. As we noted in chapter 4, each of these goals requires a form of measurement that is unique to the goal. In this chapter we will focus on measuring for content learning.

After completing this section you should be able to meet the following objective.

■ You will understand different forms of measurement of content so that, given a list of measurement items, you will identify them as production or recognition items and identify them as knowledge-level or higher levels of learning.

Evaluating Students' Acquisition of Content

The two primary forms of content taught in discovery lessons are concepts and generalizations. Both of these are abstractions—ideas people use to describe and understand the world. The value of abstractions lies in their utility in contexts outside the immediate learning situation. In other words, we teach abstractions in the elementary science curriculum because they can be transferred or used in other situations beyond the classroom and at a later time and place. In a sense, the teaching of abstractions involves teaching for future transfer to other situations.

Accordingly, the measurement items used to evaluate the learning of abstractions should focus on whether students have learned generalizable ideas rather than strings of words. *Generalizable* means that the ideas contained in an abstraction can be extended or used in other situations with examples not previously encountered.

Two Learning Levels

In constructing measurement items to evaluate the learning of science concepts and generalizations, it is helpful to differentiate between knowledge-level learning and higher levels of learning (Bloom 1956). Table 6–3 compares the two levels and how they're taught, learned, and evaluated.

Table 6–3 **Comparison of Knowledge Level and Higher Levels of Learning**

	Knowledge Level	Higher Level
How taught	Through repetition and drill	Through the use of examples and illustrations
How learned	Through repeated practice	Through the meaningful processing of data
How measured	Verbatim recall or recognition of original information	By asking students to provide or by presenting students with new or original examples to classify

Teaching at the knowledge level for the most part consists of recitation and reinforcement. To help students remember the connection between words, the teacher provides a number of opportunities for students to practice these connections and provides appropriate means of reinforcement if they are learned. Anyone who has ever tried to memorize the state capitals, a poem, or a quotation will understand what we mean by connections between words. When learning at the knowledge level is measured, the learner's primary task is to reproduce the original content in basically the same form it was taught. In the case of a concept, this could involve recalling the definition for that concept as it was defined in class or in the text. For a generalization, one would need to be able to remember the generalization as stated in class or in the text.

By contrast, higher-level learning involves the assimilation of knowledge in a more personal and sometimes idiosyncratic manner. In other words, the goal of higher-level learning is not for individuals to recite information verbatim, but rather to learn an idea so that it has meaning. A major way of judging the meaningfulness of an idea is whether the learner can relate it to the real world. Accordingly, lessons designed to teach at higher levels emphasize the importance of relating abstract ideas to concrete referents, the examples and data that characterize discovery lessons. The major focus of these lessons is to teach abstractions students can use to describe and explain their world.

A major criterion to be used in judging the success of discovery lessons is whether the learner is able to use the new ideas to understand aspects of the environment not specifically discussed in the class. Measurement items used to evaluate higher levels of learning are related to this goal. These items are designed to assess whether students can apply the ideas learned to new and original situations. A child who has learned the concept *mammal,* for instance, is able to identify examples of animals not previously encountered as mammals. A child who can apply the characteristics of mammal to a "new" animal has acquired a generalizable abstraction.

For example, if an elementary science teacher were trying to teach the concept of plant, he or she might use the following items as examples:

Grass grown in a clay pot

A tree outside the window

An ivy plant

A picture of a palm tree

A piece of moss growing on a rock

After the class had time to observe the examples and analyze them for commonalities, the teacher would evaluate whether they had learned a generalizable abstraction by providing them with *new* examples of plants and non-plants and asking them to classify them. If she used only the teaching examples he or she would be measuring whether they remembered these examples, not whether they had learned a generalizable abstraction. An alternate way of measuring for this kind of learning would be to ask students to bring in or provide their own examples of plants.

Two Measurement Items: Production and Recognition

Production and recognition items are related to the measurement of content acquisition. *Production items* ask students to provide their own definition or examples of a concept, to describe a generalization in their own words, or to provide an example of a generalization. For example, a production item used to measure students' understanding of the concept *reptiles* might ask, "List three examples of reptiles that have not been previously discussed in class." *Recognition items* provide students with a number of choices. The student's task is to recognize correct alternatives. A recognition item designed to measure the concept *reptile* would be:

Which of the following are reptiles?

salamander

crocodile

frog

iguana

(All of the options listed would be ones not previously discussed in class.)

Each type of item has advantages and disadvantages. Recognition items are slightly more difficult to prepare, but they provide more uniform information and allow the teacher to make comparisons between students and across groups. This kind of information is helpful to teachers who are trying out new teaching techniques. Production items are easier to construct, and allow the teacher to see more clearly what is going on in students' minds. Production items are generally more difficult to complete and consequently may not elicit a response from certain students.

Measuring for Concept Learning

Concept learning can occur at the knowledge level or higher levels. Two types of measurement items can be constructed to tap that learning. Items that evaluate students' knowledge of a concept at the lowest level will measure the ability to remember the *definition* of a concept, the *characteristics* of a concept, or *examples* of a concept previously presented in class. Items measuring these different aspects of concept learning in both a recognition and production format are exemplified in table 6–4.

By measuring information that was discussed in class, these items ascertain whether students remember the information in basically the same form it was presented. This knowledge alone would not ensure that the student had acquired a *generalizable abstraction.*

Measuring for concept learning at higher levels requires students to classify examples not previously encountered in the learning activity. This task can be accomplished with either production or recognition items. For example, the following production item measures the concept *carnivore:*

Name two examples of carnivores not previously discussed in class.

A recognition item to measure concept acquisition would present a list of examples and requires students to identify all of the positive examples of the concept.

In using recognition items to measure students' understanding of a concept, the teacher should take care that the selection of examples

Table 6–4 Knowledge Level Items Measuring Concept Learning

Recognition	Production
1. Definition	**1. Definition**
A carnivore is: a) An animal that lays eggs. b) An organism that eats meat. c) An animal that is warm-blooded. d) An organism that has a spinal column.	What is a carnivore? _____ _____ or Meat-eating animals are called: _____
2. Characteristics	**2. Characteristics**
Which of the following are characteristics of carnivores? a) four-legged b) warm-blooded c) have scales d) have a three-chambered heart e) eat meat	What characteristics would you find in *all* carnivores? _____ _____
3. Examples	**3. Examples**
Which of the following are carnivores? (These would be taken from a pool of examples that the class had discussed previously.) a) dog b) horse c) bear d) cow	List two examples of carnivores that were discussed in class the other day. _____ _____ _____

truly measures the concept being taught, rather than some other type of content. If the examples used are not familiar to students, the item will be measuring students' knowledge of the examples rather than their understanding of the concept. If a teacher trying to measure students' understanding of the concept carnivore provides lynx as one alternative, for example, the validity of the item would be in question. If students did not know what lynx eat, then the item would be measuring this bit of information, rather than students' understanding of the concept. One way to avoid this problem is to provide enough description in the examples to overcome any lack of previous learning. The following alternatives could be provided to students:

Which of the following are descriptions of carnivores?

1. The horse is a large domesticated animal that was brought to America by Spanish explorers. Its utility was soon discovered by the Indians and soon horses were found all over the west. Horses fed on the lush grasses found on the prairies and grew large and healthy.

2. The lynx is a member of the cat family that is found in many locations of North America. However, it isn't often seen because it tends to shy away from contact with human beings. Feeding on rodents and other small mammals, the lynx often hunts alone at night.

3. The buffalo was once in danger of becoming extinct, but is now staging a comeback. Protected from hunters, buffalo herds are now growing in a number of national parks. These parks are primarily located in the west where the buffalo once roamed over grassy prairies, grazing on the rich grasses and plants found there.

4. The weasel is a fast and efficient hunter often attacking animals almost as big as himself. Fairly small, the weasel hunts for and kills rodents and other plant eaters that are often as big as himself.

Measuring concept learning poses special problems to the early elementary teacher because many young children are nonreaders. Measuring tools often include drawings and pictures. A lesson on the concept *plants* could be followed by an art assignment in which students are asked to draw a plant different from the ones discussed in class and containing the three main parts (root, stem, and leaves). Alternatively, nonreaders could be shown pictures, then asked to color or mark all the pictures that were positive examples of animals, fish, fruits, etc.

Measuring for the Learning of Generalizations

Generalizations, like concepts, are abstractions. Many of the issues and concerns discussed in the previous paragraphs also hold true here. Although generalizations can be learned and evaluated at the knowledge level, to do so limits their value in the science curriculum. Figure 6–5 shows a number of items to measure knowledge-level learning.

The learning of generalizations can and should be evaluated at higher levels. This practice requires teachers to teach for these levels and design special items to measure higher-level learning. These measuring devices can be designed as a combination of recognition and production items.

Table 6–5 **Items Measuring the Learning of a Generalization at the Knowledge Level**

Generalization:	The evaporation rate of a liquid is directly related to its temperature.
Recognition	Recall
The evaporation rate of a liquid is directly related to its _____ a. color. b. temperature. c. depth. d. salinity.	The evaporation rate of a liquid is directly related to its _____ or How are evaporation rate and temperature related?

A recognition item, for example, would present students with a number of illustrations of the generalization and ask them to identify those to which the generalization applies. The following test question is a recognition item.

Which of the following anecdotes illustrate the generalization that the evaporation rate of a liquid is directly related to its temperature? (The hotter a liquid is, the faster it will evaporate and the colder it is, the slower it will evaporate.)

a) Ms. Jones, in hanging out clothes to dry, noticed that they dried much faster in the afternoon than in the morning.

b) Ms. Jones, in hanging out clothes to dry, noticed that thin clothes dried faster than thick ones.

c) Ms. Jones, in hanging out clothes to dry, noticed that they dried better when the humidity in the air was low.

d) Ms. Jones, in hanging out clothes to dry, noticed that they dried better when the wind was blowing.

To answer this question the student would have to analyze each of the examples and identify those that could be explained by the generalization. A production item to measure students' understanding of a generalization would ask them to provide examples of the generalization they had not previously discussed in class.

Students may also be asked to apply a generalization in a novel situation. As shown in table 6–6, the application of a generalization is actually step two of a two-step process. In step one (recognition), the individual encounters the problem and recognizes it as being an example of the generalization. In the second step, the individual takes the information in the problem and uses the generalization to solve it (production).

Table 6–6 **A Two-Step Model of Problem Solving**

Step One: Recognition	Step Two: Production
Problem is presented to student and student recognizes it as being a subset of or example of the generalization.	Student takes the data in the problem and applies generalization to solve it.

To illustrate this two-step process, consider the following items that could be used to determine if students could apply the generalization discussed in the previous examples.

■ Mr. Smith was mixing a solution of sugar water to put in his hummingbird feeder. Before he noticed what he had done, he had put in too much water. Since he had run out of sugar, he couldn't add more of that. How could he get rid of some of the water quickly?

■ Mr. Cane was hanging up a few shirts to dry in his bathroom when he received a call that his meeting was being scheduled one hour earlier than planned. He wanted to wear one of the shirts that he had washed but noticed that it wouldn't dry in time. What could Mr. Cane do to get his shirt ready on time?

Both items require students to recognize that the process of evaporation could be used here and further requires them to apply the generalization linking evaporation rate and temperature. Failure to respond correctly could be attributed to students' inability either to recognize that the problem had to do with evaporation rate and heat or to remember and apply the generalization. This suggests a need for several types of items, including ones that measure ability to remember the generalization (recall), ability to recognize situations where the generalization applies (recognition), and ability to apply the generalization (production).

The third type of item, those that ask students to apply the generalization, are perhaps the most important for several reasons. A student who can apply a generalization almost certainly can remember the generalization and recognize situations where it is applicable. Also, application-level items test whether students' science knowledge extends to the real world. A related reason for the use of such items is motivational. Students appreciate being shown how knowledge learned in the classroom relates to the world at large. When this occurs the science classroom provides a welcome change of pace from other disciplines where the emphasis is strictly on abstract verbalizations.

Our discussion of measuring for the acquisition of scientific content has been necessarily limited. Much in the evaluation process is beyond the scope of this text. A reader wishing a more detailed discussion of the measurement process is encouraged to refer to one of the texts listed at the end of this chapter.

Before going on to the next chapter answer the exercise that follows:

Directions: Examine the measurement items below and determine whether they are production or recognition items. If necessary explain your answer in terms of students' previous classroom experiences.

Exercise 6.4

1. (1) | 1 lb. | (2) | 1 lb. | (3) | 1 lb. |

   Which is more dense?
   a. block 1
   b. block 2
   c. block 3
   d. all blocks are equally dense

   Knowledge level or higher?
   Production or recognition item?

2. What is density? In your definition include an example that was discussed in class.

   Knowledge level or higher?
   Production or recognition item?

Figure 6–15
Tennis Balls

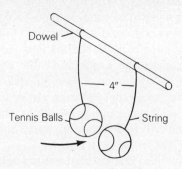

3. Which of the following is most like camouflage?
   a. A brown and gray rabbit in the snow
   b. A green snake in the grass
   c. A fish with a large eye spot on its tail
   d. A brown deer that runs faster than other forest animals.

   Knowledge level or higher?
   Production or recognition item?

4. In figure 6–15, air is blown between the tennis balls. The balls will:
   a. Come together because they are pulled in by the air moving between them.
   b. Move apart because the air moving between them forces them apart.
   c. Come together because the air moving between them decreases the pressure between them.
   d. Not move because there is the same amount of air on both sides of the balls even though some is moving.

   Knowledge level or higher?
   Production or recognition item?

5. When you pluck the strings (figure 6–16) they will all make a sound. The strings are all pulled equally tight. Which string will make the highest sound? Which will make the lowest sound?

   Knowledge level or higher?
   Production or recognition item?

Feedback

Exercise 6.1

1. Archimedes's principle is a particular form of content and as such is appropriate for the discovery model.

2. Sorting shells is a classification activity. It has a limited content goal and most appropriately fits the experiential model.

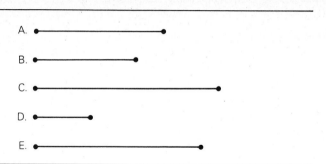

Figure 6–16
Strings

3. Factors influencing the strength of an electromagnet describe a situation most appropriately taught with the inquiry model. This topic will be discussed in detail in chapter 8. Electromagnetism is a concept, however, and could be taught with the discovery model.

4. *Camouflage* is a concept—a particular form of content—and is appropriately taught with the discovery model.

5. This is also a goal most appropriate for inquiry, but one that contains a concept, evaporation. This concept could be taught with a discovery lesson.

6. The teacher in this example is primarily interested in children's experience and as such this is most appropriate for the experiential model.

7. Lever is a concept and could be taught through a discovery lesson.

Exercise 6.2

1. One way of gathering data here would be to place candles under various sized glass containers and measure the time it takes for candles to go out. The class could also experiment with lifting the edge of the container off the surface to let in air (and the oxygen contained in it). If the teacher feels that students could not safely handle matches or candles, this activity could be done as a demonstration.

2. A number of different types of examples could be provided to teach this concept. Leaves, most animals with backbones, cars, and most articles of clothing have bilateral symmetry. After the teacher has presented a number of these, either the real items or pictures, he or she might ask class members to pick out examples of this concept in the classroom and the school yard.

3. The optimal kind of data would be the actual examples of mammals. To provide these, the teacher could bring into the classroom a dog, a cat, gerbils, mice, or white rats. These examples would allow students to see that mammals have fur and are warm blooded. Additional data such as pictures of mammals nursing their young would have to be provided so that students could understand the relationship of additional essential characteristics to the concept. Alternate ways of presenting data would be to show slides, pictures, filmstrips, or movies. If these are used it would be important again to make sure that the essential characteristics of the concept are contained in the data.

4. There are two major ways of presenting data to teach this generalization. The preferable one would be to hang a thermometer outside the class window and have class members record the temperature daily over time. Alternate methods of collecting this data would be to have students obtain this information from a newspaper, radio, or television.

5. This generalization could be taught by placing a long, weighted wooden stick in liquids of different density. The weight on the stick would make the stick float upright and thus would make it a more sensitive gauge of a liquid's bouyancy. Liquids of different densities could be made by melting sugar or salt in the water.

Exercise 6.3

1. Initial presentation of data. Mr. Kirk presented the class with the apple core and orange peels.

2. Observations. The class was asked to describe the data.

3. Additional data. This part of the lesson occurred at several points. One was where the teacher brought out the bottle, the toy, cloth, and paper. The teacher also provided additional data when he brought out the bucket of objects.

4. Additional observations. The class described the objects listed in number 3 above.

5. Inferences. The class made generalizing inferences when they tried to find names for the two categories. Some of the names they tried were plant products, nonmanufactured products and objects that fall apart.

6. Closure. Mr. Kirk tried to bring the lesson to closure when he had the class list the characteristics of biodegradable objects on the board.

7. Extension. Students classified additional objects in the bucket and placed additional objects in the bucket to see if they were biodegradable.

Exercise 6.4

1. This is an example of a recognition item because the student has to recognize the correct answer from a number of alternatives. If these particular examples had not been used previously in class, this item would be measuring above the knowledge level.

2. By contrast, this is a knowledge-level item because the definition had been discussed previously in class. It is also a production item because students are required to provide a correct definition rather than choose from a list of alternatives.

3. This item is a high-level recognition item (assuming students had not encountered these examples previously).

4. Again, the crucial variable is whether this particular example had been used to teach this generalization. If this item had been used by Ms. Sims, the teacher in the previous anecdote, it would be a knowl-edge-level, recognition item. If the example were novel, then the item would be tapping higher levels of learning, students' ability to apply a generalization.

5. This item is also a recognition item designed to measure under-standing of a generalization. It would measure higher levels of learning if the examples were not familiar to students and knowledge-level learn-ing if the example had been used previously.

References

Ahman, J., and Glock, M. *Measuring and Evaluating Educational Achieve-ment.* 2nd ed. Boston: Allyn and Bacon, 1975.

Anderson, R. C. "How to Construct Achievement Tests to Assess Com-prehension." *Review of Educational Research* 42, 2 (1972): pp. 145–170.

Bloom, B. *Taxonomy of Educational Objectives. Handbook I: Cognitive Do-main.* New York: Longmann, 1956.

Carin, A., and Sund, R. *Teaching Science Through Discovery.* 2nd ed. Colum-bus, Ohio: Merrill, 1970.

Devito, A., and Krockover, G. *Creative Sciencing.* Boston: Little, Brown, 1976

Ebel, R. *Essentials of Educational Measurement.* Englewood Cliffs, N.J.: Prentice-Hall, 1972.

Esler, W. *Teaching Elementary Science.* 2nd ed. Belmont, Calif.: Wadsworth, 1977.

Gega, P. *Science in Elementary Education.* 3rd ed. New York: Wiley, 1970.

Keislar, E., and Shulman, L., eds. *Learning by Discovery: A Critical Appraisal.* Chicago: Rand McNally, 1966.

Romey, W. *Inquiry Techniques for Teaching Science.* Englewood Cliffs, N.J.: Prentice-Hall, 1968.

Sax, G. *Principles of Educational Measurement and Evaluation.* Belmont, Calif.: Wadsworth, 1974.

Thorndike, R., ed. *Educational Measurement.* 2nd ed. Washington: American Council on Education, 1971.

This chapter is provided as a supplement to chapter 6. It is intended to reinforce your understanding of the discovery model and to provide a source of activities for use in the classroom. Activities are not only offered as possible sources of ideas for lessons, but also as springboards for your own ideas. Our goal is for you to be able to generalize from these activities to generate your own discovery activities and exercise your own creativity. It should be obvious that these examples are purposely not exhaustive of all discovery possibilities. We will have met our goal in writing this book if you can use the ideas and examples here as starting points for your own lessons. Therefore, we urge you to feel free to adapt, change, and use the ideas in the way most appropriate for your own situation.

Chapter 7   Discovery Activities

In describing the activities in this chapter, we have adopted the following format:

Content Objective

The objectives describe in behavioral terms what students should be able to do when the lesson is completed. In addition to content goals, discovery activities have process goals and goals that are related to students' understanding of the way science operates. Because these goals are common to all discovery activities, they will not be restated for each activity.

Content Background

This section is designed to provide the teacher with the necessary content background for the lesson and briefly describes the major concepts and generalizations related to the topic.

Materials

This section describes the equipment you will need to carry out the activity. It serves as a quick planning checklist before you begin an activity. Materials required for all activities are easily obtained, not only as a convenience, but also because use of common, everyday objects reinforces the idea that science is an attempt to make sense of our surroundings. It is not something that only occurs in laboratories with sophisticated equipment.

Procedures

Listed here are the series of steps a teacher would follow in implementing the activities. The steps are listed sequentially and in detail; they can be used as a lesson plan for the activity if the teacher wishes. We encourage teachers to adapt these procedures to their own needs and interests.

Related Activities

Where appropriate, we have included additional topics suitable for further investigation. These, of course, are merely suggestions; the extent to which you use them is strictly a matter of judgment. Also, we hope our suggestions will trigger investigations we have not considered. These related activities are often cross-listed with lessons in other chapters to allow teachers to plan a series of activities on the same topic.

Content Objective

Children will understand the generalization, "The longer the vibrating column, the lower the pitch of the sound" so that, when shown pairs of vibrating objects, they will be able to predict which pitch will be higher.

**Activity 7.1
Vibrations and
Sound**

Content Background

Sound results from vibrating objects causing vibrations in the air, which then travel to our ears. One factor operating in determining the pitch of a vibrating object is its length. The longer the vibrating object, the slower the vibrations and the lower the sound. For instance, long piano strings have a lower pitch than short ones. Other factors also influence pitch, such as the tension on the string and its thickness, but this activity will focus only on length.

Materials

Plastic drinking straws, soft-drink bottles, water glasses, water, stringed instrument

Procedures

This activity is described as a classroom episode in the introduction to chapter 6. It is presented here as the first activity of this section in an effort to help you make the transition from the content of chapter 6 to the activities in this chapter.

1. Give each student in the class a plastic drinking straw (that you have cut to different lengths), have them flatten one end slightly and cut the edges of the straw to make a reed. (See figure 6–2.) Have them put the straws in their mouths and try to make the cut edges vibrate against their lips like a reed instrument. It will then make a loud buzz. (Your class will enjoy this.) Some will have trouble making the noise, but with some effort they will all be able to do it.

2. Have the children listen to the sounds of the straws and describe their observations.

3. Have the children observe the length of the straws and compare the different lengths.

4. Have one student with a very long straw and one with a very short straw blow them. Compare their lengths and the sounds they make. Do this with other length combinations.

5. Discuss the notion of vibration and ask the students what is vibrating. Relate speed of vibration and length.

6. Take three glasses of water filled to different levels (see figure 7–1) and tap them on the sides with a metal object such as a pair of scissors.

Relate the sounds and the length of the water column. (Note that the water column is the vibrating object.)

7. Repeat the procedure by blowing over the soft-drink bottles until they make a sound. (Note here that the air in the bottles is the vibrating column.)

Figure 7–1
Columns of Water

8. Ask students to relate all three examples in a generalization.

9. Bring out a stringed instrument and ask students to predict what will happen when you shorten the string by placing your finger on it.

Related Activities

A prerequisite activity relating sound and vibration might be required with young children. Activities such as holding their throat while they talk, snapping a ruler over a desk edge, and plucking rubber bands would work well. The existence of sound waves could be demonstrated by tapping a tuning fork, putting the vibrating ends into water, and observing the movement of water. This lesson could also be preceded by experiential activity 5.7, which deals with sound and hearing. In addition, activity 9.6, on pitch and sounds, is a related inquiry lesson. Note also that a description of how to demonstrate transverse and longitudinal waves is presented in the activities related to activity 9.6.

Content Objective

**Activity 7.2
Evaporation**

Students will understand the concept of evaporation so that, when presented with a container of liquid, the student will describe in his or her own words what will happen if the container is left uncovered.

Content Background

Evaporation occurs when the force holding the individual molecules of a liquid together (cohesive force) is overcome by the energy of their motion (kinetic energy) and individual molecules fly away from the liquid into the air. Heat increases the molecular movement, so heat increases the rate of evaporation.

Materials

Plastic cups, water, alcohol

Procedures

This activity can be done on different levels beginning with very young children. With preschool or kindergarten children the following procedures may be followed:

1. Have the children, in groups of two or three, pour some water into four plastic cups and mark the level of the liquid on the outside with a marking pen. Leave two of the cups uncovered. Cover the other two with clear plastic wrap. Have students put one of the covered and one of the uncovered cups in sunlight near the window and the others away from a heat source in shadows.

2. At a preselected time each day or every other day, have them mark the new water levels. This process, showing some water has disappeared, illustrates evaporation. Have students record the results for later discussion.

3. After a week, compare the results from the different conditions by having students fill out a table similar to the one shown in table 7-1. Introduce the term evaporation and discuss factors that influence its rate. Ask students where the water on the sides of the covered containers comes from.

Table 7-1

Cup	Day 1	Day 3	Day 5
1			
2			
3			
4			

4. The same procedure can be followed with rubbing alcohol, as the liquid and the rates of evaporation of water and alcohol can be compared. Other substances such as soft drinks can also be added for comparison. If they are, discuss the residue that is left and ask students where it came from.

5. Give each student a wet paper towel and have a contest to see who can produce the driest paper towel in ten minutes.

Related Activities

There are a number of worthwhile related activities. For example, children may pour the remaining amount of alcohol or water into a graduated cylinder to measure the amount remaining and then graph the amount remaining, recording their observations daily. The activity is closely related to or could be modified into an inquiry activity (see activity 9.10), and may be done in conjunction with activity 7.3 on distillation.

As another activity, children could drop two drops of alcohol onto the palm of the hand and time how long it takes them to evaporate, repeating the procedure with four drops, six drops, eight drops, and so on. The results could then be graphed and if the line was not straight, the students could make inferences as to why it is not.

An additional discussion of the cooling effect of evaporation might be interesting. Have children spread rubbing alcohol on their arms with cotton balls and describe how this felt. The discussion could lead to why fans make you cooler (moving air increases evaporation and thereby increases cooling); why high humidity makes us feel warmer (high humidity retards evaporation of perspiration); and why perspiring helps us stay cool (evaporation of perspiration has a cooling effect). Evaporation could also be related to the reverse process of condensation, such as dew forming overnight and water drops forming on the outside of a cold drink glass in the summer.

Content Objective

Students will understand the concept of distillation so that, without aids, they can describe the process in their own words and explain how it can be used to purify a substance.

Content Background

Distillation involves separating two substances through the process of evaporation, and then collecting one of the substances through condensation. In its simplest form, it involves boiling a substance and collecting the steam or gas that results. In the case of water, this steam or gas is purified water. When it cools it becomes distilled water (like the distilled water you can buy in a store). Distillation is also used to separate liquids that boil at different temperatures, such as water and alcohol. If a mixture of water and alcohol, like the grain mash used to make whiskey, is heated just to the boiling temperature of the alcohol, then the only substance that evaporates is the alcohol. Its boiling point is lower than that of water. Consequently, the gas vapor that is given off is alcohol; if this vapor can be cooled and collected, pure alcohol will result.

Materials

A beaker, bunsen burner or alcohol burner (or electric hot plate), water, distilled water, salt, sugar, aluminum foil. Arrange the beaker and burner so that the steam from the beaker will be collected on the aluminum foil as shown in figure 7–2. Bend the aluminum foil so that any water vapor that collects on it will collect in a run-off pan.

This activity requires a moderate amount of apparatus, so it might best be done as a demonstration in front of the class. If children are capable of observing the safety precautions necessary around heat, however, it would be excellent as a learning center activity.

**Activity 7.3
Distillation**

Figure 7-2
Distillation Apparatus

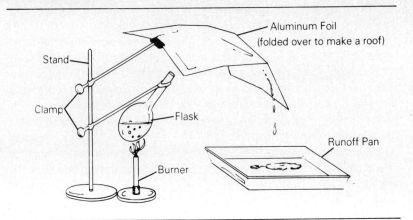

Procedures

1. Place a small amount (100 to 200 ml.) of distilled water in the distillation apparatus and have students taste it before boiling. Boil the liquid so the steam hits the foil and the condensed water runs off into the pan. Collect the distillate. Have one or two of the students taste it. Have students examine the contents of the beaker when through. (It should be clear if the distilled water was pure.)

This would be an excellent time to caution students against tasting any unknown substance. Explain to students that tasting the water in this situation is all right because you know what is in it.

2. Now do the same procedure with tap water. Have students taste the distillate and again observe the empty beaker. Discuss where the residue came from. This residue is due to minerals and chemicals in the water that either are naturally occurring or are put in to purify the water. The amount of residue left will depend upon whether your area has soft or hard water. Hard water will have lots of residue in it.

3. Repeat the experiment with salt water, then sugar water. Place a teaspoon of sugar in a cup of water. Be sure the sugar and salt are completely dissolved before heating. Have the children taste both liquids to verify the sweet and salty taste. Ask them how the water appears. (It should look no different from ordinary tap water.) After distilling the two solutions, have them taste the distilled water. Also, have them taste the residue left after the water is gone in each case. They will again taste the sugar and salt.

4. Ask students to compare the findings from the four activities and generalize about the results.

5. Take some dirt and put it in a beaker, then add some distilled water. Ask, "Suppose we wanted to drink this water. How could we make it clean enough to drink?"

Related Activities

Place a covered jar of water in a sunny window. Ask students where the drops of water on the side came from. Have students design a water purification plant for use with ocean water. Also, students could design a seawater salt plant to extract salt from the seas.

Distillation as a means of purification could lead to a discussion of other purification methods, such as filtration and the use of chemicals. A social studies lesson focusing on the economic impact of different forms of water treatment and their importance in urban areas can also be related to this lesson. This activity also relates to inquiry activity 9.10, Rates of Evaporation, and to 7.2, earlier in this chapter.

Content Objective

Students will understand the concept of buoyancy so that, when shown situations in which the densities of floating liquids vary, the student will explain how this property affects buoyancy.

**Activity 7.4
Buoyancy**

Content Background

Buoyancy refers to the ability of an object to float in a liquid or gas. The denser the object, the lower it floats; the denser the liquid or gas, the higher the object floats. This latter generalization explains why people are more buoyant in the ocean or the Great Salt Lake of Utah than they are in fresh water.

Materials

Long test tubes or vials or graduated cylinders, small wooden dowels or pencils, thread, tacks, lead weights, sugar, salt. Fasten a weight on the end of a dowel or pencil by placing a tack in one end and tying a weight to a piece of string or thread. Experiment with the amount of weight until the piece of wood floats in a test tube of water with the water line about midway on the piece of wood.

Procedures

If there is sufficient equipment, the lesson can be done with small groups. Otherwise, it can effectively be done as a center activity. The following description is for a small group activity.

1. Have the students form groups of two or three. Have each group mark a small stick or dowel with lines 5 millimeters apart. Have them put the stick in a test tube partially filled with water and have them mark the water line on the stick with a pencil.

2. Have the students add a teaspoon of salt to the water and again observe where the water line is.

3. Have students add additional teaspoons of salt, each time noting where the water line is on the stick. If possible, measure the distance between lines.

4. Repeat the procedure with sugar, again noting each time where the water line falls.

5. Have the groups compare their results by helping to fill out a table similar to table 7–2. Do the same for the sugar solution.

Table 7–2

Condition	Stick Higher or Lower?	How much?
No Salt		
1 tsp.		
2 tsp.		
3 tsp.		
4 tsp.		

6. Ask students to generalize about the results: "When the liquid has more salt in it, the stick floats higher." Introduce the idea of buoyancy and density and explain the relationship of these terms to the results of the activity.

7. Have students predict what would happen to a boat that floats to a certain level in fresh water and is then put in an ocean. (Make sure students understand that ocean water contains salt.)

Related Activities

Two identical quantities of water could be put in graduated cylinders, one with and one without salt. Have students predict which will be heavier and then which will float the stick higher. Weigh both containers and see if students' predictions were correct. Then compare hot and cold water and their ability to float objects.

As an additional activity, ask students if any of their parents make beer or wine. If they do, they will probably have a hydrometer, a device to measure the amount of sugar still left in immature beer and wine. As the sugar is converted to alcohol, the hydrometer sinks lower and lower into the solution until the proper level is reached and the liquid is bottled or drunk.

This lesson is closely related to experiential activity 5.14, on weighing and measuring and discovery activity 7.16 where students acquire the concept of density. The two activities may be done in sequence, and the results of the buoyancy activity discussed in terms of density.

Also, the activity may be performed by using wood materials of different densities if they are available. If not, the density of the dowels

Figure 7-3
Full Moon

may be modified by attaching additional weights or even more tacks or paper clips.

Another buoyancy activity calls for the placement of ice cubes in water and alcohol. Show students two glasses that appear to contain water (one in fact contains alcohol). The ice cube floats in the water but sinks to the bottom in the alcohol. Until students determine that the liquids are different, which they cannot easily tell visually but can when smelled, the activity is puzzling and a good starting point for a discussion of buoyancy.

Content Objective

Students will understand the phases of the moon so that, given information about the moon's present condition, they will be able to predict future phases and explain why.

**Activity 7.5
Phases of the
Moon**

Content Background

The moon revolves around the earth just as Earth revolves around the sun, but instead of 365 days, one revolution takes 28 days. The moonlight we see is really sunlight reflected from the moon's surface. The shape of the moon depends on how much of the moon's lighted side is exposed to the earth. When Earth, the sun, and the moon are lined up as in figure 7-3, a full moon results, because the lighted side is totally exposed to the earth.

However, when the earth, moon and sun are as in figure 7–4, we either see no moon at all or a slight sliver or crescent part of the light side.

Figure 7-4
New Moon

Figure 7–5
Half-Moon

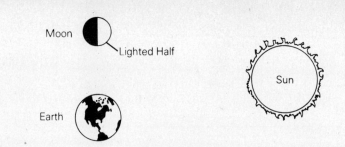

Another condition occurs when the lighted side of the moon is half visible from the earth. A half-moon results from this condition (figure 7–5).

As we said earlier, the moon revolves around Earth in a regular 28-day cycle. Consequently, there are 28 days from one full moon to the next, and from any shape of the moon to its corresponding shape in the next phase. Correspondingly, it takes 14 days to go from a new moon to a full moon or from a waxing (getting bigger) half-moon to a waning (getting smaller) half-moon. These changes are summarized in figure 7–6.

Materials

Bulletin-board calendar to record the phases of the moon, individual calendars for each student, newspaper with weather report

Procedures

1. Try to plan the activity so that it begins several days before a full moon. This will allow students to see the moon "growing" right after, or around sunset.

2. Introduce the activity to students and ask them to watch for the moon that evening. Construct a simple calendar on the bulletin board or chalkboard and draw the shape of the moon each morning. Have students do the same with their individual calendars. If skies are cloudy, consult the weather section of newspaper.

3. Have students describe the changes that are occurring from day to day.

4. Compare students' data with another calendar, which the teacher can construct for the previous month.

5. Ask students to compare the results and generalize from these. Some sample generalizations include:

- There are 28 days from one full moon to the next.
- There are 14 days from a new moon to a full moon.
- After a full moon, the moon gets smaller.

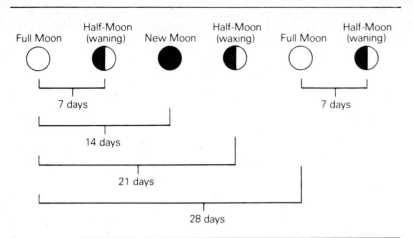

Figure 7–6
Phases of the Moon

Explain these results in terms of the relative positions of Earth, the moon, and the sun, using diagrams and illustrations.

6. Predict when the next phases of the moon will occur. Follow up when that time comes.

Related Activities

The phases of the moon can be demonstrated in class using a softball for the moon, a basketball for Earth, and a strong flashlight for the sun. In a darkened room, shine the flashlight on the softball and move the softball to different positions around the basketball (Earth). Eclipses of the sun and moon can be demonstrated by placing the light, softball, and basketball in alignments that place the softball in the basketball's shadow (eclipse of the moon) or the basketball in the softball's shadow (eclipse of the sun).

Also, if you teach in a coastal area, the moon's effects on the tides can be measured. Record tide levels as reported in the newspaper over a period of time; compare these levels to the moon's phases and its position at various times. If desired, this activity could also be integrated with experiential activity 5.4, which deals with the general topic of weather, and with discovery activity 7.24, Shadows.

Content Objective

Students will understand the generalization, "Temperature variations are related to changes in environmental conditions", so that given a description of a change in the environment, students will predict the possible change in temperature.

**Activity 7.6
Temperature
Variations**

Content Background

The temperature in our environment is influenced by a number of factors, some of which operate in a regular or predictable fashion. For example, outdoors it is usually warmer in the summer than in the spring or fall and these seasons are usually warmer than the winter. In addition, morning is usually the coolest time of the school day and late afternoon the warmest. Shade and direction of exposure can also influence the temperature, with a southern exposure generally being warmer than a northern. In the classroom, the temperature is kept fairly constant by a thermostat, but factors such as radiators, windows, and the number of people in the room can influence the temperature.

Materials

Thermometers, chart to record temperatures

Procedures

1. Have students in groups of two or three measure temperatures in the following locations and at the following times. Make sure that they leave the thermometer untouched for at least ten minutes. Stations can be assigned to different groups of students and the results shared.

a. In the room by the radiator or heat vent, early and late morning, early and late afternoon

b. In the room by a window (or away from heat source), early and late morning, early and late afternoon

c. In the room away from a heat source or window, early and late morning, early and late afternoon

d. Outdoors near the school building, early and late morning, early and late afternoon

e. Outdoors away from the school building, early and late morning, early and late afternoon

f. Same as d and e above but in a sunny site

g. Same as d and e above but in a shady site

h. Take the above readings over a week's or several months' time.

2. Place the data gathered into a chart such as the one shown in table 7-3.

Table 7-3 Time/Temperature Chart

	Location	Time	Temperature
a.			
b.			
c.			
etc.			

3. Ask students when the temperature was the highest, when lowest, and when it changed the most. Ask for reasons.

4. Ask students to generalize about the data and write these generalizations on the board.

5. Ask students to predict the temperatures between the times when they were taken and then check their predictions in a follow-up activity. Also ask students to predict what the temperature does after school and in the evening and have them check to see if their predictions are correct.

Related Activities

If possible, this lesson should be preceded by experiential activity 5.5, which teaches students about thermometers. Also, this lesson could be related to inquiry activity 9.14, which investigates factors that influence the amount of energy stored by different objects.

The activity could be expanded to different places in the school. See if students can find the hottest and coldest spot in the school. Also see what effect height has on temperature (at the floor and at the ceiling). Data from another classroom in another location in the school could be compared. Have students graph the results.

This lesson could be linked to one on energy conservation, in which students are asked to design houses for living in warm and cold sections of our country. Factors such as the number and placement of windows could be discussed.

In a related social studies activity the effects of temperature and environment in general on people's style of living can be discussed. Pictures of people from different parts of the country and the world can be shown in work and play situations, and the differences in their clothing patterns discussed. Types of houses in different countries and different parts of our country can be compared.

Content Objective

**Activity 7.7
Sterilization**

Students will understand the concept of sterilization so that, when faced with a cut or scratch, they can suggest ways to prevent the spread of microorganisms.

Content Background

Microscopic organisms exist all around us and will grow on surfaces that are moist and have nutrients, such as a cut or a scratch. A major way to prevent infections from occurring in these cuts is to sterilize the wound. This can be done with soap, heat, or chemicals such as alcohol or iodine.

Materials

Pieces of potato or apple, toothpicks, small jars or cups (baby food jars or clear plastic cups), clear plastic wrap, candle (or bunsen or alcohol burner), hand soap, rubbing alcohol, iodine solution, sterile eyedropper

Procedures

1. Have the students form groups of two or three; give each group a whole potato or apple. Explain to them that they are going to cut the foods and tell why they shouldn't touch the pieces after they are cut.

2. Have the students cut the apple or potato into pieces, touch different pieces with separate toothpicks that had been touched to or dipped into one of the following materials:

- A lighted fire
- Soap
- Rubbing alcohol
- Iodine
- The inside of the mouth
- Nothing.

3. Have the students put the pieces into the jars, touching them as little as possible, and cover the jars tightly with clear plastic wrap. Record the results as shown in table 7–4. If the pieces start to dry out, a few drops of water can be sprinkled inside with a *sterile* eyedropper to maintain the proper humidity. Sterilize the dropper by dipping it in alcohol before using.

Table 7–4 **Container/Results Chart**

Container	Results		
	Day 1	Day 2	Day 3
1			
2			
2			
3			
etc.			

After growths appear on the pieces, caution students not to open the containers or handle the contents.

4. When growths appear on most of the samples, draw a chart on the board and have the class discuss their results. Introduce the terms *sterile* and *sterilization* and ask for generalizations. Dispose of the results of the activity and wash the containers with hot, soapy water before reusing.

5. Ask students to predict what would happen if the same procedures were applied to cuts and scratches.

Related Activities

Other ways to minimize the spread of germs may be discussed. Samples could be refrigerated, frozen, and warmed to different temperatures and the results observed. A nurse or a doctor could come in and talk about sterilization procedures in an operating room.

The historical attitudes toward sterilization, infection, and illness make interesting stories, such as some of the material in chapter 1 or the practice of "bleeding" patients to get rid of illnesses.

Practices that have developed in food preservation with advanced technology also make interesting discussions (see activity 7.16). Children can be shown dried beef, for example, and the process of drying as a way of preserving food could be discussed. This can be extended to other methods such as salting, pickling, and preserving with sugar. The effect of different sterilization techniques can also be investigated in inquiry activity 9.16 on mold growth.

Content Objective

Activity 7.8 Conductors

Students will understand the concept of electrical conductor, so that, when provided with an array of objects, they will predict which are conductors and which are not, and will describe one way of testing the objects.

Content Background

Conductors are materials that allow an electrical current to flow through them. Most metals are good conductors; electrical wiring is made of metal such as copper, a good conductor, and is covered by rubber, a poor conductor that acts to keep the electrical current inside.

We can test to see if an object is a good conductor by placing it as a connecting link in an electrical circuit. An electrical circuit is a flow of electrons from a power source to a machine or a bulb. An inexpensive electrical power source is a regular D-size battery. When a battery like this is hooked up to a light as shown in figure 7-7, power flows from the battery, through the light bulb and back into the battery.

In this diagram, the ends of the wire have been stripped bare and taped securely to the top and bottom of the battery. The electrical current from the battery flows through the wires into the bulb, making it glow, and back again to the battery. If this circuit is broken in any way, the bulb goes off.

Materials

Dry-cell or flashlight D batteries, electrical tape, light electrical wiring, flashlight bulb, and socket. All of these materials should be available at a

Figure 7-7
Conductor Apparatus

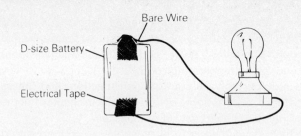

hardware store or an appliance repair shop. In the absence of a light bulb socket you can connect the wire directly to the light bulb as in figure 7-8, but the arrangement isn't as secure.

After you have the electrical circuit working, cut the wire leading away from the bulb and strip the wire of its coating. After you have determined that touching the two bare wires together will complete the circuit, you are ready to begin the activity.

Procedures

1. Have students working in groups gather a number of metallic and nonmetallic objects from around the room or home. Keys, screws, nails, pens, pencils, glass, plastic objects, paper, and coins are all excellent.

2. Have each group test the circuit beforehand to make sure it works. Then have students test the materials that they have gathered by touching the wires to opposite ends of the material as shown in figure 7-9.

3. Have students make a list of objects that will light the bulb and those that will not.

4. Assemble the class and compile a list on the board of all the substances that lit the bulb and all those that did not. Introduce the term *conductor* and explain how conductors allow the flow of electrons to pass through.

Figure 7-8
An Electrical Connection

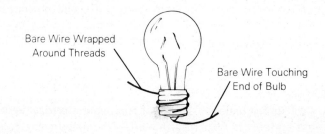

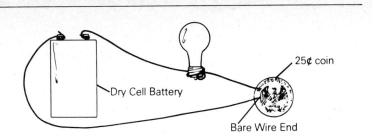

Figure 7–9
An Electrical Circuit

5. Have students observe the lists that were formed on the board and ask them to generalize about the lists (for example, plastics are poor conductors; so is wood).

6. Bring out some new objects from your desk drawer, some of which are conductors, some of which are not. Ask students to predict which are conductors and then have the class test them.

Related Activities

Ask students which of the materials tested would be good for making electrical wire and which would be good for wire coverings. See if water is a good conductor. Then add a little salt, sugar, or baking soda to three beakers of water. Did anything happen? Now add more of each until the solution is saturated (no more will dissolve). Test the solutions again.

With advanced students, this activity may be followed by activity 7.18, Series and Parallel Circuits. Fourth, fifth, and sixth graders can read about and discuss semi-conductors and the implications they have had for modern stereo equipment, television, and computers.

**Activity 7.9
Magnetic
Attraction**

Content Objective

Students will understand the generalization, "A magnetic field will pass through nonmagnetic objects, but not through magnetic ones" so that, when provided with a group of objects, students will predict which objects will allow passage of the magnetic field.

Content Background

Magnets are objects that attract iron, nickel, and cobalt metals. (Iron is the most common of these metals and will be the basis of discussion here.) Their attraction is caused by a magnetic field that surrounds the magnet. Magnetic objects such as nails or pins entering this field absorb the magnetic force; nonmagnetic objects such as wood or paper allow the field to flow through them.

Figure 7-10
Magnetic Attraction Apparatus

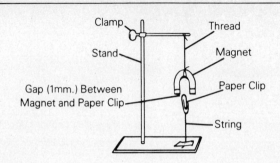

Materials

Stand, clamp, a powerful magnet, paper clips, paper, aluminum foil, cloth, pane of glass, piece of clear plastic, lid from a tin can of fruit or vegetables.

Set up the magnet so that it is hanging from a clamp on the stand, and the paper clip, which is attached to the base by a piece of string, is pulled upward by the magnet. A space about 1 cm. wide exists between the clip and the magnet (figure 7-10).

When magnetic objects are carefully eased through the gap, they absorb the magnetic field so that the paper clip, no longer attracted to the magnet, falls. When nonmagnetic objects are slid into the gap, the magnetic field passes through them and the paper clip remains attracted to the magnet.

Procedures

1. Have students form small groups and have them construct the apparatus as illustrated. After students have set up their materials, ask them to explain what is happening and why the paper clip and string are upright.

2. Have students test the different materials by placing them in between the magnet and the paper clip. Have them observe and record their results.

3. Make a chart on the board and ask students to share their data by listing their results in two columns: Paper clip fell/Paper clip did not fall.

4. Ask students to make a generalization about the materials in the two columns.

5. Have students test the materials in both columns with the magnet. Ask students about the relationship between the two sets of materials. (Objects that are attracted to magnets don't allow a magnetic force to pass through.)

6. Bring out some new objects to test—cardboard, a leaf, a piece of thin lead, and a piece of thin iron, for example—and ask the students to

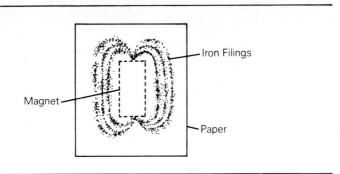

Figure 7–11
**Iron Filings to Illustrate a
Magnetic Field**

predict what will happen. First touch each object to the magnet, then place it between the magnet and the paper clip.

Related Activities

This activity would nicely follow an introductory lesson on magnetic attraction, where students would merely test a large variety of objects to see if they are attracted to magnets.

Another related activity is to use iron filings to illustrate a magnetic field. Place a magnet on a desk, cover it with paper, and sprinkle iron filings on the paper. The filings will tend to line up with the lines of force in the magnetic field, as shown in figure 7–11.

As part of a unit the activity could be related to inquiry activity 9.11 and the related activities described there.

Content Objective

Students will understand the concept of geotropism so that, when provided with seedlings in different orientations, they will correctly predict the direction the roots and stem will grow.

**Activity 7.10
Geotropism**

Content Background

A tropism is an involuntary orienting response in living organisms. Geotropisms (from the stem word *geo,* meaning Earth) are orienting responses to Earth's gravitational pull. Geotropisms in plants cause the roots to point down into the soil and the leaves and stem to point up toward the air and sunlight.

Materials

Seeds (pea, bean, or corn), potting soil, clear panes of glass or plastic, paper towels, paraffin, sewing needles, bulbs (tulip, onion, or gladiolus).

Figure 7-12
**Demonstration of
Geotropism**

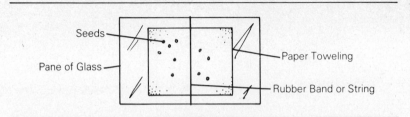

Have the students plant some of the seeds in containers with potting soil. Make sure these containers have holes punched in the bottom for drainage and plant the seeds about 1 or 2 cm. deep. Keep the soil moist but not wet. Tilt some of the containers to a 45° angle. Seeds should sprout in a few days.

Take some other seeds and place them with two layers of paper toweling between two panes of glass. The glass can be held together with string or rubber bands as shown in figure 7-12.

Wet the paper toweling and keep it moist. (A plastic bag can be placed over the panes of glass to prevent them from drying out on weekends.) Prop up on a ledge until seeds start to sprout. When they do, rotate the panes a little each day so that the roots are horizontal with the ground. Soon, they will adjust their growth to point downward. Keep on rotating the panes every day in the same direction.

Place a needle in a paraffin base with the sharp end up. Impale one of the seeds on the sharp end and place in a pan of water. Cover with a glass as shown in figure 7-13. The water in the pan will provide enough moisture to allow the seed to sprout. As the seed sprouts, realign it so that the root sprout is pointing upward.

Procedures

1. Have the students carefully uncover the seeds in the dirt containers after they have sprouted.

2. Ask for observations. Ask about the roots and establish which direction the roots are pointing.

3. Focus students' attention on the seed impaled on the needle. Ask for observations. Ask why the water in the bottom of the pan is necessary. Call attention to the root sprout. Ask why it is growing the way it is. Ask how the two groups of seeds examined so far are similar or dissimilar.

4. Call students' attention to the seeds in the panes of glass. If the seeds have not yet sprouted, ask students to predict which direction they will grow. If they have sprouted, ask students what would happen if the pane were moved so that the roots were pointing up. Would they continue to grow that way? If they did, what would happen to the plant?

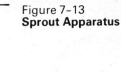

Figure 7-13
Sprout Apparatus

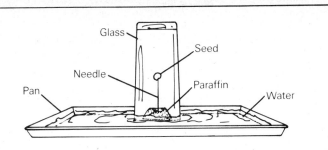

5. Summarize the activity by asking students what the three activities had in common. Write the word geotropism on the board and relate it to the activities.

6. Show the class one of the bulbs you brought in. Ask where they think the root will develop. Ask what will happen if the bulb is planted upside down. Plant some of the bulbs about three or four centimeters deep in potting soil. Place some of the bulbs with the roots down and some with the roots up and dig up in about two weeks to see what happens.

Related Activities

This activity could be part of a unit on plants that included activity 5.3 on seeds, 5.16 on vegetables, 7.10 on tropisms, 7.12 on overcrowding, 7.20 and 7.23 on nutrients and water, and 9.7 and 9.8 on germination and sunlight.

As an evaluation item for this lesson, students may be asked to draw a picture of a seed growing on a steep mountainside. Which direction will the roots go? What would happen if seeds were sprouted in outer space where there is no gravity? You may also wish to investigate other tropisms, such as hydrotropism (orientation to water) and heliotropism (orientation to the sun), by growing seeds in different conditions.

Content Objective

Students will understand the generalization, "In a balanced lever, weight times distance from a fulcrum on one arm of a lever equals weight times distance on the other arm of the lever" so that given a condition (weight and distance) on one arm of a lever, the student will describe how to balance it with various weights and distances on the other arm.

Content Background

A lever is a simple machine with two arms balanced by a central point or fulcrum. The weight times the distance on one side of a balanced lever

**Activity 7.11
Levers**

Figure 7–14
A Simple Lever

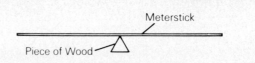

always equals the weight times the distance on the other side. For any given configuration of weight and distance on one side, any number of combinations of weight and distance can be used to balance the other side.

Materials

Metersticks, triangular pieces of wood scraps for fulcrums, and pennies or washers for weights. The levers can be made in either of two ways. The simplest method uses a small piece of wood as the fulcrum, as shown in figure 7–14.

The other type of lever is more difficult to construct, but will prove easier to work with. Push a tack into the center of a meterstick and suspend it by a piece of string attached to the tack. A small paper cup to hold weights is attached to each end of the stick by a loose loop. Figure 7–15 illustrates.

Procedures

1. Break students into groups and explain how levers work and how the two sides should be balanced. Then introduce the following types of problems and have students solve them by experimenting with their levers.

Table 7–5

Right Side Distance	Weights	Left Side Distance	Weights
10 cm.	3	10 cm.	?
15 cm.	4	15 cm.	?
20 cm.	5	20 cm.	?

2. Discuss the results of the activity, then introduce another set of problems. Have the students solve them by experimentation.

Table 7–6

Right Side Distance	Weights	Left Side Distance	Weights
5 cm.	2	?	1
10 cm.	4	?	2
20 cm.	6	?	3

Note that the second group of problems requires compensation of length for weight.

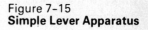

Figure 7-15
Simple Lever Apparatus

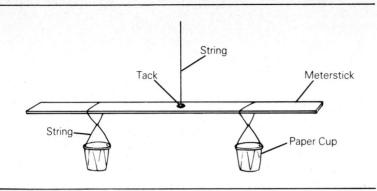

3. Discuss these results and then present another set of problems, which require compensation of weight for length. Have students experiment with the levers to solve the problems.

Table 7-7

Right Side Distance	Weights	Left Side Distance	Weights
10 cm.	2	5 cm.	?
20 cm.	4	10 cm.	?
10 cm.	4	20 cm.	?

In order to simplify the experimentation process, tell the students to put all the pennies or washers on the same point when they experiment. For instance, in the third arrangement above, two washers at the 20 cm. point will be required to balance the four washers at 10 cm., although the four washers could also be balanced by 2 washers at 10 cm. and one washer at 20 cm. Combinations can become complex, so, in initial experimentation at least, we encourage students to keep the balancing washers on the same point.

4. Have students analyze all of the data and ask if they have discovered a way to balance the two sides without actually weighing and measuring.

5. Present additional problems for students to solve. Ask them to first solve them in their heads or with pencil and paper and then check with their levers.

Related Activities

The concept of simple machines and how they assist us in our work relates well to this activity. Students can be asked to cite examples of levers found in the home—hammer, broom, car jack handle, scissors— and ask how they help with work. As the concept of work is discussed, the concept of mechanical advantage can be introduced. This notion can be used to explain the use of a crowbar for lifting heavy objects or a bottle opener for prying off caps. The use of balanced levers as scales (activity 5.14) can also be discussed.

Activity 7.12 Overcrowding

Content Objective

Students will understand the effect of overcrowding on organisms so that, given descriptions of different conditions of crowding, they will predict what effect these conditions have on growth.

Content Background

In any environment, organisms compete for the available sunlight, water, and nutrients. When the space between organisms is sufficient to allow each to grow to its full capacity, there is no negative effect from other plants or animals. When this space is insufficient, however, overcrowding develops and growth suffers.

Materials

Milk cartons, potting soil, and radish seeds

Procedures

1. Have students form groups and plant seeds. Have groups of students plant three different milk cartons with radish seeds. In one carton, put one or two seeds; in another, plant the seeds 2 or 3 cm. apart; in the third, plant the seeds 0.5 to 1 cm. apart. Plant all the seeds at the same depth (1 cm.) and water all the seeds with the same amount of water. (Make sure the milk cartons have holes in the bottom for drainage.)

2. Have students measure the plant growth in the different containers and record the results for later sharing. In addition to measuring the height of the plants, students may also want to describe qualitative differences between pots in terms of number of leaves and strength of stem.

3. Have students share their data by putting it into a table, as shown in table 7–8.

Table 7–8

Pot	Height of Plants			Description of Plants
	1st week	2nd week	3rd week	
1				
2				
3				

4. Ask students to generalize about the data in the chart. Also ask them to comment on the relative changes occurring in each subsequent week. Typically, the effect of overcrowding becomes more pronounced as the plants get bigger. You may wish to graph these results with height on the vertical axis and time on the horizontal axis.

5. Show students the directions on seed packages. Ask why they think they recommend spacing seeds as they do. Ask students how seed manufacturers find out what the optimal spacing is.

Related Activities

Step 5 in the procedures is fertile with discussion topics for the students. The optimal spacing as described on a seed package is actually a generalization derived from trying a variety of spacings. The process in arriving at the generalization is the same as the process in forming any generalization. It is a regularity or pattern and relates to the description of scientists' search for patterns as well as any other regularity. The value of discussing this with students is that it provides another example for them of science in operation in our everyday world.

The activity may also be repeated with other types of seeds to see if they respond to crowding in the same way as the radish seeds.

Pull up some plants and weigh them, trying to determine what type of spacing gives a maximum yield per area. Try to find out the effects of adding extra fertilizer and water on overcrowding. The results of the experiment with water and fertilizer could lead to a discussion of how farmers can minimize the effects of overcrowding and maximize their yields.

The activity also relates to inquiry activity 9.7, in which crowding can be one of the variables investigated in an activity on plant growth. One hypothesis could be: "The more plants are crowded, the less they grow." Several crowding conditions could be set up to test the hypothesis.

Activity 7.13
Air Expands When Heated

Content Objective

Students will understand the generalization, "Air expands when heated and contracts when cooled" so that, given a description of a situation involving the heating or cooling of air, students will predict the outcome.

Content Background

The air around us is composed of invisible molecules that are constantly in motion. When these molecules are heated, their motion increases; consequently, they exert more pressure on the walls of the container they are in. If the container walls are flexible, the container will expand. If a container is heated without a cap, some of the molecules of air escape through the opening. If the opening is then sealed tightly and the container cooled, the molecules inside (because some escaped) are fewer than those on the outside and have less energy to push against the walls of the container (because there are fewer of them than on the outside).

Consequently, the air pressure from the outside will cause the walls to bend inward.

Materials

Soda bottle, balloons, bunsen or alcohol burner or hot plate, ice, plastic milk carton (gallon size) with cap, empty gallon turpentine can with cap

Procedures

1. Place a balloon over the top of a soda bottle and heat over a bunsen burner or hot plate until the balloon expands. After the balloon has expanded, allow the bottle to cool until you can touch it, and then plunge the bottle in a bath of ice water. Discuss what happens.

2. Have students blow up balloons and measure their length or circumference or both. Then place them in ice water for a few minutes and measure them again.

3. Half-fill the gallon milk carton with boiling water. Swirl the water around to heat up the air inside the carton. Empty the water and immediately put the top on tightly. Then place the container in ice water. Have students observe and discuss the results.

4. Heat the turpentine can over a flame or on a hot plate with the lid *off.* After the can is hot, remove from the heat and immediately put the cap on tightly. Be careful not to burn your hands. Then, as students watch, pour ice water over the walls of the container. If the can was heated sufficiently and the cap is fastened tightly, the can should crumple.

5. Ask students what the four activities have in common and ask them to form a generalization about the data. Introduce the term *air pressure* and ask why the two containers crumpled.

6. Ask students to predict where the warmest part of the room is and explain why. Ask why most clothes are loose at the bottom and tight at the top. Ask where heat registers should be placed in a room for maximum effectiveness.

Related Activities

The generalization in this activity actually describes only one of the characteristics of air. Air has other characteristics: it takes up space, it exerts pressure, and it has weight. A number of activities can be performed to demonstrate each of these characteristics. For example, hang two balloons on the end of a makeshift balance, then inflate one balloon as shown in the figure 7–16.

Another activity involves a card and glass of water (figure 7–17). When the glass is turned upside down, the water doesn't fall out as a result of air pressure. (Practice this one beforehand!)

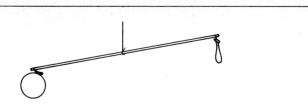

Figure 7–16
A Balance

In another demonstration that air takes up space and exerts pressure, have the students cover the end of a clear plastic straw with a finger and put it down into water (figure 7–18). Because the air occupies space in the straw, it doesn't allow the water to reach a higher level.

The same can be done with a glass or cup that has a paper towel crumpled and pushed into the bottom of it (figure 7–19).

The towel remains dry, demonstrating that air exerts pressure and takes up space.

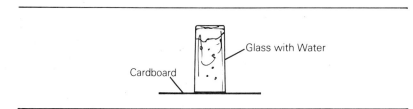

Figure 7–17

Glass with Water

Cardboard

Content Objective

Students will understand how a candle burns so that, when shown a diagram of a burning candle, they can in their own words describe the factors that determine how a candle ignites and burns.

**Activity 7.14
The Burning
Candle**

Content Background

A candle burns when, as it is touched with a match, some of the solid wax liquifies, moves up the wick by capillary action, vaporizes (turns into a gas), and ignites. The flame, then, is caused by burning wax in a gaseous state. The wick actually burns too, but the primary cause of the flame is the burning wax vapor. Capillary action is caused by the attraction of the liquid (wax) for the solid (the candle wick). Capillary action also causes water to rise above the water level when a sponge or paper towel is placed halfway into a glass of water.

Figure 7-18

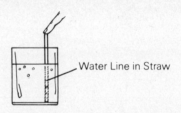

Water Line in Straw

Materials

Candles, pieces of heavy string, paper towels, water glass, glass plate (square of glass about 6×6 cm.)

Procedures

This lesson can be done as a large-group activity with the teacher providing the directions at each step, or, if the children can read and follow directions, it could be done as a center activity. The choice depends on the teacher's goal and the children's background.

1. Divide the class into groups of two or three. Each group should have a candle, string, paper towel, water glass, and plate.

2. Have each group fill the water glass about two-thirds full, then roll the paper towel into a cylinder and put it into the water (see figure 7–20).

Have them record their observations every two to three minutes during the course of the activity. (They will observe that the towel gradually gets wet above the water line, demonstrating capillary action.) Do the same with the piece of heavy string. If students are having trouble seeing the results of capillary action, add a few drops of food coloring to the water.

Figure 7–19

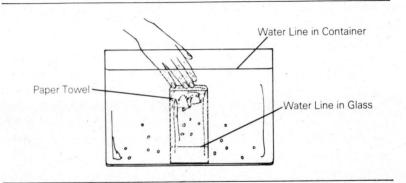

Water Line in Container

Paper Towel

Water Line in Glass

Figure 7-20

Paper Towel

3. Have students chip some pieces of wax from the candle and have them try to ignite the solid candle wax. They should record their observations. (Solid wax won't burn.)

4. Have the children melt the solid wax by heating the wax chips on the glass plate over the candle flame. Have them try to ignite the liquid wax. (Liquid wax also will not burn.) Have them record their observations.

5. Have them try to ignite the string. It will, perhaps, burn with a dull flame but will not resemble a candle flame. Again, record their observations.

6. Now each group should light its candle and observe what happens to the wax at the top.

7. Have the children incorporate observations of their attempts to ignite solid wax, liquid wax, and the string (wick), together with their observations of the paper towel in the water to form a description of how the candle burns. The summarizing of the activities and forming the description may require a large-group discussion with some prompting from the teacher.

Related Activities

This activity relates closely to exercise 4.2 from chapter 4, an experiential activity, and activity 9.3, an inquiry activity. The three lessons show the development of activities through the three phases of science. If done in sequence, they illustrate how science develops.

Content Objective

Students will understand the concept *camouflage* so that, given pictures of animals in a natural setting, they will be able to identify those that are camouflaged.

**Activity 7.15
Camouflage**

Content Background

Camouflage is a means of protection in which animals are difficult to see because their shape, color, or texture causes them to blend in with their background. Camouflage is a relative phenomenon in which environment is an important factor. For instance, a zebra is camouflaged in the underbrush at dusk; during midday on an open plain it is not.

Materials

Color pictures or slides of animals, some of which are camouflaged and others are not. Pictures can be obtained from books or magazines like *National Geographic, Audubon,* or *National Wildlife.*

Procedures

1. Show the students a picture of an animal in its natural setting. In this activity it is probably better to start with an uncamouflaged animal to add to the discovery process. The animal chosen could be an antelope on an open plain, a brown seal on an ice floe, or an elephant in the open.

2. Ask the children to describe the picture. You can add an experiential dimension to the activity by spending practice time describing observations about the picture (see related activities).

3. Show the students another picture, of either a camouflaged or an uncamouflaged animal. Have the students compare and contrast the pictures.

4. Continue the procedure of showing camouflaged and uncamouflaged animals, prompting the children to state that when the animals are camouflaged, their color, shape, and/or texture makes them hard to identify.

5. If possible, show an animal in one setting where it is camouflaged and in another setting where it is not, to illustrate that camouflage depends on the animal's immediate environment.

6. Have the students state a definition of camouflage.

Related Activities

This activity can be done as an experiential activity with young children (see activity 5.15), in which the emphasis would be on making observations of the animals and comparing and contrasting their features. A number of related incidental generalizations can also be derived from the activity, such as, "Small animals tend to be camouflaged more than large animals," and "Animals who protect themselves by fleeing tend to be long-legged." The activity can be extended to a discussion of other forms of protection such as changing color (snowshoe rabbits and ptarmigan), emitting odors (skunks), and protective coats (armadillos and porcupines). A trip to a zoo, aquarium, or aviary could serve as the culmination for the lesson.

In another lesson, students can investigate the effect that color, size, and shape have on our ability to see objects. Have students cut out equal numbers of pieces from disferent-colored construction paper. Make some of the pieces very small (like a grain of rice), medium (like a raisin), and large (like a penny). Make some round, some square, and some long and thin. Mark off a meter-square area on a green lawn and sprinkle the pieces in this area. Record which pieces were found within the first minute, the second minute, and so on. Discuss the results and generalize from the findings. Do the same activity in a different environment (such as dry brown grass) and compare the results with the first activity.

Finally, a discussion of animals' color blindness might be interesting. Because animals in general are color blind, why would an animal such as a tiger evolve to be so brightly colored? The same question can be raised for other animals. Hunters take advantage of this phenomenon by wearing red jackets, which are visible to humans but not to deer and other color blind animals.

Activity 7.16 Density

Content Objective
Students will understand the concept *density* so that, given the size and weight of different objects, they will be able to tell which is most dense.

Content Background
Density is a concept that describes the weight of an object in a certain amount of volume. For example, suppose two identical glasses were filled with equal volumes of water and sand, respectively. The glass of sand would weigh more than the glass of water, so we say sand is denser than water. Scientists typically describe density as the number of grams each cubic centimeter of a substance weighs (g/cm^3).

Materials
Water, rubbing alcohol, cooking oil, salt, sugar, sand, rectangular block of wood, small centimeter ruler, balance (see activity 7.4) and gram weights, several identical containers (small paper cups, cylinders)

Procedures
This activity might well be done at a learning center, unless students have already built balances. If done as a group activity, the lesson should be performed in groups of two or three.

Figure 7–21
**Determining the Density
of Irregular Materials**

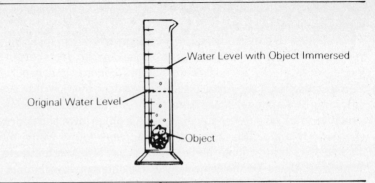

1. Have the children fill each of the small containers respectively with equal volumes of water, alcohol, oil, sand, sugar, and salt.

2. Have them put one container on each arm of the balance, for example, water on one side and alcohol on the other. Continue this until all materials have been compared and they can be ordered (classified by weight) from the heaviest to lightest. Since all volumes are the same, the heaviest object is the most dense.

3. If the volume of the container is known, the density can be calculated. A small paper clip weighs about 1 gram, so paper clips can be used as weights if standard weights are unavailable. Density can be calculated by dividing the substance's weight by its volume.

4. Bring out a baseball-sized ball of cotton and piece of string. Weigh both together on the balance and then ask students what will happen to the weight of the cotton if it is wadded up and wrapped tightly with the string. Ask the same about its volume. Then wad and wrap it up and weigh again.

5. Have the children try to apply what they have learned by determining the density of the wood block. (They will have to measure the block, calculate its volume, and find its weight.)

Related Activities

This lesson could be taught in conjunction with experiential activity 5.14, on weighing and measuring, and with discovery activity 7.4 on bouyancy. This activity can also be related to math activities in multiplying length times width times height to find the volume of the block and then dividing to find its density. It can be extended by determining the density of several objects of different shapes, such as spheres or cylinders, depending on the background of the children. Also, the density of irregularly shaped materials could be determined by immersing them in a graduated cylinder as shown in figure 7–21, and measuring how much the water level is raised. This would be used to determine their volume.

The weight of these objects could be determined by placing them on a balance beam and balancing them with paper clips or other standard weights. Note that this method of computing density only works with objects that sink in water.

Content Objective

Students will understand that the rate of swing of a pendulum is determined by its length so that, given pendulums of varying lengths, they can serial order them from fastest-swinging to slowest-swinging.

Content Background

A pendulum can be made from a piece of string and a paper clip. Its rate of swing, that is, how fast it swings from one side to the other and back again, is determined by its length and not the weight of the object on the end.

Materials

String, masking tape, paper clips, marking pen

Procedures

1. Give each child a length of string and a paper clip. The pieces of string can be cut in advance to ensure a variety of lengths ranging from short (20 cm.) to quite long (100 cm.).

2. Direct students to tie a small knot in one end of the string, and a small loop in the opposite end, and hook the paper clip into the loop.

3. Have them hold the string by the knot (to be certain they hold the string in the same place each trial); when you say "go" have them count the number of complete cycles in a certain time period—about 15 to 20 seconds.

4. Repeat the timing and counting two or three times to see if they get the same number of swings each trial. Emphasize that the search for patterns or regularities in science, one form of regularity is consistency within our own trials.

5. When everyone has consistent measurements, place a strip of masking tape on the wall or board and tape the knot of each pendulum to the tape, in order, according to the number of swings in the time period. Make sure that the knots in the strings are all on the same level. Your display will look approximately like figure 7–22. Displayed like this, the pendulums actually form a physical graph that is very concrete for students and obviously shows the relationship between length and rate of swing. Students should be asked to generalize about the data.

Activity 7.17
The Pendulum

Figure 7–23a
A Pendulum

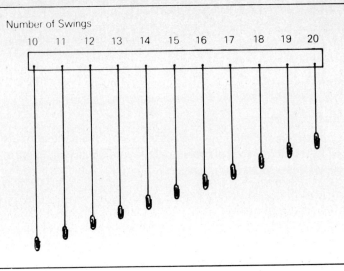

Number of Swings

6. Examine the data in the graph and determine if there are any gaps in the data (for example, no pendulum that swung thirteen times in a given time period). If there is a gap, ask students how they could make a pendulum that would swing at that rate. If no gap exists, ask students to extend the graph downward or upward. In either case, verify their prediction with a newly constructed pendulum.

Related Activities

This lesson is closely related to exercise 8.4, which shows how a related pendulum problem could be done as an inquiry activity.

The idea of using a simple pendulum as a clock can be introduced; students can be asked to design a pendulum that swings exactly once every second or two seconds. Students might use this "clock" to measure their pulse rate (activity 9.9) and compare their results with the clock in the room. For more advanced students, the pendulum might serve as a starting point for a discussion of kinetic and potential energy, as demonstrated in figure 7–23b. (Kinetic energy is energy in motion. Potential energy is stored energy.)

**Activity 7.18
Series and Parallel
Circuits**

Content Objective

Students will understand series and parallel circuits, so they will be able to cite examples of each and describe their effect on the electrical circuit.

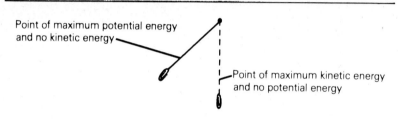

Point of maximum potential energy and no kinetic energy

Point of maximum kinetic energy and no potential energy

Figure 7–23b
Kinetic Energy

Content Background

An electrical circuit is a pathway for electrons to flow from the battery to the bulb (or other machine, like a radio) and back to the battery again. To work, electrical circuits must provide a complete path for the electrons to flow out from the energy source and back again. When the circuit is not complete, a light bulb will not shine and machines will not work. For example, when the switch is open, the circuit is not complete; when the switch is closed, the circuit is complete because there is a complete path for the electrons to travel on (figure 7–24).

In a series circuit, there is only one pathway for the electricity (see figure 7–25). In a parallel circuit, there are two paths for the flow of electrons (see figure 7–25).

In a series circuit, if one bulb burns out, the circuit is broken and all bulbs go out; while in a parallel circuit, if one bulb burns out, the electricity still has a pathway and the other bulbs do not go out. Old-fashioned Christmas tree lights used to be organized in a series in which one bulb failure would cause the whole chain to go out.

Materials

Dry-cell or flashlight batteries with holders, wire, small bulb holders, and flashlight-type bulbs

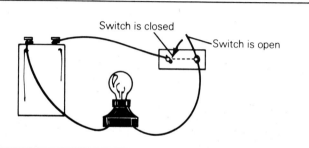

Switch is closed

Switch is open

Figure 7–24
A Simple Circuit

Figure 7-25
Electrical Circuits

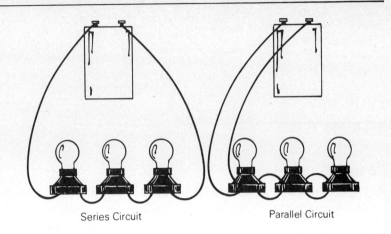

Series Circuit   Parallel Circuit

Procedures

1. Give the children a dry cell, wire, bulb holder, and bulb and tell them to try and make the bulb light.

2. Watch them work and prompt those children who are having considerable difficulty. To light the bulb, the wire must afford a path from the battery to the light bulb and back again to the battery (a complete circuit).

3. After they successfully light the bulbs, have them connect a second bulb in series with the first and observe the brightness of the bulbs. Have them disconnect one of the bulbs and observe what happens.

4. Have the children make several arrangements of batteries and bulbs (see figure 7-26) and observe the brightness of the bulbs in each case. For instance, they could use the following arrangements:

- Two bulbs in series
- Two bulbs in parallel
- Two batteries in series with each bulb arrangement
- Two batteries in parallel with each bulb arrangement

5. With each arrangement, have the children unscrew a bulb or disconnect one wire from the battery and observe the results.

6. Have them generalize about series and parallel circuits.

Related Activities

The activity can be related to household wiring. The children can be asked if house lights are wired in series or parallel and how they

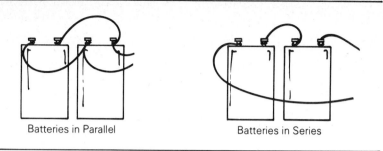

Figure 7–26
**Different Arrangement of
Batteries**

Batteries in Parallel   Batteries in Series

know. (If one bulb burns out the others stay on, so house lights are wired in parallel.) They can also look at other equipment such as flashlights and decide if the batteries are in series or parallel. The relationship of electrical circuits to conductors (activity 7.8) and insulators (7.21) could also be investigated.

Content Objective

Students will understand the concept of friction so that, when provided with an array of objects and an inclined plane, they will predict which objects will encounter the least friction and slide down the plane the fastest.

**Activity 7.19
Friction**

Content Background

Friction is the resistance to motion between two bodies. In general, smooth hard surfaces rubbing against each other cause less friction than soft, rough, or uneven surfaces. Stated positively, friction allows us to grip and hold things; stated negatively, friction causes moving parts that rub against each other to wear out and generate heat.

Materials

A wooden board, spring balance, blocks of wood that are approximately the same size. Some of the blocks of wood should be sanded smooth, some left or made rough by making shallow cuts with a hand saw, some should be covered on one side with a piece of sandpaper, and some oiled with any kind of oil or petroleum jelly. Set up an inclined plane by placing the wooden board at an angle to the floor. The exact angle should be determined by sliding the sanded blocks down the plane.

Procedures

1. Set up the inclined plane so that the sanded blocks will slowly slide down the inclined plane.

2. Place the rough-cut block on the board so that the rough surface is facing down. Ask students why it wouldn't move or why it moved so slowly. Pass the block around for students to feel.

3. Do the same with the sandpaper and oiled blocks.

4. Make a chart as shown in table 7–9 and ask students to fill in the values.

Table 7–9

	Block	How it felt
Fastest		
Slower		
Slower		
Slowest		

5. Introduce the term friction and ask *students* to make a generalization about friction and speed.

6. Have students set up their own timed experiment, in which the sliding times for the different blocks are timed and compared. Arrange the slope so that the slowest block just makes it down the board.

Related Activities

Have students rub their hands together and ask what they feel. Put lotion on their hands and then compare with the hands dry. Also, try putting round dowels, pencils, or marbles between the hands and ask how they help. Examine a set of wheels (bicycle, wagon, or roller skate wheels would do) and discuss how the ball bearings in the wheels help reduce friction.

Compare rolling friction to sliding friction by pulling a heavy box over the floor and then placing dowels under the box and comparing the effort needed. Effort can be measured by hooking up a spring balance to the weights.

Situations in which friction is desirable and those in which it is not can be discussed. The discussion can be extended to ways we reduce friction, such as engine oil in cars. (See activities 5.10, 9.12 and 9.13.) This lesson can also be related in a social studies lesson to the invention of the wheel and its effect on human activity.

The initial activity may also be altered by pulling the blocks up the inclined plane with spring balances if they are available. Use the balances to measure the force required to move the blocks; compare starting friction to moving friction.

If spring balances are not available, large rubber bands and meter sticks may be used in their place (figure 7–27).

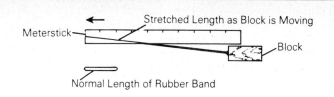

Figure 7-27
**Apparatus to Measure
Force**

The extension of the rubber band is a measure of the force required to move the block. Activities might include putting a second, identical block on the first and comparing the required force. Students could then be asked to investigate if twice the weight required twice as much force.

Content Objective

Students should understand that plants need food to grow and that they get this food from various sources, so that, provided with a description of a growing situation, students will state whether the plants will have the necessary nutrients.

Content Background

Plants need to obtain minerals and chemicals from their environment in order to grow. Usually these nutrients are obtained through the roots, which absorb them from the water in the ground and the soil itself. Certain planting mediums, like vermiculite, are for the most part non-nutritive and need to be supplemented with other nutrient sources. The amount of chemical and mineral nutrients present in water will vary with the location. Distilled water has no nutrients, soft water few, and hard water the most.

Materials

Potting soil, vermiculite (obtained quite inexpensively at any garden shop), distilled water, fertilizer, and seeds (bean, pea, or corn)

Procedures

1. Have students in groups plant seeds in one container of regular potting soil and three containers of vermiculite. Water all the plants, using distilled water for two containers of vermiculite and for the potting soil. Use tap water for the remaining container of vermiculite. Fertilize one of the distilled water vermiculite containers, but not the other.

2. Have students observe the containers daily and record when the seeds first sprout, their height, and number of leaves.

**Activity 7.20
Plants and
Nutrients**

3. Have the groups compare their results by putting the data into a table as shown in table 7–10.

Table 7–10

Condition	Days to Sprout	Height	# of Leaves
Soil			
Vermiculite + distilled water			
Vermiculite + distilled water + fertilizer			
Vermiculite and tap water			

4. Ask students to generalize about the data. Also, ask them to explain any trends in the data. Introduce the term nutrients and ask students where the plants in each condition got their nutrients.

5. Start some slips of ivy, coleus, or philodendron in distilled water and regular water and ask students to predict what will happen. Buy some industrial or construction sand from a building materials store and plant seeds in it. Ask students what should be added to the sand to help the plants grow.

Related Activities

Write a letter to the water purification plant in your area, asking them to identify the chemicals in your tap water. Obtain a book on hydroponics (gardening in a water medium) and plant a small-scale hydroponic garden. Bring in some empty fertilizer bags from a plant nursery and discuss the different percentage of nutrients found in each. Write the county agricultural agent, asking for materials on soil characteristics in your area.

This activity also relates closely to inquiry activity 9.7, in which other factors in plant growth are considered. Experiential activity 5.3 is also related; in this activity children can gain valuable experience in measuring and organizing data.

**Activity 7.21
Insulation**

Content Objective

Students will understand the concept of insulation so that, given descriptions of different types of insulators, students will predict what effect each will have on heat loss.

Content Background

Heat energy causes molecules to move faster. When heat is added to a substance, the molecules move faster; when a substance cools, the molecules move more slowly. Heat loss occurs when molecules in a substance transfer their energy to the molecules around them. Insulators prevent this process by slowing down the transmission of heat energy from the object to its environment.

Materials

Thermometers (purchased fairly inexpensively in large lots from a school supply firm), plastic tumblers (at least six for each group) hot water, aluminum foil, paper, thin cotton cloth, and heavier wool cloth

Procedures

1. Have students form groups of two or three and have each group cover the sides of several plastic tumblers with different materials: aluminum foil, a layer of paper, four layers of paper, thin cotton cloth, and heavier wool cloth. These coverings can be taped on. Leave one glass uncovered.

2. Heat water on a hot plate to about 70°C. Check to make sure that the water won't melt the plastic cups.

3. Have them immediately measure the temperatures in each container, leaving the thermometers in for at least a minute to get a true reading. Ideally, there should be enough thermometers for each of the containers. Measure each container again at regular intervals every two minutes or every five minutes.

4. Collect the data from the individual groups, average it, and put it in a table such as the one shown here for the class to see and discuss.

Container	Immediate Temperature	Temperature at 5 min.	Temperature at 10 min.	Temperature at 15 min.

5. Ask the students to generalize about the data. Also, ask them why some containers lost heat faster than others.

6. Have a contest to see who can devise the most efficiently insulated container with the materials. Discuss with students why and how they think their designs would work.

Related Activities

Try the same activity with ice water and compare results to those of the heat activity. Try different types of bottoms and tops on the containers

Figure 7–28
**Heat Loss of the
Containers**

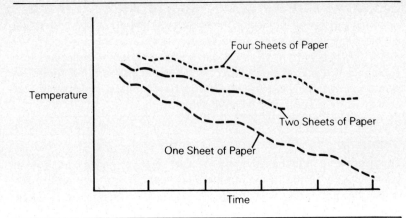

such as aluminum foil or cloth to see what effect they have on temperature gain or loss.

The activity also relates closely to experiential activity 5.5 on thermometers and to inquiry activity 9.14, in which materials that absorb and store energy are investigated.

Students can gain valuable experience in working with data in this activity when they average the data from their trials. Students may also be asked to graph their data as in figure 7–28.

This experience can emphasize that scientists, in doing experiments, gather large quantities of data and then graph and average results and look for trends in the data. Trends amount to patterns or regularities; graphs help us see these patterns more clearly.

**Activity 7.22
Symmetry**

Content Objective

Students will understand the concepts of bilateral and radial symmetry that, when presented with an array of objects, they will select those that illustrate each type of symmetry.

Content Background

All living things are organized in some systematic fashion. Two of the most common methods of organization are bilateral and radial symmetry. In bilateral symmetry, the object or organism is organized so that a line down the middle would separate the object into two separate but equal parts. For example, imagine a line running from the head to the toes through the middle of our bodies. Radial symmetry involves circular organization, in which the object or organism is organized around a central point like a starfish. Note that an object that has radial symmetry also has bilateral symmetry.

Materials

Paper, pictures from magazines, mirrors, objects with bilateral symmetry (toy car, chair, leaves, fish), objects with radial symmetry (wheels on toy car, bowl, umbrella top, orange cut in half)

Procedures

1. Arrange the materials on the floor or on a desk for all the students to see.

2. Ask students to make observations and then ask them to classify the objects. Accept any classification systems they suggest, as long as they are consistent.

3. Arrange the materials in two groups on the basis of one type of symmetry. Ask students to make observations and have them try to infer the basis for the grouping. Spend time in discussion and prompt students if necessary. Do the same with the other type of symmetry.

4. When appropriate, introduce the terms *bilateral symmetry* and *radial symmetry* and explain how the terms relate to the objects in the groups. Show students how mirrors can be placed on the central axis of bilaterally symmetrical objects to check whether or not they are symmetrical.

5. Have students look around the room and discover other examples of bilateral and radial symmetry in the room (waste basket, light fixture, windows, and so on).

Related Activities

Ask students to cut pictures from magazines and mount them as illustrations of the concepts. Show students some letters (O, A, and H) and some words (tot and tat) that have bilateral symmetry. Ask if they can suggest others.

An interesting and somewhat entertaining activity is to group students in pairs. Ask them to study each others' heads and faces to determine if we are truly bilaterally symmetrical (in general, we are not). Close observation will generally show one eyebrow higher than the other, a slightly bent nose, one ear lower than the other and so on. These findings can be amusing if handled in the proper spirit. (Of course, you will have to judge the advisability of this activity if you have a student with an obvious unique physical characteristic about which he or she might be sensitive.)

This activity also relates to experiential activity 5.6, in which mirrors are used to create additional images of objects.

Activity 7.23
Plants and Water

Content Objective

Students will understand how water flows through plants so that, when given a picture of a plant, the student will trace the movement of water through the plant and describe factors that influence this movement.

Content Background

Water is an essential ingredient for the growth of all plants. It enters the plant through the roots, travels through the stem, and is lost to the environment through the leaves. When transplanting plants, it is often advisable to trim back some of the foliage (leaves) to minimize the amount of water lost by the plant and thus avoid damage.

Materials

Bean plants, approximately 5 cm. tall (they should have four to six leaves), potting soil, milk cartons with drainage holes in the bottom

Procedures

1. Have students form groups of two of three and prepare several potting containers. These are prepared by punching holes in the bottom of milk cartons and filling them two-thirds full with potting soil.

2. Have each group transplant several bean plants into different pots. The first group should transplant the beans as usual, being careful to disturb the roots as little as possible. The second group should remove all the fine root hairs before transplanting. Have the third group do the same to the roots, but also pinch off all but one or two leaves. Have the fourth group leave the roots intact but pinch off all but one or two leaves. Give all the plants equal amounts of water and put in indirect sunlight.

3. Observe the plants over the next two or three weeks and have the students describe their observations in writing.

4. Share the results as a group activity in which each group has input into the construction of the data, as shown in table 7-11.

Table 7-11

Plant Condition	Observations			
	Day 2	Day 4	Day 6	Day 8
First Group				
Second Group				
Third Group				
Fourth Group				

5. Ask students to generalize about the results and make explanatory inferences about their findings.

6. Ask what people should do when they transplant bushes and shrubs to prevent damage to the plant.

Related Activities

Vary the activity by putting some of the plants in each group in direct sunlight and some in shade. Or cover some of the pots and plants in each group with a plastic bag to maintain high humidity and thus reduce moisture loss from leaves.

The activity may be related in discussion to inquiry activity 9.10, where surface area is considered as a factor in evaporation. While not exactly the same phenomenon, the plant's water loss is reduced when leaves are removed because the surface area of the plant is reduced.

Content Objective

Activity 7.24
Shadows

Students will understand how the position of the sun affects the shadows that are cast so that, when given a drawing of the sun and an object, they will describe the changes that occur in the shadows during the day.

Content Background

As the sun moves through the sky, the shadows it casts vary with its height and position. In the morning it is low on the horizon and casts a long shadow. At noon it is directly overhead and casts a short shadow, and in the late afternoon the shadows become long again. The position of the sun also changes from day to day, rising earlier and setting later in the spring and rising later and setting earlier in the fall. In addition, the sun also is lower on the horizon in fall and winter.

Materials

Wooden stakes, crayons, butcher paper

Procedures

1. Have students drive a wooden stake into the ground so that approximately 30 cm. are above the ground. Give each group of students a meter-long piece of butcher paper to put on the ground so the shadow from the morning, noon and afternoon sun falls on it. Placement of the paper may have to be experimented with for a day or two before the actual measurements are taken. Mark the four cor-

Figure 7-29
Investigation of Heat Intensity

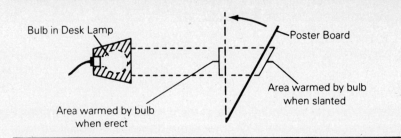

ners of the paper with stick markers so the identical location can be found the next day to allow the paper to be taken into the schoolroom after each measurement.

2. Have students outline the shadow cast by the sun at nine o'clock, noon, and three o'clock, but be sure they do not fill in the shadowed area.

3. Repeat this procedure every few days over a period of several weeks.

4. Discuss the results as a group. Ask why the shadows are changing and if there is any pattern to the changes. Have the students generalize about their findings.

5. Ask students to predict what their shadow drawings will look like in two weeks by sketching in an outline with a pencil. (They can predict this by inferring from the changes that have already occurred.) Also, have students simulate the shadow changes in a darkened classroom with a flashlight and a ruler stuck in clay.

Related Activities

Repeat the activity during a different season and compare the results. You may wish to integrate this lesson with the experiential activity on weather (5.4).

In an additional related activity, have students investigate the intensity of the heat received on a certain area when the sun is at an angle or aimed directly at the area. This activity may be simulated with a light bulb and a piece of poster paper, arranged as in figure 7-29.

The longer shadows in the morning and afternoon help explain why it is warmer at noon and also why it is warmer in the summer when the sun's rays are more direct. We are actually farther from the sun in winter than summer, so directness of rays is the determining factor in affecting temperature.

We began this book by describing science as a search for regularities, then showed how this search pervades the elementary science curriculum. In the primary grades, it is characterized by heavy emphasis on the processes of observation and classification and by "hands-on" activities that allow children to gather data through sensory experiences. We then showed how the experiential model, a teaching strategy for promoting this type of activity, corresponds to the early stages of a developing branch of science.

As we progressed, we used a dual framework, the cognitive development of the child and the development of science. As a learner moves into the middle elementary grades, there is a shift away from an emphasis on experiential activities for their own sake and a shift toward activities that lead to the formation of essential concepts and generalizations.

Chapter 8 The Inquiry Model: An Experimental Teaching Strategy

The discovery model, presented in chapter 6, is a strategy for helping children learn these forms of knowledge. While experiential activities are still important, they become a means for learning concepts and generalizations, rather than ends in themselves. This trend in the curriculum parallels the progress of science as it moves from the stage of information gathering to one in which information becomes organized into patterns in the form of concepts and generalizations.

We are now ready to move into the third stage of the development of science, in which controlled experiments are used to form generalizations about the world at large. We call this the inquiry phase, and in this chapter the inquiry model will be presented as a strategy for teaching children these skills. In inquiry activities, students become active investigators by searching for regularities through the process of experimentation. In these activities students not only learn content but also learn how to structure situations to produce their own knowledge. In a sense they are learning to learn. The inquiry model is essentially a sequential teaching strategy with the following steps:

- A problem or question is identified.
- Hypotheses are formed relevant to the problem.
- Data is gathered to test the hypotheses.
- A confirmed or revised hypothesis is formed, based on the data gathered.

The activity begins with the identification of a problem or question that is of interest to the class. After the problem has been clearly defined, students attempt to form hypotheses or tentative solutions to the problem. Data is then gathered to test each hypothesis, and the hypothesis is accepted or rejected depending on its ability to account for the data. We will illustrate this process in the paragraphs that follow.

After completing this section of the chapter you should be able to meet the following objective:

- You will understand the basic format of an inquiry activity so that, given a description of an inquiry lesson, you will identify the four major steps.

The Inquiry Model in the Classroom

Ms. Norris, fourth-grade teacher, wanted to provide her students with experiences in inquiry and the analysis of problems.

She began her activity by asking, "How many of you have ever flown a paper airplane? Good, just about everyone has. Well, today we're going to study about paper airplanes and answer the question 'What determines how far a paper airplane will fly?'"

With that she wrote the question on the board for all to see and asked if anybody had any ideas.

The class pondered the question a moment and finally Susan said, "It will fly farther if it isn't too big."

"That's a possibility, Susan," replied Ms. Norris. "Now try to put your statement in general terms."

Susan struggled and was uncertain of how to begin.

Ms. Norris then prompted, "Which will fly farther, big or little airplanes?"

Susan then said uncertainly, "Small ones fly farther than big ones."

"Excellent, Susan!" encouraged Ms. Norris, and she wrote this hypothesis on the board.

"Now, how about some other ideas? Anybody?" She waited a few moments without a response from the students. Finally she asked, "What effect do you suppose the size of the wing would have on the distance the plane will fly?"

Bobby responded, "It will fly farther if the wing is big."

"Good, Bobby, could you say that in a general sentence the way Susan made her statement?"

"I know, I think," Bobby continued. "The bigger the wing the farther the plane will fly."

"Good. Any other ideas?"

No one responded, so she went on, "That's fine, everyone. We may think of some new ones later, but for now let's see if we can figure out a way to test these to see if they check out."

"I know, I know!" Chuck said excitedly. "Let's build some airplanes and fly them."

"Okay," Ms. Norris smiled. "Let's think about how they have to be built to test our ideas."

John raised his hand tentatively, "If we wanted to test our first idea, we could build some small ones and some big ones and see which will fly farther."

"Good, John. Let's test this idea by each making a plane. I have some pieces of paper in three different sizes. Each of you take one of each size."

Ms. Norris passed out the papers and guided the children through the process of constructing the paper airplanes. Finally, each student had three airplanes of different sizes.

"Let's look at the planes we've made and see how they're similar. Anyone?"

After a short pause Carol volunteered, "They're all white."

Jim added, "They all look alike except some are smaller."

"Good, Jim. What do we know about the shape or design of the planes based on what Jim said?" After receiving no response she added, "Are the shapes the same or are they different?"

"They're the same," Jim said.

"So what have we done?"

"We have different-sized planes but have kept the shape the same."

"Fine. We might also say we've kept the design the same in each case," Ms. Norris added, rewording Jim's statement a bit further.

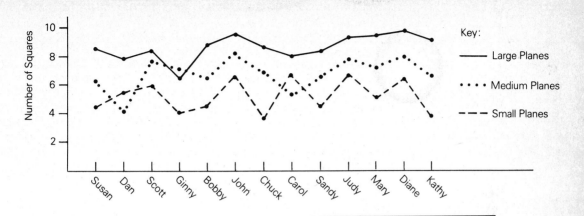

Figure 8–1
The Effect of Airplane Size on Flying Distance

She then had the children line up and throw each of their airplanes twice, measuring the distance after each throw. They were instructed to throw the planes with the same effort (if possible) in each case. She had a tile floor in her classroom, so she had the children count the number of tiles for each throw as a measure of the distance the planes traveled.

As the children gathered their data, they recorded the numbers on a section of the blackboard that the teacher had prepared for the activity. Then they talked about ways to graph the data to help them decide whether their hypothesis was acceptable or not. The graph they made can be seen in figure 8–1.

"You've done very well," Ms. Norris said. "Now let's look at our results."

"The line for the bigger planes is higher than it is for the smaller planes."

"That means we were wrong," Margy said fretfully.

"Oh, don't worry about that," Ms. Norris responded quickly. "Our suggestion represented our best idea at the time we thought of it. We found, however, that the data we gathered when we threw the planes didn't support the idea, so we have to reject it. The idea was fine. We really don't want to worry about right and wrong but whether the information we gather supports or doesn't support our original idea. Now, who could summarize our results in a general statement, Bill?"

"The larger the paper airplane the farther it will fly," replied Bill, after a moment's hesitation.

"Excellent, Bill! That's a good generalization. Class, do you think this generalization will always be true?"

The class didn't reply.

"Well, can you think of some situation where the generalization wouldn't be true? Jim?"

"If the paper airplanes got real big they might get too heavy, and then they wouldn't fly farther."

"That's a good answer, Jim."

"Now," she went on, "let's check our second idea. We should have learned some techniques from our first experiment."

After a pause she prompted, "What do we know about the design in this case?"

"I know!" Bobby jumped up. "We'll change the design so the wings of one plane are bigger than the wings on the other."

"But we'll keep the size of the airplane the same," Joan added.

"Excellent, class," Ms. Norris replied. She then handed each of the students three identical pieces of paper and showed them how to build planes with three different designs. Again she had them line up and throw the planes, using the same procedure.

"Now," she went on, "how can we record our information?"

"We could make a graph like before," Betty suggested, "to compare the effects of the different wing designs."

"That sounds fine," Ms. Norris replied.

The students then recorded the information and looked at the results on the graph.

Brenda began, "It looks like our idea was okay because the ones with the biggest wings flew the farthest."

"Yes, that means we can accept our idea," Jerry added.

"Now, who can summarize these results in the form of a generalization? Mary?"

"The bigger the wings the farther a paper airplane will fly?" offered Mary.

"Very good," Ms. Norris praised.

"There is something I don't understand," Karen questioned. "Didn't the ones that were bigger in the beginning also have bigger wings?"

"Go on," encouraged Ms. Norris. "Why might that be important?"

"Well, we don't know if the big airplanes flew longer because of their size, or the size of the wings."

"That's an excellent point, Karen!" Ms. Norris responded. "Could you suggest how we might investigate this problem?"

The class then prepared to study the problem more closely by designing planes of different overall sizes but with the same-sized wings.

The Four-Step Procedure

Let's stop now and discuss the relationship between Ms. Norris's activity and the inquiry model. The activity began with the teacher presenting the question, "What determines how far a paper airplane will fly?" to the class (step one). In response to the question the students initially formed two hypotheses, which Ms. Norris referred to as "ideas" (step two). The first was the statement relating the size of the plane and the distance it will fly, and the second was the hypothesis relating the wingspan and distance. Each of these hypotheses became the focal point for subsequent data gathering (step three). The students gathered data by throwing the planes and measuring the distance each plane traveled.

This was followed by an analysis and the ultimate rejection of the first hypothesis and acceptance of the second (step four). The activity is summarized in table 8-1.

Table 8-1 **Inquiry Steps Being Implemented**

1. Question or problem	What factors determine how far a paper airplane will fly?
2. Hypotheses	Small planes fly farther than large planes. Planes with big wings fly farther than planes with small wings.
3. Data gathering	The children threw the planes and summarized the data in graphs.
4. Analysis of the hypotheses	The class rejected the first hypothesis and accepted the second.

The Student's Role

In this activity, the students took a more active role in forming and investigating their hypotheses than they did in the other models. In an inquiry activity, the regularity (hypothesis) is proposed in advance, then tested with data. In a discovery activity, data is presented first and then a concept or generalization is formed. One result of this difference is that an inquiry activity generally is more demanding of the learner than either of the other types.

The students were processing information when they set up procedures to test their hypotheses, when they actually gathered the data and placed it into charts and graphs, and when they analyzed the data in terms of their hypotheses. In a very real sense they were "doing" science. The level of sophistication was obviously different from that of scientists working in laboratories, but the process was the same.

While processing data the students were also learning important inquiry skills and concepts. They were learning how to form hypotheses, how to gather data, and how to analyze the data in terms of the hypotheses they had formed. These skills are valuable not only to a scientist but also to people in the everyday world who have problems to solve and decisions to make.

Let us look a bit more closely at the concept of *hypothesis.* A hypothesis is essentially a generalization that is presented in advance of an investigation and is used as the basis for gathering data. For example, in Ms. Norris's activity the first hypothesis was *Small planes fly farther than big ones.* (Notice that when Susan suggested, "It will fly farther if it isn't too big," Ms. Norris encouraged her to reword the statement in the form of a generalization.) The students then used the hypothesis as the basis for gathering their data by making paper airplanes of different sizes to see if the hypothesis would be supported by the data. The class found that their first hypothesis had to be rejected but their second could be accepted.

In the course of the activity, the teacher also made an important point regarding the acceptance or rejection or the rightness or wrongness of hypotheses. Hypotheses are tools to help us in our inquiry investigations and as such aren't really "right" or "wrong." It is important that students do not feel that the hypothesis unsupported by data is "wrong." Rightness or wrongness is never a consideration in forming hypotheses. Rather, students should be helped to understand that a hypothesis that was rejected was just as good as one that was accepted and that the whole purpose of an inquiry activity is to discover things about the world rather than "proving" something right or wrong.

Variables in an Experiment

In her activity Ms. Norris used, but did not explicitly label, the concepts of independent, dependent, and controlled variable. An *independent variable* is some factor in an experiment we are interested in investigating. We focus on the independent variable because we think that it affects or influences the outcome of the experiment. In the first experiment the independent variable was the size of the plane. The students selected plane size as an independent variable to investigate because they thought it would make a difference in how far the airplane would fly. In the second experiment the independent variable was the wing design. Again this factor was selected for investigation because the class thought that design would make a difference in the experiment.

The *dependent variable,* on the other hand, is the factor in the experiment that is being influenced or changed. For example, using an illustration from chapter 3, if we wanted to find out which kind of dog food was best for puppy growth, puppy growth measured in height and weight would be the dependent variable because it was influenced by the kind of food, the independent variable. In the lesson at the beginning of the chapter, distance was the dependent variable in both experiments.

A third type of variable in an experiment, the *control,* assures that the experiment is a fair one. In experiments we try to keep everything else the same for different experimental conditions *except* the independent variable. All the variables that are kept the same are called controlled variables. In the first airplane activity, the design of the planes was controlled; in the second, the size of the plane was controlled.

At the end of the activity, Karen noted that the size of the wing was different when the overall size was different, suggesting it was an uncontrolled variable in the activity. Uncontrolled variables often exist in experiments and investigators try to control them as much as possible to make their experiments fair. As Ms. Norris's activity ended, her class was involved in preparing a method for investigating the size of the wing as an independent variable, which would then solve the problem Karen raised. More will be said about independent, dependent, and controlled variables in the planning section of this chapter.

Directions: Read the following teaching episode and answer the questions that follow.

Exercise 8.1

Ms. Taylor was teaching a unit on the human body. Part of the content included a section on the circulatory system and how it works. To teach analysis skills and provide variety she decided to try an inquiry activity.

She began by saying, "Who knows what your pulse rate is? Lynn?"

"It's how fast your heart goes," Lynn replied.

"Good," Miss Taylor encouraged, "and who knows how we can count that? Jan?"

"The doctor can do that by listening to your chest," Jan responded.

"Fine, can anyone think of another way? Mary?"

"You can hold your wrists like this and feel the bumps going through your veins."

"That's good, Mary. Let's everyone try and see if you can feel your pulse," directed Ms. Taylor.

She then went around the room helping students find the pulse and showing how to time it using the clock on the wall. After everyone could count their pulse rate she continued by writing the following question on the board: *What makes your pulse rate beat faster?*

"Everybody look at what I've written on the board," Ms. Taylor instructed. "Does anyone have any ideas? Andy?"

"Exercise could do it," Andy offered.

"Being scared, too," added Mary. "When I get frightened my heart really beats fast."

"Good, let's look at one of those for now and see what we can find out. Who can give me a hypothesis to test that has exercise in it? Jane?"

"Ummh, how about this? The harder you exercise, the faster your pulse rate."

"Good," Ms. Taylor said, "and who has some ideas of how we could test this hypothesis? Ken?"

"We could all do some exercises and see what effect this has on our pulse rate," offered Ken.

With that the class broke up into groups and measured their pulse rates while sitting. Then they walked around the room for a minute and jumped rope for a minute, checking their pulse after each activity. As each group completed their task, they put their results on a poster the teacher had prepared.

The next day, the first part of the science period was devoted to graphing the data. The graph they constructed is shown in figure 8-2.

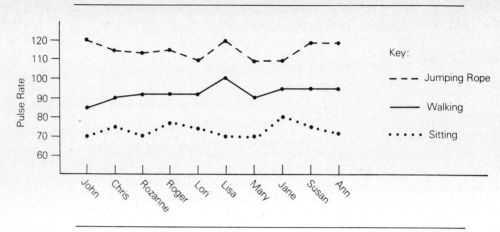

Figure 8–2
**The Effect of Different
Types of Exercise on Pulse
Rates**

"What can we say about our data in terms of the hypothesis we formed? Anyone? Jill?"

"The graph shows that our hypothesis can be accepted. The more we exercise the faster our pulse rate goes."

"Good Jill," replied Ms. Taylor. "That was a good answer. Do you think this is true for all people? Sally?"

"I think so, but the graph might look a little different if we just used people who exercised a lot."

"Hmm, that's an interesting idea. Maybe we could investigate that tomorrow when we have science again."

Identify the four phases of the inquiry model in Ms. Taylor's activity.

1. Statement of problem.
2. Hypotheses.
3. Data gathering.
4. Data analysis.

Feedback for this and other exercises in this chapter can be found at the end of the chapter.

Planning Inquiry Activities

After reading this section of the chapter you will be able to meet the following objectives:

■ You will understand the goals of inquiry so that, given a list of questions, you will identify those appropriate for inquiry activities.

■ You will be able to plan inquiry activities so that, given a topic, you will design a problem that can be implemented with an inquiry procedure.

■ You will be able to design inquiry activities so that, given a selected topic, you will suggest possible hypotheses that could be suggested by students.

■ You will understand the concept *variable* so that, given a description of an activity, you will identify the dependent, independent, and controlled variables in the activity.

■ You will understand developmental factors that influence inquiry activities so that, without aids, you can suggest several ways to start students out in an inquiry activity.

Goals of Inquiry Activity

A first step in planning any activity is a consideration of goals. Inquiry activities are typically designed to teach three types of interrelated goals: to familiarize students with the way science operates, to sharpen process skills, and to teach science content.

By analyzing questions, forming hypotheses, gathering data, and forming conclusions, students have first-hand experiences with science. They actually become scientists, experiencing the same kind of problems and working out solutions in the same way scientists do in the real world. Through involvement in these processes, students not only improve their thinking skills but develop an understanding of science as a human endeavor marked by setbacks and advances but ultimately designed to help us find regularity in the world around us.

Process skills, in addition to observation and inference, include the ability to define a problem, to form testable hypotheses, to gather data appropriate to the hypotheses, and to evaluate that data. These skills, the four steps of the inquiry model, are best taught by direct involvement. Through practice and feedback from the teacher, students eventually develop proficiency. In Ms. Norris's activity, for example, the students were asked to form hypotheses and were prompted to reword them in the form of generalizations. They also graphed the information and made decisions about the hypotheses based on the data. Students develop these process skills through practice such as this.

Students also learn content through their involvement, although this goal may be a bit less important than the other two. When content is the primary goal, the discovery model may be more appropriate for the activity. Nevertheless, children can and do learn content through inquiry. Ms. Norris's students learned concepts of airplane design and the effects of wingspan and size on airplane flight. Ms. Taylor's children learned how to find their pulse and how pulse rate is related to exercise. So, while they learned about science and developed their process skills, students were also learning science content.

Identifying Appropriate Topics

Not all content is appropriate for this teaching model. One way of determining if a topic is appropriate for inquiry is to see if it can be investigated with a question describing a *cause-and-effect* relationship. Ms.

Figure 8-3
Pendulum Apparatus

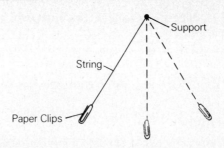

Norris began the lesson by asking "What determines (causes) how far a paper airplane will fly?" Cause was what the students were trying to determine; effect was the distance the planes flew. In Ms. Taylor's activity, cause was the amount of exercise and effect was the heart rate. Notice, by the way, cause is the independent variable while effect is the dependent variable.

By contrast, the question, "What is a nocturnal animal?" is not suitable for an inquiry activity. While the question also appears to be in the form of a problem, the task is one of defining the concept *nocturnal animal,* rather than identifying a cause-effect relationship. The answer would be more appropriately taught with the discovery model, whose primary focus is the teaching of concepts and generalizations.

Let's consider another example. Look at the diagram of a simple pendulum, shown in figure 8-3. It can be constructed from string and paper clips. The paper clip is pulled to the side to keep the string tight, then released, allowing the string and paper clip to swing freely.

An inquiry activity investigating the workings of this simple pendulum might begin with the question, "What determines how fast a pendulum will swing?" Or, we could say, "What factors cause the pendulum to swing faster?" This is an appropriate problem for an inquiry activity, because it involves determining cause and effect.

Topics for inquiry activities often arise from other lessons. Students in Mr. Peterson's class in chapter 6 noticed that some soils were wetter than others, then decided to investigate factors that caused this to happen. A similar type of spin-off lesson occurred in the class that was learning the concept of biodegradable objects. When the class wondered what factors influenced the rate that objects would decay, the teacher suggested an inquiry activity to investigate these factors.

Opportunities like this occur frequently in the science classroom, and teachers should attempt to take advantage of them whenever they can. The practice allows students to see science as a human search for regularities, determined in large part by where the data lead us.

Turn now to the following exercises, which are designed to reinforce your understanding of appropriate content goals for inquiry.

1. What objects sink and what objects float?
2. What kind of objects are attracted to metals?
3. What determines how strong an electromagnet will be?
4. What makes plants grow?
5. What does it mean when we say an animal is camouflaged?
6. What factors affect the rate of evaporation of a liquid?

Data Gathering: The Need for Planning

In order to use class time efficiently, the teacher must anticipate some possible hypotheses and the variables involved in each case. In an inquiry activity the students are attempting to investigate how changing the value of the independent variable will affect the dependent variable. They attempt to keep all other variables constant or controlled. For example, if we wanted to find out what effect different amounts of water (the independent variable) had on plant growth (the dependent variable), we would want to keep other factors, such as sunlight, soil, and fertilizer, constant or controlled. Then if we observed some difference in plant growth we would feel confident that it was due to the water and not some other factor.

In planning for inquiry activities the teacher needs to consider what the independent, dependent, and controlled variables will be, as they determine what data will be gathered and consequently what materials need to be prepared prior to the activity. Ms. Norris anticipated design and size as variables and had pieces of paper prepared for the students. Because she considered size as a possible variable she brought along pieces of paper of different sizes. In considering design as a variable she anticipated different ways of making the airplane out of the same size paper. She might have considered weight as an additional variable and could have planned for it by bringing paper clips that could have been fastened to the planes to change their weight.

One way to make this planning process easier for the teacher is to plan for the activity to occur over a period of several days. In this way, the problem and hypotheses can be considered in one day and the actual data gathered in another. Sequencing the activity in this manner also allows students to have input in how the data should be gathered and provides experience in this aspect of inquiry.

To reinforce the ideas of independent, dependent, and controlled variable, consider the problem, "What determines how fast a simple pendulum will swing?"

Exercise 8.3

Directions: Consider the hypothesis, "The longer the string on a pendulum, the slower it will swing." Identify the independent variable, the dependent variable, and two variables that must be controlled to investigate this hypothesis.

1. Independent.
2. Dependent.
3. Controlled.

Exercise 8.4

Directions: Identify two more hypotheses that might be suggested to answer the question, "What determines how fast a pendulum will swing?" For each hypothesis list an independent, dependent, and two controlled variables.

H_1.
H_2.

Exercise 8.5

Directions: Outside of class, investigate each of the three hypotheses and graph the results.

Controlling the Length of the Activity

Each of the activities we have described has been designed to be completed in a class period or less. In situations like this, the data gathering would be short enough to allow completion of the activity in a relatively short time. Consideration of the time students will need to gather data is important in planning inquiry lessons. Many activities cannot be finished in a single class period and appropriate adjustments are needed in class schedules. Suppose the problem is, "What factors affect the growth rate of plants?" Students would plant the seeds under different conditions and measure the different heights of plants to determine the growth rate. This growing period would be several days at a minimum, and could actually take several weeks or months.

Another example of a problem requiring long-range data gathering would be, "What determines how fast a liquid will evaporate?" Students could investigate this problem by observing liquids in various-shaped containers or by placing different types of liquids (water, alcohol, and cooking oil) in the same-sized containers. Either of these approaches would require observations by students over an extended period of time, well beyond the length of one class period. When extended data gathering is necessary, the teacher will have to plan how long the activity will take each day, who will be responsible for gathering the data, and how the students will record information so it can be analyzed later. These procedures will be discussed in more detail in the implementation section of the chapter.

Directions: Suggest three possible hypotheses that could be investi-   **Exercise 8.6**
gated to solve the plant growing problem.

H_1. _____

H_2. _____

H_3. _____

Directions: Identify two hypotheses that could be investigated to solve   **Exercise 8.7**
the evaporation problem.

H_1. _____

H_2. _____

Developmental Differences

As we have seen, students at different levels of development approach learning tasks in different ways. We have described the formal operational child as one who can think theoretically and control variables in an experiment. Most children do not reach that stage until eleven years of age or later, although there is a good deal of room for individual differences in development. Other factors, however, such as familiarity of materials and the complexity of the learning situation, influence students' ability to engage in inquiry activities. It is our position that children throughout the elementary school can and should engage in inquiry activities, if the proper modifications are made. These modifications are the subject of this section.

Structure for Younger Students

In introducing young children to inquiry activities, it is important to structure the event more specifically than for older children. For example, in investigating what effects different amounts of water have on plant growth, the teacher might want to bypass a general statement of the problem and hypotheses and ask instead, "How can we find out if water affects plant growth?" or, "How can we find out how much water plants need?" When setting up the experiment, the teacher should also help students control variables, explaining while doing so that this is important for a fair test. Younger students may also encounter difficulties in interpreting the data; the teacher may have to help them phrase the results in the form of a generalization. At some point in their science experiences, students should certainly be encouraged to perform all these functions themselves; early introduction to these ideas is probably the best way of learning these processes.

Use of a Model

Another factor that can help younger students understand inquiry activities is a simple demonstration using familiar objects. The problem of factors that influence how high a tennis ball will bounce is an excellent way of introducing students to inquiry activities. By seeing and practicing the activity with a simplified topic and with teacher guidance, students soon learn how to design and implement these activities themselves. This activity can then be followed by another one taken from the unit under study at the time, thus reinforcing the idea of inquiry and showing how it can be applied to another topic.

Familiarity and simplicity are important for younger children. The more familiar they are with the data, the easier it will be to extract meaning from these activities. As for simplicity, it is helpful if the teacher considers only one hypothesis at a time.

Finally, don't be discouraged if students do not pick up the ideas immediately. Remember, a major goal of inquiry activities is to teach these processes. Students learn by trying out the processes and by experiencing success and failure. Trial-and-error learning is an important component of inquiry activities.

To review, the teacher has three primary tasks in designing inquiry lessons: to identify a problem to serve as the focus for the experiment, to anticipate some possible hypotheses to guide the data gathering, and to consider the duration of the data-gathering activities. In the paper airplane and pendulum problems, the lessons could be planned for a single class period; the data gathering process for the plant and evaporation problems would span several weeks.

Implementing Inquiry Activities

After reading this section of the chapter you will be able to meet the following objectives:

You will understand how to implement inquiry activities so that, given a particular topic, you will describe the actions of the teacher in each of the four inquiry steps.

You will know how to organize data graphically so that, given the results of an experiment, you will construct a graph, correctly labeling it and the axes.

Statement of the Problem

The beginning point in an inquiry activity is very simple. The teacher merely states the problem or asks the questions. Ms. Norris asked, "What factors determine how far a paper airplane will fly?" With the pendulum problem, the teacher could begin by asking, "What causes a pendulum to swing fast?" The presentation of the problem tells students the focus of the activity and provides a starting point for forming hypotheses.

Inquiry problems such as these typically occur after conscious planning and preparation by the teacher. As we've mentioned, however, sometimes an activity could develop as an outgrowth of a previous problem. This happened in Ms. Norris's class when Karen questioned whether the size of the wing wasn't also changed with the size of the plane. Another problem could have arisen spontaneously if a student had suggested weight as a factor in the distance a plane will fly. When a situation like this occurs, a teacher should make every effort to follow through with the activity if possible. The motivational advantages of pursuing a self-generated problem, plus the opportunity for students to see how science proceeds in uncharted leaps and bounds, more than outweighs the management problems of such an investigation. As a teacher gains experience with this mode of teaching, spontaneous investigations such as these will be welcomed rather than feared.

However a problem is identified, it is important that it is placed on the board or an overhead transparency for the whole class to see. This allows everyone to participate in the activity and provides a focal point for the hypothesis phase of the activity.

Forming Hypotheses

After the problem has been presented, the teacher asks the students for statements of hypotheses or solutions to the problem. For example:

Small airplanes fly farther than big ones.
The bigger the wing, the farther a plane will fly.

These are not the only possible hypotheses. The class might also have said, "The smaller the plane, the farther it will fly," or even "The larger the plane, the farther it will fly." The content of the hypothesis is important only in the sense that it provides direction for data gathering. Whatever the content, students should be encouraged to state their hypotheses in general rather than specific terms. For example, in the lesson on paper airplanes Susan began by saying that "It will fly farther if it isn't too big," and Ms. Norris then encouraged her to change the description slightly to make it a general statement. This relates to the concept of hypothesis discussed earlier, in which a hypothesis was described as a generalization that is tested with data. Students often initially find it difficult to state hypotheses this way, but quickly pick up the idea after they have been given some practice. Initially, the teacher may need to prompt, just as Ms. Norris did.

The formation of clearly stated hypotheses is as important in the classroom as it is the science laboratory because of the direction it provides for data gathering. Without the hypothesis relating to size in Ms. Norris' lesson, the students would have been gathering data essentially at random and without a sense of direction. Because their hypothesis relating size and flying distance was clearly stated, the students purposely built airplanes of different sizes to measure this variable.

Teaching Students to Form Hypotheses

There are several ways to begin to teach students how to form hypotheses. One is to form hypotheses as a group activity, but this practice has a major disadvantage. The students who typically volunteer hypotheses in a large group are those who already have mastered the skill; those who choose not to participate actively in the activity often do so because they don't know how. If students are asked to develop hypotheses in small groups, and the results are compared with the group as a whole, the more timid students are not placed in a threatening situation. It also provides more students an opportunity to participate in the activity. Another way is to ask each student individually to write out his or her hypothesis and then anonymously critique these as a class.

Whatever method is used, the hypotheses should be stated in such a way that they will be of value in the gathering of data. To illustrate, we have compared a number of hypotheses in table 8–2.

Table 8–2 **Appropriately Stated Hypotheses**

Inappropriately Stated	More Appropriately Stated
The weight will influence the swing rate of a pendulum.	The heavier the weight, the faster the pendulum will swing.
Water temperature affects the melting rate of ice cubes.	The hotter the water, the faster ice cubes will melt.
Sunlight will make plants grow.	The more sunlight plants receive, the faster they will grow.

Each of the hypotheses on the right are stated in such a way as to suggest a direction for data-gathering efforts. In the first example, data gathering would consist of comparing the swing rates of several pendulums of different weights. In the water temperature example, the appropriate hypothesis more clearly outlines the procedures for investigating the relationship between temperature and melting rate than the inappropriate hypothesis. When hypotheses are precisely stated, the procedures stem directly from the hypothesis; loosely stated hypotheses do not make this as obvious. The inappropriate hypotheses have far less value as a directional guide to data gathering. Remember, however, that the hypotheses on the left are not "incorrect"; rather, those on the right provide more direction for students and are therefore more useful to them.

Directions: Rewrite the hypotheses appearing below to make them more appropriate for data gathering.

Exercise 8.8

1. Water affects plant growth.
2. Hot water makes sugar dissolve.
3. Heat makes water evaporate.

Gathering Data

After the problem is presented and the students form hypotheses, the class is ready to begin gathering data. Ideally, the teacher will have anticipated some of the hypotheses during the planning phase of the activity and will have prepared materials for the investigation of key variables. If not, the class can plan for gathering these materials and they can do the activity the next day. Science in the laboratory does not operate by strict timetables. When doing inquiry activities, faster is not necessarily better. Remember, though, that younger children have shorter attention spans, and plan accordingly.

The most efficient way to begin the data-gathering phase is to have students examine the hypotheses and consider how they might be tested. Essentially, this step involves stating specifically what will be done to measure the independent and dependent variables. Ms. Norris's students suggested that large and small airplanes be built and flown to test their first hypothesis. They defined their dependent variable (distance) by counting the tile squares.

To illustrate further, consider the following hypothesis: "The more bean plants are watered, the taller they grow." Several considerations affect the gathering of data to measure this hypothesis. First, the dependent and independent variables need to be identified by the class. The independent variable is the amount of water; plant growth is the dependent variable. Defining the independent variable in this case is fairly straightforward; the unit of measurement can be milliliters, tablespoons, or ounces. Deciding how to measure the dependent variable presents a few more options. Height could be defined as either the total height of the plant, the height to the bottom leaf, the height to the top leaf, or the number of leaves on the plant. Each of these measures has advantages and disadvantages and there actually is no "right" way to define the variable. Because this type of decision is one scientists continually wrestle with, allowing students to struggle with such problems provides insights into the process of science. It reinforces the idea that *people* make science what it is.

An additional consideration for data gathering is the control of other variables. In the plant growing activity, the students should be encouraged to consider factors such as the amount of sunlight, the size of the pot, and the type of soil. If these variables are not held constant, the students cannot conclude that differences in plant growth are due to differences in the amount of water.

Exercise 8.9

Directions: Identify two other variables that would have to be controlled to investigate the height of bean plants compared to the amount of water they are given.

As an additional example of controlling variables consider the hypothesis: "The heavier the pendulum, the slower it will swing." In order to carry out this investigation, the students would need to identify the weight as the independent variable and the speed of the swing as the dependent variable. The independent variable could take on different values as different numbers of paper clips are placed on the string; the dependent variable could be defined as the number of times the pendulum would swing in a 30-second period (or any time length agreed upon by the class). In addition, other variables, such as length of the string and the height from which the pendulum is dropped, would need to be controlled. Once these variables are defined and considered, the pendulum is put to motion, making the data gathering a simple process.

Exercise 8.10

Directions: To reinforce your understanding of the data-gathering process, read each of the problems and hypotheses below; identify the dependent, independent, and controlled variables; and describe how the data would be gathered.

1. Problem: What determines the size of a plant?

   Hypothesis: The larger the seed, the larger the plant.

   Independent _____

   Dependent _____

   Controlled _____

   Description _____

2. Problem: What factors influence the temperature of the contents of a can?

   Hypothesis: The darker the can, the warmer the contents.

   Independent _____

Dependent   _____

Controlled   _____

Description   _____

3. Problem: What factors affect the strength of an electromagnet?

Hypothesis: The more times a wire is wound around a piece of metal, the stronger the magnet.

Independent _____

Dependent   _____

Controlled   _____

Description   _____

Interpretation of Data

The next step in an inquiry activity takes place when students are ready to compare the data to the hypothesis. In doing this, they will determine if the hypothesis can be accepted or needs to be rejected. To make adequate comparisons, the data must often be organized or ordered in some way, especially if there are large amounts of information or the data gathering took a long time. One way to order the data is to graph it, as was done in Ms. Norris's activity. Another way is to chart the information. Charts allow easy comparisons between different values of the independent variable.

Graphing the data with the class provides excellent opportunities to teach students a new skill—how to construct and read graphs. When graphing data with students, several points should be followed. Generally, the independent variable is placed on the horizontal axis and the dependent variable on the vertical axis. In addition, the graph should be clearly labeled so that a reader can tell from the title what is being described. Examples of these ideas being implemented can be seen in figures 8-1 and 8-2.

In comparing data to hypotheses, students should not be reluctant to discard hypotheses that are not supported. When Ms. Norris's students found that large airplanes actually flew farther than small ones, it was counter to the hypothesis they had formed. With the teacher's guidance, the class rejected the old hypothesis and formed a conclusion based on the data they had gathered. As in science, the ultimate authority is the data. This process—hypothesis formation, data gathering, and hypothesis acceptance or rejection—is an integral part of science, and students can gain experiences with this process through inquiry activities.

As students analyze their data, they should be encouraged to generalize about their results. This procedure places the information they have gathered in a form that will be useful in future situations. Ms. Norris's class did this when they concluded, "The bigger the wings, the farther a paper airplane will fly." This generalization summarizes the data gathered and provides students with something they can use at a later time.

As students form these generalizations, they should also be encouraged to think about the limits of their validity. Questions such as, "Is this always true?" "Will what you say always hold true?" and "Can you think of a situation where this wouldn't be true?" will help students think about the limits of the generalizations they have formed.

Once the data has been analyzed, the implementation phase of the model has been completed. It remains for the teacher to evaluate what students have learned from the activity. Before proceeding to the next section, evaluation, complete the exercises below.

Exercise 8.11

Directions: Consider the following hypotheses that appeared in exercise 8.10 and sketch a rough outline of a graph for each hypotheses. Label the graph and each axis.

1. The larger the seed, the larger the plant.
2. The darker the can, the warmer the contents.
3. The more times a wire is wound around a piece of metal, the stronger the magnet.

Evaluating Inquiry Activities

After the inquiry activity is completed, evaluation procedures will show if students have acquired the basic content and skills taught in the lesson. We will discuss evaluation of content acquisition first and evaluation of skill development and understanding of inquiry next. Because evaluating for content has already been discussed in chapter 6, our discussion here will focus upon particular concerns in evaluating content acquisition in inquiry lessons.

Content Acquisition

Evaluation of students' understanding of science content can take a number of different forms. Rather than comparing true-and-false items to fill-in-the-blank items, however, we will discuss ways of measuring different levels or degrees of understanding concepts and generalizations.

Recognition Items

At the lowest level of understanding, students are able to recall or recognize the major findings of an activity. For example, a multiple-choice item measuring students' ability to recognize the results of an activity dealing with pendulums might look like this.

Which of the following best summarizes the finding from our pendulum activity?

- The heavier the weight, the faster a pendulum swings.
- The heavier the weight, the slower a pendulum swings.
- The longer the string, the faster a pendulum swings.
- The longer the string, the slower a pendulum swings.

This item measures students' ability to recall the generalization formed during a class period and would be considered to be a knowledge-level item in Bloom's Taxonomy (Bloom 1956).

Production Items

A higher-level measure of students' understanding of the content of an inquiry lesson is to ask them to apply the generalization to a new situation. For example, the following item could be used to measure students' understanding of the generalization, "The larger the surface area, the faster the rate of evaporation."

You've just been hired by the Sea-Salt Company to design a salt producing apparatus. The evaporation tank that you make will make salt by evaporating ocean water. The best design for the evaporation tank is:

- Tall, narrow, and long.
- Tall, wide, and narrow.
- Shallow, wide, and long.
- Shallow, narrow, and long.

Another way of measuring students' understanding of an abstraction is to ask them to solve a problem. For example, the teacher in the lesson at the beginning of the chapter might use the following item to evaluate her students' ability to apply the content learned in the lesson:

You are going to build a glider to enter into the First International Glider Contest. The first prize is $1,000 for the glider that can fly the longest distance. What material would your glider be made of? What would it look like?

Here the measurement item can be used to tell whether the information gained in a school setting will transfer to the real world—our ultimate aim in teaching any school subject.

These examples of measurement items are obviously not complete or exhaustive. A more complete discussion can be found in some of the texts in measurement and evaluation listed in the reference section of this chapter.

Skill Development and Understanding of Inquiry Activities

Evaluating students' acquisition of process skills involves measuring their ability to do something, whether forming hypotheses, controlling variables, or interpreting data. Students' ability or inability to perform a certain skill, however, may arise from their lack of knowledge about that skill. Students who do not know what a controlled variable is would not be able to design an experiment in which critical variables are controlled. This suggests a two-step method of evaluation in which the teacher measures students' understanding of a skill before asking students to apply the skill itself.

Production Items

Alternative ways of measuring students' understanding of a skill-related concept are to ask students to define the concept, to identify a correct definition from a list, or to identify an example of the concept. For example, the following production item asks students to identify examples of independent and dependent variables. It could be used to measure students' understanding of these concepts.

> Researchers were trying to determine which kind of dog food was better for young puppies, Puppy Yummies or Puppy Chow. To do this, they took ten beagles and fed half of them Puppy Yummies and half Puppy Chow. They gave all of them the same amount of water and exercise. Then they weighed them after four weeks.

What is the dependent variable?

What is the independent variable?

Recognition Items

A multiple-choice (recognition) item to measure understanding of a process-related concept would ask students to select the best answer from a list of alternatives, as follows:

> The Florida Honeybee Club said their honeybees could produce more honey than the Alabama honeybees. They set up an experiment to see which group of honeybees was the best honey producer. Which of the following is an example of a control variable?

- The Alabama honeybees have strong wings.
- The Florida honeybees have lots of flowers from which to get nectar.
- Each group got to use 100 bees for the experiment.
- Florida is under Eastern Standard Time; Alabama is under Central Standard Time.

Application to New Situations

Another important dimension of students' acquisition of process skills is the ability to apply the processes in new situations. This can be measured in a number of ways. The most open-ended is to pose a problem to students and ask them to design an experiment. An example of such an item is the following.

> Design an experiment about the differences between fifth-grade boys and girls. Identify the independent, dependent, and controlled variables.

Parts of this measurement item may be too difficult for students to answer, however, and because of this difficulty students may fail to answer the question at all. When this happens, teachers have little specific information about what students know and do not know. One way to remedy this situation is to place some students in more structured situations, such as the following:

> Scientists are trying to decide which kind of toothpaste is better at preventing cavities, Clean or White. In conducting their experiment, they are going to have fifty boys and girls brush with one kind of toothpaste and fifty boys and girls brush with the other. After one year, dentists will check all the boys and girls for new cavities. What are two variables that need to be controlled to make this a good experiment?

Because of the built-in structure, student error is easier to diagnose and necessary remedial work is easier to define.

Judging the Validity of Generalizations

Perhaps the most sophisticated example of measuring for process exists when the students are required to interpret data to make decisions about inferences based on observations. This is an extremely useful skill in the real world because it involves the ability to analyze the statements and claims of others and critically judge their validity. For example, consider table 8–3.

Table 8–3

Breed of Cow	Weight	Feed	Pounds of Milk per Year
Holstein	190	Corn	4800
Holstein	2200	Corn	5200
Holstein	2500	Corn	5600

The generalization most supported by the information is:

■ The more you feed cows, the heavier they become.

- Holstein cows thrive on corn as feed.
- The weight of a cow determines the amount of milk.
- The more milk a cow gives, the better she is fed.
- All generalizations are equally well supported.

This and similar items measure students' ability to judge the validity of others' generalizations. An alternative format is to provide students with the same data and ask them to make a generalization. Although these two process skills are closely related, the latter places a greater demand on the learner. Students must actually produce a generalization, rather than just evaluate someone else's. Additional items related to the table could be:

1. The controlled variable(s) is/are:

- Pounds of milk, types of feed, and breed of cow
- Breed of cow, weight, and type of feed
- Breed of cow
- Breed of cow and type of feed
- Weight of cow

2. The independent variable(s) is/are:

- Breed of cow, type of feed
- Weight and pounds of milk
- Weight
- Type of feed

3. The dependent variable(s) is/are:

- Breed of cow, weight, feed, and pounds of milk
- Breed and feed
- Pounds of milk
- Weight
- Feed

Exercise 8.12

Directions: Identify the correct choice in each of the multiple-choice questions above.

As another example of items designed to measure students' ability to analyze data consider the following item. Look at the data in table 8-4. The experimenters hypothesized, "Fertilizer from salt water sources is better than commercial fertilizer in promoting plant growth."

Based on the data the hypothesis should be:

- Accepted
- Rejected
- Cannot tell from the data given

Table 8-4

Plant	Type of Fertilizer	Gallons of Water/Day	Hours of Sunlight/Day	Tomatoes/Bush (pounds)
Tomato	Fish meal (salt water source)	2 gal.	6	9.7
Tomato	Vigaro	2 gal.	6	8.3
Tomato	Weed and Feed	2 gal.	6	9.8
Tomato	Whale bone (salt water source)	2 gal.	6	8.5
Tomato	Quick Grow	2 gal.	6	9.2
Tomato	Super Feed with cod liver oil (salt water source)	2 gal.	6	8.0

If the students haven't seen this data before responding to the item, they are required to use their process skills in order to respond correctly.

It is our hope that teachers will use items like these not only as a means of evaluating student learning but also as a means of producing such learning. One way to do this is to use these items as class exercises. An alternative way is to discuss test items thoroughly when they are handed back to students. By discussing these items, not only do students learn correct responses, but teachers also have an opportunity to find out what is going on in students' heads.

Exercise 8.1

Feedback

1. The statement of the problem occurred when the teacher wrote the following question on the board: "What makes your pulse rate beat faster?"

2. The hypotheses formed by the class were "Exercise affects pulse rate" and "Being scared affects pulse rate." The class investigated the exercise rate hypothesis.

3. Data was gathered by having each member of the class measure his or her own pulse rate after various types of exercise.

4. The data was analyzed by first placing it on a graph. After doing this the class generalized about the data and concluded that "The more you exercise, the faster your pulse rate."

Exercise 8.2

The following topics could be appropriate starting points for inquiry activities:

   3. What determines how strong an electromagnet will be?

   4. What makes plants grow?

   6. What factors affect the rate of evaporation of a liquid?

Each of these topics involved cause-and-effect relationships. The other topics dealt with the formation of concepts and would be more appropriately taught using the discovery model. Rewritten in cause-and-effect terms, these questions might look like this:

   3. What causes an electromagnet to be strong?

   4. What causes plants to grow?

   6. What factors cause the rate of evaporation of a liquid to vary?

Exercise 8.3

The independent variable in this activity is the length of the string. The dependent variable is the rate of swing. Two variables that should be controlled are the weight of the pendulum and the height that the pendulum is lifted to start it in motion.

Exercise 8.4

Two more hypotheses that might be investigated are:

A. The heavier the weight on the end of the pendulum, the faster it will swing.

B. The higher the pendulum is lifted to start it in motion, the faster it will swing.

   In (A) the independent variable is the weight of the pendulum and the dependent variable is the rate of swing. Two variables that would have to be controlled are string length and starting height.

   In (B) the independent variable is the starting height and the dependent variable is the rate of swing. Two variables to be controlled are the length of the string and the weight of the pendulum.

   Don't be concerned if your answers do not exactly match ours. Several variations could occur. What is important is that you begin to develop an idea of these concepts.

Exercise 8.5

No feedback required.

Exercise 8.6

Some possible hypotheses include:

- The more plants are watered, the faster they'll grow.
- The more sunlight plants receive, the faster they'll grow.
- The blacker the soil, the better plants will grow.
- The larger the container they're grown in, the faster plants will grow.
- Plants that are put in pots with drainage holes will grow better than plants put in pots with none.

Some possible hypotheses for this activity include:

Exercise 8.7

- The lighter the substance, the faster it will evaporate.
- The broader the surface area of the liquid, the faster it will evaporate.
- The darker the holding container, the faster the liquid in it will evaporate.

The following hypotheses would provide more direction for subsequent data-gathering efforts:

Exercise 8.8

1. The more plants are watered, the faster they grow.
2. The hotter the water, the faster sugar will dissolve.
3. The hotter the water temperature, the faster it will evaporate.

Some other variables that would have to be controlled are:

Exercise 8.9

- Type of seeds
- Depth the seeds were planted
- Amount of fertilizer

In controlling these variables, students would want to ensure that all the plants they were growing received the same amount of fertilizer, were planted at the same depth, and came from similar seeds. If they found that certain plants grew better than others, they could then conclude that this was because of the *independent* variable and not something else.

1. To investigate this problem, different-sized seeds could be planted in pots and their growth measured over a period of time. The independent variable is the size of the seed; the dependent variable is the growth rate, which could be defined as plant height. If this problem were investigated, we would want to make sure that all the seeds were placed in similar pots and soil, at the same depth, and given the same amounts of water and sunlight. These are the *controlled variables.*

Exercise 8.10

2. In this problem, the independent variable is the color of the can and the dependent variable is the temperature as measured by a thermometer. In investigating this problem, you could fill different-colored cans with sand, place a thermometer in each and put them in the sun. Some variables that would need to be controlled are the size of the can, the substance (for example, sand, dirt, and so on) placed in each can, and the amount of sunlight received by each of the cans.

3. The independent variable in this problem is the number of times a wire is wrapped around a piece of metal and the dependent variable is the strength of the magnet. The dependent variable could be defined as the number of tacks or the weight of a piece of metal that could be lifted. Some variables that would need to be controlled are the kind of wire used to make the magnet and the kinds of batteries used.

Exercise 8.11

Note that each graph (figures 8-4, 8-5, and 8-6) is labeled with the independent variable on the horizontal axis and the dependent variable on the vertical axis.

Figure 8-4
The Effect of Seed Size on Plant Size

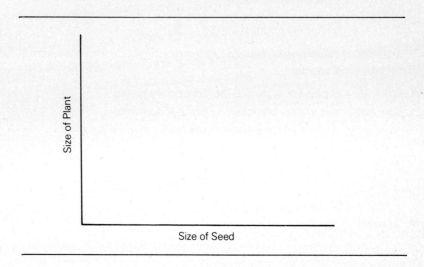

Figure 8-5
The Effect of Color on Temperature of a Can

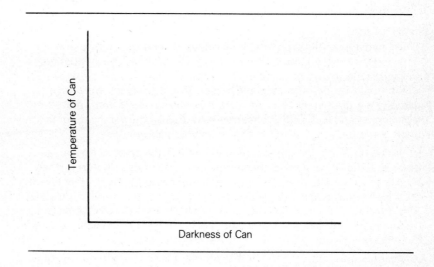

Exercise 8.12

The correct answers are 1D; 2C; and 3C.

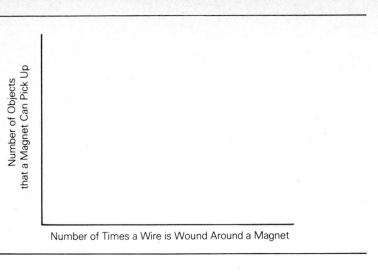

Figure 8–6
**The Effect of Wire Loops
on Magnetic Strength**

Number of Objects that a Magnet Can Pick Up

Number of Times a Wire is Wound Around a Magnet

References

Ahman, J., and Glock, M. *Measuring and Evaluating Educational Achievement.* 2nd ed. Boston: Allyn and Bacon, 1975.

Brown, D. *Appraisal Procedured in the Secondary Schools.* Englewood Cliffs, N.J.: Prentice-Hall, 1970.

Carin, A. and Sund, R. *Teaching Science Through Discovery.* 2nd ed. Columbus, Ohio: Merrill, 1970.

Devito, A. and Krockover, G. *Creative Sciencing.* Boston: Little, Brown, 1976.

Ebel, R. *Essentials of Educational Measurement.* Englewood Cliffs, N.J.: Prentice-Hall, 1972.

Eggen, P.; Kauchak, D.; and Harder, R. *Strategies for Teachers.* Englewood Cliffs, N.J.: Prentice-Hall, 1979.

Esler, W. *Teaching Elementary Science.* 2nd ed. Belmont, Cal.: Wadsworth, 1977.

Gega, P. *Science in Elementary Education.* 3rd ed. New York: Wiley, 1970.

Joyce, B., and Weil, M. *Models of Teaching.* Englewood Cliffs, N.J.: Prentice-Hall, 1972.

Kuhn, T. *The Structure of Scientific Revolutions.* Chicago: University of Chicago Press, 1962.

McCain, G., and Segal, E. *The Game of Science.* Monterey, Cal.: Brooks Cole, 1973.

Sax, G. *Principles of Educational Measurement.* Belmont, Cal.: Wadsworth, 1974.

Suchman, J. *The Elementary School Training Program in Scientific Inquiry,* Research project 216. Washington, D.C.: U.S. Office of Education, 1962.

Suchman, J. *Inquiry Development Program: Developing Inquiry.* Chicago: Science Research Associates, 1966a.

Suchman, J. *Teacher's Guide: Inquiry Development Program in Physical Science.* Chicago: Science Research Associates, 1966b.

Suchman, J. *Inquiry Box: Teacher's Handbook.* Chicago: Science Research Associates, 1967.

Suchman, J. "A model for the analysis of inquiry," in *Analysis of Concept Learning.* Herbert Klausmeier and Chester Hauss, eds. New York: Academic Press, 1966.

Thorndike, R., ed. *Educational Measurement.* 2nd ed. Washington, D.C.: American Council on Education, 1971.

Victor, E. and Lerner, M. *Readings in Science Education for the Elementary School.* 3rd ed. New York: MacMillan, 1975.

This chapter is written as a supplement to chapter 8. Ideas found here are intended to reinforce your understanding of the inquiry model and to provide a source of activities for use in the classroom. These activities, offered as possible sources of ideas for lessons you may wish to teach, are intended as springboards for your own ideas. Our goal is for you to generalize from these activities to generate your own inquiry activities and exercise your own creativity. It should be obvious that these examples are purposely not exhaustive of all inquiry possibilities. We will have met our goal in writing this book if you can use the ideas and examples here as starting points for your own lessons. Therefore, we urge you to feel free to adapt, change, and use the ideas in the way most appropriate for your own situation.

In describing the activities we have adopted the following format:

Chapter 9   Inquiry Activities

Purpose

The purpose describes a *content* goal for the lesson. As you read the descriptions of the activities, keep in mind that all the activities also have process goals and goals that are related to students' understanding of the way science operates. These goals, as outlined in chapter 8, include teaching students to investigate hypotheses on the basis of data and to understand how the process of experimentation can be used to develop and refine our scientific knowledge. Because these goals are common to all inquiry activities, they will not be restated for each activity.

Content

This section briefly describes the major concepts and generalizations related to the topic. For instance, in activity 9.3, "The Burning Candle," a description of how a candle burns is provided; in activity 9.11, however, the content simply describes what an electromagnet is.

Question or Problem

This is the question, posed by the teacher, that serves as the starting point for the inquiry lesson. In each case, the teacher can use the problem in a form that would be more meaningful to a particular group of students. For example, in activity 9.11 you might say: "Today we are going to study electromagnets. Someone tell me what an electromagnet is."

At this point, electromagnets would be discussed enough to ensure that the students understood what they are and how they work. You could then describe the problem by saying: "I have a problem we need to solve about electromagnets. The problem is, 'What determines how strong an electromagnet will be?' " After hearing the problem, the students would be prepared to propose hypotheses.

Possible Hypotheses

The hypotheses are suggestions the students may propose as solutions to the problem or answers to the question. If the students have difficulty with hypothesizing, you may wish to suggest a hypothesis as a possible starting point for the data gathering process. If after considerable prompting the students still cannot suggest hypotheses, you may not have provided sufficient background prior to stating the problem, or the content may simply be too sophisticated for your students. In either case, additional time would need to be spent on developing and explaining the content involved so that students could offer meaningful hypotheses and participate in the activity.

As we discussed in chapter 8, students may experience initial difficulty in stating hypotheses in usable forms, instead using phrases such as: "How strong the battery is," or "How many times you wrap the wire."

In these cases, you would encourage the students to rephrase the statement as: "The stronger the battery, the stronger the electromagnet," and "The more wraps around the nail, the stronger the electromagnet." With practice they will be able to state hypotheses with little difficulty.

The hypotheses we are presenting are only suggestions. You and your students will probably think of a number of others that would be appropriate for investigation.

Materials

This section describes the equipment you will need to carry out the activity. As such, it serves as a quick planning checklist for you before you begin an activity. Materials required for these activities are easily obtained, not only for convenience, but also to reinforce the idea that science is an attempt to make sense of our surroundings, not something that occurs only in laboratories with sophisticated equipment.

Possible Data Gathering Procedures

Procedures are presented as ideas you might use to help students gather data to investigate their hypotheses. If students propose alternate data gathering procedures, we encourage you to follow them. As students gain experience with the process of inquiry, suggestions such as these from the teacher may become unnecessary.

We noted in chapter 5 that many experiential activities can be done on an independent basis and are appropriate for use in learning centers without a great deal of teacher direction. Inquiry activities, on the other hand, usually require considerable direction, at least initially. As children become more experienced they can become more independent in their investigations. We are assuming, in describing the following activities, that they will be teacher-directed with the data gathered in groups of two or three students.

Possible Conclusions

These are some possible results that you and your class might expect to find from the hypotheses studied. However, these "conclusions" should be viewed with caution and should not be misinterpreted as "right answers." As discussed in chapter 1, one characteristic of science is that it is based on observable data. When the data that you and your students gather do not agree with the possible conclusions offered here, *do not* conclude that your data is wrong. The procedures and equipment you used in gathering your data could influence your results. When a discrepancy like this occurs, suggestions for more data gathering and more careful observations might be appropriate, but telling students they got the "wrong" results is inconsistent with the spirit of science.

Related Activities

Where appropriate, we have included additional topics that would be suitable for further investigation. These, of course, are merely suggestions; the extent to which you use them is strictly a matter of judgment. Also, we hope our suggestions will trigger investigations we have not considered.

A final comment regarding the possible hypotheses is in order. We have purposely worded some of the hypotheses in such a way that the data will cause them to be rejected. If all hypotheses proposed by students are later accepted, students come to develop the view that hypotheses are meant to be correct. When they must be rejected students conclude they have made a mistake in hypothesizing. This is an incorrect view of hypotheses and a false notion of how science proceeds. By providing experiences in which students make, test, and ultimately reject hypotheses, teachers can do much to dispel this incorrect view.

Activity 9.1
Dissolving Candy

Purpose

To help children understand the concept *dissolve*

Content

Dissolving is a physical change that occurs when a solid melts into or merges with a liquid. Stirring or heating a liquid speeds up this process, as does breaking up the solid into smaller pieces to increase its surface area.

Problem

What determines how fast a piece of candy will dissolve?

Possible Hypotheses

1. The harder the candy, the faster it dissolves.
2. The more the water is stirred, the faster the candy dissolves.
3. The hotter the water, the faster the candy dissolves.

Materials

Clear plastic glasses, candy (lemon drops, jelly beans, chocolate bars), hot plate, thermometer

Possible Data Gathering Procedures

1. Place equal amounts of several types of candy such as lemon drops, jelly beans, and chocolate bars in water. Observe the candy periodically (once or twice a day) and record when they are dissolved.

2. Put a piece of candy (the same type of candy) in each of three containers. Leave one alone, stir the second slowly, and stir the third rapidly; observe which dissolves first.

3. Put a piece of candy into cold water, room temperature water, and hot water. The temperatures could be chilled with ice for the cold temperature and warmed with a hot plate for the warm water. Measure the water temperature with a thermometer. Observe and see which dissolves first.

Possible Results

1. The results will depend on the type of candy. The hypothesis may be accepted or rejected.

2. Typically, stirring increases the rate of dissolving, so this hypothesis would probably be accepted.

3. Heat in general increases the rate of dissolving, so this hypothesis would probably be accepted.

Related Activities

This topic could be expanded to investigate solubility in general (the extent to which a substance like sugar dissolves in a fluid like water). Students could investigate hypotheses such as the heavier the solute (the material being dissolved), the *more* will dissolve; for example, salt versus sugar. They could also investigate fluids dissolving in other fluids (oil will not dissolve in water but vinegar will) or the effect of different types of solutions, such as alcohol or vinegar, on dissolving rates.

**Activity 9.2
Rate of Erosion**

Purpose

To help students begin to understand the concept *erosion*

Content

Erosion is the removal of the topsoil in a land area. Topsoil is the layer of Earth's crust that contains plant and animal matter and supports all plant

Figure 9-1
Runoff Troughs

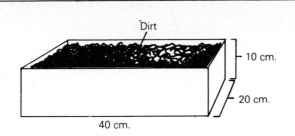

life. It is the layer we walk around on, and it can vary from a few inches to many feet in depth. Without topsoil an area is incapable of growing plants. The two most common ways topsoil is removed (eroded) is through wind or running water.

Problem

Under what conditions does soil erode the most rapidly?

Possible Hypotheses

1. The more material soil has in it, the faster it erodes.
2. The steeper the grade of land, the faster the soil erodes.
3. The wetter the soil, the faster it erodes.
4. The heavier the rainfall, the faster soil erodes.

Materials

Seed boxes made from orange crates and lined with aluminum foil, potting soil, grass seed, water sprinkler, straw or leaves, run-off pans (cooking pans will do), protractors and a hot-plate

Possible Data Gathering Procedures

To investigate each of the hypotheses, you can prepare soil in three or four large boxes or run-off troughs (as shown in figure 9-1). Then sprinkle water on the soil with a bottle and stopper (figure 9-2), or with a hose equipped with a spray nozzle.

1. Plant different amounts of grass seed in the different containers. Leave one bare; plant another lightly; plant a third heavily with seeds. Water carefully until all the seeds have sprouted and developed roots. Or take different containers of soil and mix straw and plant material in with the soil. Or leave the material on top, without mixing in, and investigate what effect this has on the erosion rate.

Figure 9–2
Water Sprinkler

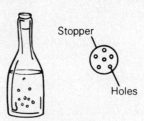

Whatever procedure is used, water each container with the same amount of water and (slant at the same angle). Collect the runoff and compare the amounts of water from different conditions. Students can also analyze the runoff for different kinds of particles and weigh the soil that is contained in the runoff. (Evaporate the water on a hot plate before weighing.)

2. Prepare flats as described in 1 above and then use protractors to set these flats at different angles. Collect and analyze the runoff as in 1 above.

3. Arrange soil in the flats so it has the same slope and is covered by the same vegetation. Leave one dry, dampen a second, and saturate the soil of a third. Sprinkle each and observe the results.

4. Arrange the soil in the pan so that slope, vegetation, and moisture content is the same in each. Sprinkle one gently, one moderately heavy, and a third very vigorously (keeping the amount constant). Observe the results.

Possible Results

1. Most types of materials, such as vegetation, help prevent erosion of soil. This probably will be observed in the activity causing the students to reject the hypothesis.

2. Soil erodes faster from steeper slopes than from more gentle slopes, unless the soil is packed tighter or the vegetation is different. (When setting up the activity, be careful to control these factors.) The students would, therefore, accept the second hypothesis.

3. The wetness of the soil is a complex variable to investigate. In many types of soil, the dryer the soil, the more moisture it will absorb and consequently, the less runoff and erosion. However, some soils, like clay, tend to pack together when moist, causing water to drain off with little or no erosion. The students may accept or reject the hypothesis depending on the type of soil used.

4. Heavy rain typically erodes soil faster than light rain, so the students will probably accept the hypothesis.

Related Activities

The topic can be extended by using a fan to investigate the effects of wind erosion. Also, the effect of different types of plowing patterns can be investigated by planting rows of seeds horizontal and vertical to the tilted boxes. The effect of erosion runoff on aquatic animal life could be investigated by allowing the runoff to go into a quart or gallon jar with snails, seaweed, and guppies, and observing the results.

The activity could be coordinated with a social studies lesson where soil quality in different parts of the country or world could be studied, and the economic effects of erosion might be considered. This lesson could also be coordinated with experiential activity 5.8, which looks at different rock and soil types.

Purpose

To help students understand factors that affect ignition and burning

**Activity 9.3
The Burning
Candle**

Content

When a candle is lit, candle wax liquifies and moves up the wick by capillary action. The wax vaporizes or turns into a gas. When this gas becomes hot enough, it combines with oxygen in the air and a flame occurs. Therefore, gaseous wax is what supports the flame in a burning candle.

As the oxygen in the air combines with the wax from the candle, carbon dioxide (CO_2) is formed as a by-product. (The carbon in the CO_2 comes up from the candle.) When all the oxygen is used up, or turned into carbon dioxide, the candle goes out for lack of oxygen.

When carbon dioxide is formed, it is warmer than the rest of the air and therefore rises. Consequently, a candle placed at the top of a container may go out more quickly than a shorter candle because of the accumulation of warm carbon dioxide at the top. (This is the reason they tell people in fires to crawl along the floor, where the air has more oxygen and less carbon dioxide.)

Problem

What determines how long a candle will burn?

Possible Hypotheses

1. The more air available in a closed container, the longer a candle will burn.
2. The thicker the candle, the faster it will burn.
3. The more nearly still the air, the faster a candle will burn.

Figure 9–3
**How Long Will These
Candles Burn?**

Materials

Candles, different-sized jars or beakers, clock with second hand

Possible Data Gathering Procedures

1. Place candles of equal length and width under inverted beakers (glass containers) of varying sizes, as shown in figure 9–3. (The length and width of the candles are controlled variables.) If necessary, measure the volumes of the containers with a graduated cylinder and water. Four or five sizes would be a reasonable number. Measure the length of time it takes for the candle to go out. Plot the results on a graph.

2. Take several candles of different widths and measure the length of time it takes for them to burn down one inch or any arbitrary length. As an alternative, you could simply light the candles, place them side by side, and see which one burns down fastest.

3. Place candles in different places in the room, light them, and watch them burn under conditions such as the following:

■ See how long it takes the candle to burn down one inch (or any arbitrary length) when the air is still.

■ See how long it takes for the candle to burn down an arbitrary length as you wave your hand (a) slowly (b) moderately fast and (c) rapidly (but not so fast that the flame goes out) over the flame.

Possible Results

1. The students will find that candles under large beakers will burn longer than those under smaller beakers. (Though your students will probably see that this is not a linear function; that is, a candle placed in a 500 ml. container will not burn twice as long as one placed in a 250 ml. container.) You and your students may wish to investigate why this happens. The hypothesis, as stated, would probably be accepted.

2. Thicker candles typically burn longer than thin candles because there is more wax available to burn. This would cause the hypothesis to be rejected.

3. Faster air increases the rate of burning (unless the candle is blown out), so the candle in the still air may burn the longest. This hypothesis would then be rejected.

Related Activities

Recall the discovery lesson on the burning candle described in chapter 6. The discovery lesson would nicely precede this inquiry activity just described.

Another variable to investigate is the height of the candle in a container. Because the warm carbon dioxide rises in the container, a tall candle is likely to go out sooner than a short one. Investigate this idea by putting candles of different heights in containers of identical sizes.

Students can also investigate the effect of carbon dioxide on burning time. Light a candle in a tall jar that has a small amount of vinegar in the base (the amount contained in paper nut cup will do). Once the candle is burning, sprinkle some baking soda on the vinegar and quickly put the lid back on. The vinegar and baking soda chemically unite to make carbon dioxide, which puts out fires.

The activity can also be extended with a lesson on safety in handling fires and perhaps safety in general.

Other activities related to burning that would help students understand concepts such as *spontaneous combustion, kindling temperature,* and so on, can also be done.

Purpose

To help students understand how the environment affects the behavior of organisms

**Activity 9.4
Fish Behavior**

Content

Every organism has an optimal environment, which can be described in a number of ways, including the properties of temperature, humidity, light, and the presence or absence of food. Human beings alter their environments by heating or cooling their homes, putting on or taking off their clothes, and running humidifiers or dehumidifiers. Animals cannot do this, so they adapt to living conditions by moving (migrating) to more favorable environments.

Problem

What factors influence where fish choose to live?

Possible Hypotheses

1. Goldfish like to live near the top of the water near the middle of the tank.

2. Goldfish like to live in darker water.

3. Goldfish like to live in warmer water.

Materials

Aquarium, goldfish, lamp, heating pad, thermometer

Possible Data Gathering Procedures

1. Set up an aquarium in the room and place several goldfish in it. (Usually, someone in the class has an aquarium that is not being used. This will avoid the cost of buying one.) When you buy the fish, select ones that differ in size, shape, or color, to make them easier to distinguish when the class starts observing. Divide the aquarium up into visual sections with marks on the side (quarters, sixths, or eighths will do). Have the class observe the fish at regular intervals during the day and record on a chart where they found each fish.

2. Collect natural or baseline data as in H_1 above. Then move an uncovered light bulb about six inches or a foot from one end of the aquarium. Make sure the heat from the bulb does not affect the water temperature. Observe the fish for a few days and record the data. Then move the light to the opposite end and observe what changes occur.

3. Set up the aquarium as in 1 above and observe the fish naturally for several days. Measure the temperature with an aquarium thermometer (purchased inexpensively from most pet stores) and record the temperature over several days. Then tape a heating pad to one end and put it on low. (Be careful that the water doesn't heat too rapidly or become too warm—the temperature shouldn't rise more than about 5° C at the heated end.) Observe the fish and note where they are located at various times of the day. Measure the temperature of the water at different locations in the tank; chart this information on a graph.

Possible Results

1. Where fish live in an aquarium depends on a number of factors, like the temperature of the water, how brightly the aquarium is lit, and what kind of hiding places (shells, miniature houses, and plants) are found in the water. All of these factors interact, so it is hard to predict where the fish will be found.

2. Generally, fish tend to avoid bright sunlight if they can. The fish in your aquarium will probably tend to stay in darker places if they are available.

3. Every species of fish has an ideal temperature in which they would prefer to live, though most fish can live in a range of temperatures. Where your fish will tend to stay will depend on the temperature gradients in your aquarium.

Related Activities

Other variables, such as the breathing rate of fish (a dependent variable that can easily be observed by watching the movement of the gills) can be compared to water temperature (an independent variable); this information can be graphed.

    Also, the activity can be extended to other cold-blooded animals such as small lizards, frogs, or toads. A discussion of the influence of environment on all species of animals could lead to library research or further investigation. This lesson could also be combined with inquiry activity 9.5, on insect behavior, and experiential activities 5.11 and 5.15, focusing on birds and animals, to form the major components of a unit on animals and their behavior.

Purpose

To acquaint students with factors that influence animal behavior

Activity 9.5
Insect Behavior

Content

Meal worms are the larval form of a species of beetle used by fishermen for bait and by owners of lizards and frogs for food. Like other organisms, meal worms have an optimal environment they prefer, growing best in warm, moist but not wet, dark places.

Problem

What factors influence the behavior of meal worms?

Possible Hypotheses

1. Meal worms tend to seek a moist environment.

2. Meal worms tend to avoid commonly used preservatives.

3. The cooler the temperature, the more slowly worms will change into their adult forms.

Materials

Meal worms (obtained inexpensively from most pet stores), gallon jars, shredded newspaper, corn—or oatmeal, sponges, bread pans, aluminum foil, sugar, salt, vinegar, rubbing alcohol, thermometer

Possible Data Gathering Procedures

1. Set up a meal worm growing culture by alternating layers of shredded newspaper sprinkled with corn or oatmeal in a one-gallon jar. Moisten these layers slightly as you go along. Punch holes in the top of the jar to let in air and moisten a piece of sponge and place on the top of the layer to maintain the moisture of the growing medium. Place meal worms in the jar and keep the sponge moist (not wet). Meal worms can be kept in a medium like this indefinitely.

Take bread pans and prepare as described above. Place a moist sponge in one end and keep the other end dry. Place ten to twenty meal worms evenly around the top. Cover with aluminum foil punched with several breathing holes. Let the pans sit for a day or two and then search through the pans, locating the meal worms and measuring the average distance from the water source. Replicate this with other pans and graph the data.

2. Prepare the bread pans as in 1 above, placing the sponge on the top in the middle of the pan. Spread ten or twenty meal worms across the top of the medium and cover and let sit for several days. Locate the meal worms and record this data. (This may be an excellent time to introduce the idea of coordinates in graphing.) Then mix a small amount of some commonly used preservative in one end of the pan. (A teaspoon of sugar, salt, vinegar, or alcohol would be about right.) Cover and let the medium sit for a day or two and then relocate the meal worms.

3. Prepare three bread pans (or any other convenient growing containers) as in 1 above, place ten or twenty meal worms in them, and cover with foil as described above. Place one container in a warm part of the room (near a radiator or heating vent, for example). Place another container in a cool part of the room and a third in a refrigerator. Measure the temperatures of each medium by placing a thermometer in each for an hour before recording. Make sure that all containers are kept equally moist. Let the containers sit for two or three weeks and then examine for beetles (the adult form of meal worms).

Possible Results

1. As with most animals, there is an ideal type of environment in which meal worms like to live. The exact place in your medium will depend on how moist different locations are in your pans. Whatever results you get, try to replicate these with another pan and growing medium.

2. Meal worms, like other insects, will tend to avoid certain chemicals in certain concentrations. However, if these concentrations are too low, they may actually be attracted to small amounts of sugar. If this occurs, you may wish to design an experiment in which you vary the amount of sugar and attempt to determine when this substance becomes noxious to meal worms.

3. The metabolism of insects, like all cold-blooded animals, is dependent upon the heat in their environments. Generally, the warmer the environment, the faster meal worms will develop into beetles. This

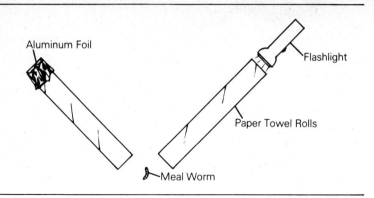

Figure 9–4
**The Effect of Temperature
on Meal Worms**

growth may not occur if the temperature becomes too warm. Graph the data and see if there is a direct relationship between temperature and rate of development.

Related Activities

The effect of temperature on meal worms can be further investigated by placing one end of a growing pan near (but not too near) a heat source and then observing where the meal worms congregate. The reaction of meal worms to light can be investigated by placing a meal worm at the mouth of two empty paper towel rolls as shown in figure 9–4. Cover the far end of one with aluminum foil to make it dark; place a flashlight in the other. Observe what happens when the meal worm is free to crawl.

Meal worms' reaction to rough and smooth surfaces can be investigated by giving them a choice of crawling over sandpaper or clear plastic. Also, their reaction to slopes can be investigated by placing a meal worm on the center of a 45° slope and observing whether they crawl downwards or upwards. Encourage students to compare their findings in this activity with the preceding one focusing on fish behavior. Ask them to explain similarities and differences in the two species.

Purpose

To help students understand what factors influence the pitch of a vibrating instrument

**Activity 9.6
Sound Pitch**

Content

All sound is created when an object vibrates, and the vibration is transmitted through some medium (like air). The vibration then hits our ears and makes our eardrums vibrate and we hear the sound. Sound, unlike light, must have a medium to carry it. For example, no sound could pass from here to the moon, although light obviously does. How high or low a sound is depends on how fast the object vibrates; the slower the rate of vibration, the lower the sound. Factors such as length of the vibrating column and the thickness and tightness of the string all influence the rate of vibration and, therefore, the pitch.

Problem

Why do different stretched rubber bands make different sounds?

Possible Hypotheses

1. The thicker the rubber band, the deeper the pitch.
2. The longer the rubber band, the higher the pitch.
3. The tighter the rubber band, the higher the pitch.

Materials

Rubber bands of varying thickness, cigar boxes, or boards with nails

Possible Data Gathering Procedures

1. Collect rubber bands of different thickness but of the same length and place them around an empty cigar box or over nails pounded in a board at equal distances. Pluck the rubber bands and listen to the sound that the vibrations make.

2. Locate rubber bands of different lengths that are similar in thickness. Stretch them over nails pounded into a board. Make sure that all the rubber bands are stretched to approximately the same tightness. (Thickness and tension are controlled variables.) Pluck the rubber bands and observe the different sounds.

3. Select rubber bands that are of similar length and thickness. Arrange them over nails pounded in boards so that one is stretched very tight, one moderately tight, and a third somewhat loose. Pluck the bands and listen for any differences.

Possible Results

1. If length and tension are kept constant, the thicker rubber bands should have deeper pitches.

2. A longer vibrating column produces a deeper pitch. Consequently, the hypothesis as stated would probably prove false.

3. This hypothesis should be supported by the data if the length and thickness of the bands are kept constant.

Related Activities

This activity can be expanded into an entire unit. Experiential activity 5.7 on sound and hearing and discovery activity 7.1 on vibrations and sound could be added to this unit. Topics such as the speed of sound; the speed of sound compared to the speed of light, and how fast sound travels through different media can be discussed. (Sound travels much faster through a railroad track than it does through air, for example.) Seeing a bass drum struck in a distant marching band, then hearing the sound later, is a good illustration of the different speeds of sound and light. Lightning and thunder also illustrate this idea. Other topics, such as longitudinal and transverse waves, can be demonstrated with a Slinky toy. Shake the toy up and down to illustrate transverse waves. Then place it on the floor, squeezing a few coils together, and watch the "pulse" go through the Slinky to illustrate longitudinal waves.

The lesson also relates nicely to music, where tone and pitch are discussed. Bring in a number of instruments and have students try to figure out how different sounds are made. Discuss the concepts of pitch, tone, and loudness; have students describe how each is produced by a given instrument.

Purpose

To have students understand what factors affect the process of seed germination

Activity 9.7 Germinating Seeds

Content

Plant seeds are designed to sprout (germinate) in conditions conducive to subsequent plant growth. Consequently, seeds that are placed in a dry or cold environment will not sprout. Dry, cold environments do not encourage subsequent plant growth. In wet, warm environments, however, seeds sprout quite readily.

Problem

What factors affect seed germination? (What makes seeds sprout?)

Possible Hypotheses

1. Placing seeds in soil will cause them to germinate.
2. The warmer the temperature, the faster seeds will germinate.
3. The wetter the seed, the faster seeds will germinate.

Materials

Seeds (grass, radish, pea, or bean), potting soil, growing pots made of milk containers with drainage holes in the bottoms, paper towels, clear plastic glasses

Possible Data Gathering Procedures

1. Place any type of available seed in containers of *dry* soil. Place similar seeds in a container without soil as a control. Do not water the seeds. Examine a few every day to see what happens.

2. Place seeds in clear plastic glasses in layers of paper towel that have been saturated with water. Put one container in a refrigerator. (The school cafeteria will usually allow you to use theirs.) Warm one container with a heating pad so that it is about 5 to 10°C warmer than the room. Keep the other at room temperature. Cover all containers with clear plastic to keep moisture in, and water them daily so that the towels are moist but not wet. Plant the same number of seeds in each container and count the seeds that sprout daily. Graph the results.

3. Place a similar number of seeds in four identical containers filled with soil. Water one container heavily, one moderately, one lightly, and one not at all. Count the number of seeds that sprout.

Possible Results

1. Soil by itself is usually not enough to make seeds germinate. If the seeds in the soil do sprout, there was probably moisture in the soil. Moisture can be eliminated by placing the soil without the seeds on a cookie sheet and drying in an oven (110° C).

2. Generally, the warmer the temperature, the faster seeds sprout. For this to happen the seeds need to be kept moist.

3. Within limits, the wetter the soil, the faster seeds will germinate. Some seeds react negatively to being kept totally immersed in water, however, and may rot before sprouting.

Related Activities

This activity is closely related to activities 5.3, 5.16, 7.10, 7.12, 7.20, 7.23, and 9.8, all of which focus on plants and their products. Related activities described in those lessons are also appropriate here.

Also, students can investigate the effect that light has on germination. Different types of sprouting seeds (bean, alfalfa) can be purchased from a health food store, with a contest to see who can make the most efficient sprouter. Let students taste the results.

Purpose

To introduce students to factors that influence the growth of plants

Content

As discussed in chapter 7, plants have various tropisms, or orienting responses, that help them adapt to their environment. One of these, *heliotropism,* is an orienting response to the sun. Most plants orient themselves toward the sun to take advantage of maximum sunlight. Plants sprouted in shade or darkness put most of their energy into finding sunlight; conseque ıtly, they appear weak, spindly, and pale from lack of chlorophyll. Plants grown in sunlight, on the other hand, will channel much of their energy into making leaves, which are then used to gather and store the sun's energy.

Problem

What effect does sunlight have on plants?

Possible Hypotheses

1. The more sunlight plants get, the taller they will grow.

2. The more sunlight plants get, the more leaves they will have.

Materials

Pea or bean seeds, potting soil, growing pots

Possible Data Gathering Procedures

1. Plant pea or bean seeds in milk carton containers filled with dirt. Place some of the containers in direct sunlight; others in sunlight for part of the day; others in room light, and place a fourth group in a cabinet or closet where they'll receive no sunlight. Water the plants every other day with the same amount of water and measure their growth with rulers or tape measures.

2. Follow the same procedures as in 1, but count the number of leaves as the dependent variable.

Possible Results

1. Counter to what most students predict, the plants in the dark generally grow the tallest. (Ask students why this may be valuable for plants growing in thick ground cover.) If the sun is too intense, it may hamper the growth of the plants in full or partial sunlight.

2. Generally, the more sunlight plants get, the bushier they are and the larger their leaves. Sometimes, however, plants grown in darkness may have many leaves, but they will be small. (This is an excellent opportunity to discuss the inadequacy of number of leaves as the dependent variable. Students might suggest using leaf surface area as an alternative.)

Related Activities

This lesson could easily be expanded to a unit on plant growth. Other variables, such as amount of water, type of water, type of soil, amount of fertilizer, and depth of seed, can be investigated. A discussion of the plant that grew in the dark might lead to concepts such as photosynthesis and the food-producing cycle in plants.

The activity can be related to art activities and the environment of the schoolroom. Children can help decorate the room with plants and discuss the various ways plants are used to decorate.

The children may also plant a garden as a follow-up activity. Students can be made responsible for maintenance of the garden and can see the cycle through to production of edible foods.

An additional investigation can center around growing plants under different color lights and measuring their growth rate. This can be done by purchasing different colored lights or by shining the light through tinted cellophane or glass.

The concept of *operational definitions* can be developed with this activity. An operational definition describes variables in terms of the procedure the investigator uses to measure each variable. For instance, plant growth could be operationally defined as: the distance from the soil to the bottom branch; the distance from the soil to halfway between the top and bottom branch; the total number of leaves; the average width of the leaves; or any other arbitrary measure. Choosing the "best" of these measures is an important decision scientists must make. In any case, through a discussion of this process, students will have a chance to learn that operationally defining is an important process in science.

Activity 9.9 Heart Rate of Students

Purpose

To introduce students to factors that influence heart rate

Content

The heart is the pumping organ of our body; it works to circulate blood to various parts of the body. The circulating blood performs two major functions: it carries oxygen and nutrients *to* the cells of the body and carries *away* carbon dioxide and other waste products.

Our pulse rate gives us an indirect measure of how fast our heart is pumping. The more strenuous the activity that we engage in, the faster the heart needs to beat to pump oxygen and other nutrients to the muscles. The heart is a big muscle. The more it is exercised the more efficient it becomes and the less it needs to pump during exercise. A person who exercises a lot should have a lower pulse rate than one who does not, especially after strenuous activity.

Problem

What determines the heart rate of students?

Possible Hypotheses

1. The heavier the student, the faster the heart rate.
2. The taller the student, the faster the heart rate.
3. Girls' heart rates are slower than boys'.

Materials

Clock with second hand, stethoscope borrowed from school nurse

Possible Data Gathering Procedures

1. Have the students find their pulse and measure it. Then weigh each person. Graph the heart rate (dependent variable) compared to weight (independent variable).
2. As with 1 above, record the heart rate and the height and graph the results.
3. Record the girls' heart rates and compare to those of the boys. Perhaps use the average rates for both.

Possible Results

This activity is rich with characteristics involved in scientific investigations. The results may generate discussions of uncontrolled variables, operational definitions and optimal ways to handle the data. For example, the amount of exercise a student gets and the student's general health influence the pulse rate. Neither of these factors is controlled, and the discussion might focus on the problem of controlling variables in an investigation. Also, the graphical results will be far from smooth, and the students will see that in science the results are generally rough. Scientists must look for trends in data as opposed to finding neat, clear or smooth patterns. For example, the trend in the heart rate compared to weight might be as illustrated in figure 9-5.

Figure 9–5

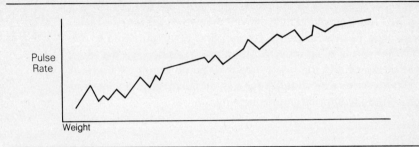

Pulse Rate

Weight

In this case we see a slight upward trend which means the hypothesis would be accepted.

On the other hand we may see the opposite trend in figure 9–6.

Figure 9–6

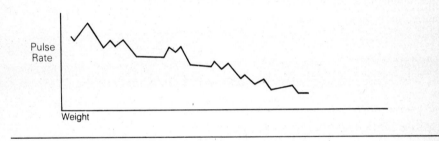

Pulse Rate

Weight

In this case, the trend is downward, which would lead to the hypothesis being rejected. In either case, the data provides a realistic picture of the kind of data science has to work with.

Additional factors, such as sample size (too few students in the class), might also be considered and discussed.

These considerations apply for all three hypotheses, depending on the nature of the class.

Related Activities

This activity can be greatly expanded. Students can bring in data taken from their parents and other relatives. Factors such as weight, smoking, drinking, and amount of weekly exercise can be investigated, and factors affecting health in general could be discussed. If facilities are available, students can check their blood pressure and compare the results to heart rate. Also have students listen to their heart beat and discuss why it goes "lub-dub."

There is also considerable opportunity here for application of computational skills, with averaging and other operations required to summarize data.

Purpose

To acquaint students with factors that affect the rate of evaporation

Content

The primary difference between the gas and liquid forms of a substance is the amount of energy they possess. If this energy level is high enough to allow molecules of the substance to fly off into the air, evaporation occurs. Any type of physical change that encourages the molecules to fly off into the air will influence the evaporation rate. Heating a liquid, fanning it, or exposing more of its surface to the air, all increase the rate of evaporation.

In general, the lighter the weight of a liquid, the easier it is for a molecule of that liquid to zoom into the air (evaporate). Because of their chemical composition, however, the molecules of certain substances are attracted to each other more than others, and so these substances evaporate more slowly.

Problem

What determines how fast a liquid will evaporate?

Possible Hypotheses

1. The larger the surface area, the faster the liquid will evaporate.
2. The heavier the liquid, the faster it evaporates.
3. The warmer the liquid, the faster it evaporates.

Materials

Water, cooking oil, rubbing alcohol, various-sized containers with dif-ferent-sized openings, thermometer

Possible Data Gathering Procedures

1. Put the same amount of water into each of several containers with different-sized openings. For instance, a cake pan, a large-mouthed bottle, and a small-mouthed bottle may be used. Measure the amount of liquid in each container each day by pouring it into a graduated cylinder or measuring cup; record the results.

2. Use three different types of liquids and put in identical containers. Put cooking oil in one, alcohol in the second, and water in the third. Weigh all three containers. Measure the amounts of liquid each day and record the results.

Figure 9-7
An Electromagnet

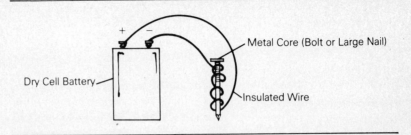

3. Put water into each of three identical containers. Place one in the refrigerator, one in a dim corner of the room, and one in the window. Record the temperature of each, each day. Measure the amounts each day and record the results.

Possible Results

1. Liquids evaporate faster when a large surface area is exposed, so the hypothesis would probably be accepted.

2. The alcohol will probably evaporate the most rapidly, and water the next most rapidly. Water is the heaviest, however, and alcohol is next heaviest, so the hypothesis would be rejected.

3. Typically, the warmer a liquid, the faster it evaporates; this hypothesis would be accepted.

Related Activities

Students can be encouraged to explore other variables, such as amount of wind and evaporation. Also, discuss why alcohol rubdowns are given to patients with fevers. Ideally, this lesson should be preceded by some experiences with thermometers and some exposure to the concept of evaporation. Experiential activity 5.5 and discovery lesson 7.2 would be appropriate here. Also, this lesson could be related to activity 7.3, which deals with the topic of distillation.

**Activity 9.11
Electromagnets**

Purpose
To introduce students to the relationship between electricity and magnetism

Content
An electromagnet is formed when a coil of insulated wire is wrapped around a metal core, and the wire ends are connected to a battery such as a flashlight battery or dry cell. The flow of electrons through the wire causes the object to become magnetized. Figure 9-7 represents the arrangement.

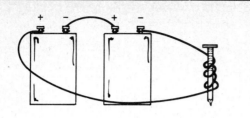

Figure 9–8
**Strength of
Electromagnets**

Problem

What determines the strength of an electromagnet?

Possible Hypotheses

1. The stronger the battery, the stronger the electromagnet.

2. The more times the wire is wound around the core, the stronger the electromagnet.

3. The bigger (thicker) the core, the stronger the electromagnet.

4. The closer the wraps of wire are wound to each other, the stronger the electromagnet.

Materials

Several dry-cell batteries, flashlight batteries, light electrical wiring, bolts or large nails, paper clips. (Electrical equipment can be obtained from a hardware or electrical appliance store.)

Possible Data Gathering Procedures

1. The hypothesis can be investigated by connecting cells in series as shown in the diagram (figure 9–8), by comparing two different-sized batteries, or by comparing the same-sized batteries that differ in strength. Strength may be ascertained by attaching them to a flashlight and comparing the brightness.

The strength of the electromagnet may be operationally defined as the number of paper clips it will pick up end to end or the total number of pins or nails it will lift up. The strength of the electromagnet can first be measured with one cell, then two cells, then three, and so on, and the results can be graphed. With flashlight batteries, the arrangement in figure 9–9 can be used. The wire ends can merely be held against or taped to the batteries to make the electromagnet.

2. The hypothesis can be investigated by increasing the number of wraps such as shown in the diagram (figure 9–10).

Figure 9-9

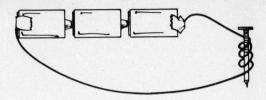

Data that could be graphed would result, with number of paper clips as the dependent variable and the number of wraps the independent variable.

3. The core can be changed by using nails and wrapping the wire around one nail, then two, then three, and so on as shown in figure 9-11. Here the number of wraps is a controlled variable.

4. This hypothesis is a bit more difficult to measure quantitatively, but can be measured at at least three levels (tight, intermediate, and loose) as shown in figure 9-11.

Possible Results

1. The stronger current resulting from a stronger battery will result in a stronger electromagnet; the hypothesis would be accepted.

2. More windings of an electromagnet will increase its strength; the hypothesis would be accepted.

3. Increasing the size of the core will increase the strength of the electromagnet; the hypothesis will probably be accepted.

4. Wrapping the wire so that individiaul turns are closer together should not increase the strength. The hypothesis will probably be rejected.

Related Activities

This activity can be included in a larger unit on electricity and magnetism. For instance, students might first be introduced to magnets,

Figure 9-10
Number of Coils in Determining the Strength of Electromagnets

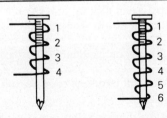

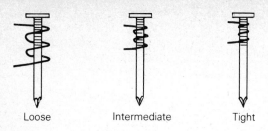

Loose   Intermediate   Tight

Figure 9–11
**Different Coil Wraps in
Determining the Strength
of Electromagnets**

polarity, and magnetic and nonmagnetic substances through discovery activity 7.9. (Magnets attract materials made of iron, nickel, or cobalt. Iron and steel are by far the most common magnetic substances.) Activity 7.8 could be used to introduce the topic of electrical conduction, which could be followed by lesson 7.18 which deals with parallel and series circuits.

If some pieces of equipment are available, the relationship between electricity and magnetism can be shown. For instance, a coil of wire attached to a battery will deflect a compass needle as shown in figure 9.12.

Students might switch poles of the battery and notice what happens to the compass.

If an ammeter (an instrument for measuring current) is available, a bar magnet thrust through a coil of wire will deflect the meter, showing that a current has been briefly created. Figure 9–13 illustrates.

As another related activity, children may be asked to try and find devices in the home that employ electromagnets, possibly even taking them apart (an old doorbell, for instance) and finding the electromagnets in them. Older children can study and build simple electric motors and generators.

Purpose
To introduce students to properties of liquids (viscosity)

**Activity 9.12
Flow of Liquids**

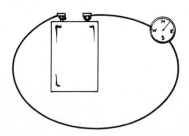

Figure 9–12
Electricity and Magnetism

Figure 9-13
Current Created by a Magnet

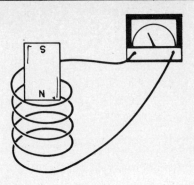

Content

The viscosity of a liquid is a measure of its flowability. A viscous fluid, such as molasses, does not flow easily. A non-viscous fluid, such as water, flows very readily.

Problem

What determines the flowability of a fluid?

Possible Hypotheses

1. The heavier the fluid, the faster it flows.
2. The warmer the fluid, the faster it flows.

Materials

Medium-sized tin cans, nails, hammer, board, different weight motor oils (10W, 20W, 30W, and 40W), hot plate, thermometer

Possible Data Gathering Procedures

1. Take a small container, such as a vegetable can, and make a small nail hole in the bottom, using the board as a pounding surface. Measure the same amount of several different weights of motor oils, as listed above, into different containers. Pour the measured amount of the 10W through the hole, timing it. Wipe the can out with a paper towel or use a different can and repeat with the other weight oils. The results could then be graphed.

2. Take a single grade of oil, such as 30W. Heat it to different temperatures, from 0° C upward. (One quart of oil measured into a variety of small containers would be ample.) For safety and convenience, the oil could be heated over a hot plate in a water bath (figure 9-14).

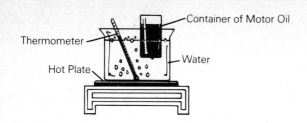

Figure 9–14
Apparatus to Heat Motor Oil

Possible Results

1. Heavier grades of oil tend to be more viscous (flow less well), so the hypothesis as stated would be rejected.

2. Heating a substance such as oil makes it flow easier, so the hypothesis would be accepted.

Related Activities

This activity is related to experiential activity 5.10 on liquids, as well as activity 9.10, Rates of Evaporation. This activity could be extended by comparing evaporation rate to viscosity. Oil does not readily evaporate, however, and if students discovered this fact when trying to evaporate the oil, a discussion of why oil is a lubricant could follow. A good application question would ask students to decide on what grade of oil to use in cars in the winter and why.

The discussion on lubricants could lead to investigations of friction and factors affecting friction, as discussed in chapter 5.

Activity 9.13
Coasting a Bicycle

Purpose

To introduce students to the concepts of *momentum* and *friction*

Content

The term momentum is used colloquially in sports and other areas. Technically, the momentum of a moving object is its mass (weight) times its speed. This means that a heavy object moving at the same speed as a lighter object has more momentum than the lighter object. The speed of the object is influenced by the friction between it and the surface it interacts with, so friction affects momentum.

Problem

What determines how far a bicycle will coast?

Possible Hypotheses

1. The lighter the person on the bicycle, the farther he or she will coast.
2. The higher the tire pressure, the farther the bicycle will coast.

Materials

Students' bicycles, tire pump, air pressure gauge

Possible Data Gathering Procedures

1. Have the children bring their bicycles to school and select two that are similar. (Many children have bicycles nearly identical to each other.) Have the children weigh themselves and then have two children ride on identical bikes at the same speed to a line and then coast. Then have one of the children ride with a third person, and so on, until a number of students have been compared in pairs. Then compare the distances the students coast to their relative weights (heaviest, second heaviest, and so on). If a bicycle has a speedometer, the procedure could be simplified by having children of different weights ride at the same speed and then coast.

2. Find two similar bicycles and two children of the same weight. Inflate the tires of the bicycles so one has only half the pressure of the other. Have the children ride together, coast, and measure the distance they coast.

Possible Results

1. The heavier child at the same speed will have more momentum than the lighter child and should coast farther; the hypothesis would be rejected.

2. The more fully inflated tire will have less friction than the less fully inflated one. The former would coast farther. The hypothesis, therefore, would probably be accepted.

Related Activities

The topic can be extended to discuss the family car and the need to keep tires properly inflated. Momentum might also be discussed in terms of football players colliding.

The activity might lead to further study of friction (activity 7.19) and a discussion of lubricants, as discussed in activity 9.12. Friction and heat could be demonstrated by rubbing palms together, rubbing smooth and rough wood blocks together, and so on. Children may then discuss why car tires get warm after a car is driven.

Advanced students can extend their concept of momentum to develop an understanding of kinetic energy (the energy of motion), researching the topic in reference books in the library.

Purpose

To introduce children to heat storage and absorption

Activity 9.14 Storing Solar Energy

Content

Certain substances give off or transmit heat much more rapidly than others. For example, a metal frying pan transmits heat from a stove to your hand more rapidly than a glass dish. By the same token, the frying pan cools off more quickly than the glass dish, so we say the dish stores heat better than the frying pan. The same principle applies to land and sea temperature at different times of the day. Water warms more slowly than land but also cools off more slowly, resulting in temperature differences between ocean and adjacent land. These differences result in the sea breezes that are found around coastal areas.

Problem

What kind of material retains heat best?

Possible Hypotheses

1. The heavier the material, the better it retains heat.

Materials

Empty cans, salt, sugar, water, sand, scale, thermometer, boxes covered with black construction paper

Possible Data Gathering Procedures

1. Divide the class into groups. Have them fill four cans respectively with regular dirt, washed sand, salt, and sugar in the same amounts. Weigh each container. Determine the density of each. (To review density, see activity 7.3.) Place each can in a box painted black on all sides. Use the same size box in each case. Place a thermometer in each of the cans. Leave the boxes with the cans inside in the sun for several hours to ensure a uniform temperature in each can. Bring the cans inside and check the temperature of each can every few minutes and record and graph the results.

Possible Results

The temperature drop will not be smoothly related to the density of each substance so the hypothesis will probably be rejected.

Related Activities

This lesson is rich with related possibilities. For example, water could be added as another substance. The procedure could be changed by taking the cans out of the boxes and measuring which one warms the most rapidly. Containers of different colors, all containing the same substance, could be compared as to how rapidly their temperature rises in the sunlight. (A heat lamp could be substituted for sunlight if necessary.)

An investigation of the heat-retaining property of liquids can be related to the rate of flow and evaporation. (Do the experiment with the different engine oils described in activity 9.12.)

The entire activity can serve as a launching pad for a discussion on energy and the different types of energy. Materials that make good heat insulators (activities 7.8 and 7.21) can be compared as electrical insulators and conductors.

The different rates of heating and cooling can lead to a discussion of sea and land breezes and to the formation of summer thundershowers. The differential heating effects of the sun at different times of the year could also be integrated with activities on the weather (5.4) and shadows (7.24).

Activity 9.15
Melting Ice

Purpose

To acquaint students with factors that affect the melting rate of ice

Content

Ice is nothing more than water that has had the heat energy removed. The lack of heat energy allows the water molecules to move very close to each other and to attach to each other in crystalline formation. When these molecules are heated again, they separate out from this crystalline structure and become free-moving water molecules. Conditions that allow heat to be absorbed quickly by ice molecules will result in rapid melting.

Problem

What factors affect the melting rate of ice cubes?

Possible Hypotheses

1. The bigger the ice cube, the longer it takes to melt.

2. The denser the melting medium, the faster ice melts.

3. The hotter the melting medium, the faster ice melts.

Materials

Ice cubes, melting pans, rubbing alcohol, salt or sugar, hot water, thermometers

Possible Data Gathering Procedures

1. Take two ice cubes; put one on top of the other. Break another cube into two pieces and separate the pieces. Leave one ice cube whole. Record the time it takes for all three arrangements to melt.

2. Prepare several melting baths by pouring an equal amount of water in one, alcohol in another, and sugar or salt water (one teaspoon per cup) in another. Make sure all are at the same temperature. Weigh the samples to establish which is most and least dense, and then put ice cubes of equal size in each and record the time it takes for each to melt.

3. Take three identical melting pans and put identical amounts of hot, warm, and cool water in each. Then place ice cubes in each of the containers and measure how long it takes for each to melt.

Possible Results

1. Smaller ice cube pieces have more surface area exposed to the warm air environment and consequently melt faster. Hypothesis would be accepted.

2. The denser the melting medium, the faster ices cubes melt; this hypothesis would be accepted.

3. Ice cubes melt faster in a hotter melting medium. The hypothesis would be accepted.

Related Activities

Have students graph the results of activity 9.3. Discuss the shape of the curve and have students hypothesize what the melting times would be for temperatures between the known values and beyond the known values. Basically, these estimations are types of interpolation and extrapolation. *Interpolation* involves estimating values between numbers and *extrapolation* involves estimating values beyond numbers. Then check the estimates by melting ice cubes in water at the different temperatures.

Another activity can investigate the effect of stirring or melting rate. In one condition don't stir at all; in another stir once every minute; in another, stir twice every minute; and so on. Other related lessons include 5.5 on thermometers, 7.6 on temperature variations, and 7.21 on insulation.

Activity 9.16
Mold Growth

Purpose
To help students understand factors that affect mold growth

Content
Molds are plants that belong to the fungus family. They are related to mushrooms, mildews, and plant rusts. Molds need warm, moist environments to survive and reproduce by means of spores. Unlike other plants, molds lack chlorophyll and consequently must obtain their energy from the surfaces they grow on.

Problem
What factors influence the growth rate of molds?

Possible Hypotheses

1. The darker the growing environment, the faster mold growth occurs.
2. The warmer the growing medium, the faster mold growth occurs.
3. The moister the growing medium, the faster mold growth occurs.

Materials
A loaf of bread, water, sandwich bags, tape, thermometer

Possible Data Gathering Procedures

1. Place a slice of bread in each of three "baggies" and sprinkle with equal amounts of water until damp but not wet. Seal each of the bags tighty with tape to prevent the loss of water and to prevent the spread of the molds once they begin to grow. Place one of the sealed bags in a dark closet, another in partial shade, and the third in direct sunlight. Measure the temperature of each with a thermometer. The molds should begin growing in three or four days. Have students cut out pieces of quarter-inch graph paper to the size and shape of the pieces of bread. Use the graph paper to measure the amount of mold growth by placing the graph paper over the piece of bread and counting the number of squares that have mold on them. Keep a daily record of the growth rate of the molds.

2. Prepare the mold-growing containers as in 1 above: place one in a refrigerator, one near a radiator, and one in a place where the temperature is the same as the average room temperature. Measure the temperature of each place with a thermometer, and record the growth rate of the mold as in 1 above.

3. Prepare the mold-growing containers as described above, but this time seal one tightly, seal a second tightly and punch two or three pencil holes in it, and prop the mouth of the third bag open. Place all three in a warm, semi-dark environment and measure the growth of the molds. Caution students against handling the molds when measuring for growth.

Possible Results

1. Molds grow best in warm, dark, moist environments. The results of this experiment will depend upon the temperature. If the temperatures in the three places are approximately equal, then the mold should grow faster in a dark environment.

2. Like most organisms, there is an optimal temperature range for mold growth. In general, the warmer the temperature the faster mold grows, but if the temperature becomes too hot, this may retard mold growth.

3. Molds need moisture to grow and will not thrive on dry environments. If the pieces of bread dry out before mold growth begins, there probably will not be any growth at all on the dry pieces of bread.

Related Activities

Students can investigate the effect of common household antiseptics and preservatives on mold growth. Prepare the packages as described above, but this time sprinkle a small amount of the following materials on the bread before sealing: rubbing alcohol, iodine, salt, and sugar. Compare the growth rate of these containers with a control. Also try varying the amounts of the above materials. Different ways of preventing mold growth could be discussed in terms of the general topics of food preservation (5.16) and sterilization (7.7).

Purpose

To acquaint students with factors that affect the boiling temperature of water

Activity 9.17
Boiling Water

Content

The evaporation of water is caused by the motion of the water molecules overcoming the attraction that the molecules have for each other. When heat is added, the molecules' motion increases and more molecules fly off into the air as water vapor or steam. At 100°C the motion of these molecules becomes quite rapid and boiling occurs. This figure is only accurate for pure, distilled water at sea level. Water that has impurities in it will boil at a higher temperature, and water at *higher* elevations will boil at a *lower* temperature. In addition, a covered pan of water will boil at a higher temperature than an uncovered one.

Problem

What factors affect the boiling temperature of water?

Possible Hypotheses

1. The shape or size of the pan influences the boiling temperature; the bigger the pan, the higher the boiling temperature.

2. Distilled water boils at the same temperature as tap water.

3. Lids will not influence the boiling temperature of water.

4. Impurities in water will cause water to boil at a higher temperature.

Materials

Distilled water, various size pans with lids, sugar and salt, heat resistant thermometers (most will be, but check for plastic components that might melt)

Possible Data Gathering Procedures

To investigate each of the hypotheses, you can set up electrical hot plates or bunsen burners to boil the water.

1. Place water in different-sized and different-shaped pans. Bring to a boil and record the temperature.

2. Take two pans of identical size and shape; boil distilled water in one and tap water in the other. Record the boiling temperature of each.

3. Take three identical pans. Cover one part way and another completely; leave the third uncovered. Record the boiling temperature of each.

4. Take three identical pans of water. Put one teaspoon of salt or sugar in one, two teaspoons in another, and nothing in the third.

Possible Results

1. The shape or size of the pan should not affect the boiling temperature of water. This hypothesis would be rejected.

2. The results of this activity will depend upon the amount of chemicals and minerals in the tap water. If they are significant, the tap water may boil at a higher temperature.

3. Putting a lid on boiling water makes it harder for the molecules to escape from the water and thus, raises the boiling temperature.

4. Sugar or salt in water should raise the boiling temperatures of water and the more impurities in the water, the higher the boiling temperature.

Related Activities

An ideal sequence of lessons would introduce students to the topics of thermometers and heat, followed by this lesson and lessons on evaporation (7.2), and distillation (7.3). Students can also investigate how various factors such as size of pan, kind of pan, amount of water, and temperature of water affect the time it takes for water to boil. Also, students could compare the temperature of water when it first boils to when it is rapidly boiling.

Appendix A

National Elementary Science Curriculum Projects

The history of the national science curriculum projects can be traced to the early sixties, when educators in all areas were revising their curricula in response to criticism. Russia's successful 1957 launching of Sputnik spurred severe criticisms of the teaching of science, mathematics, and language instruction in the United States. Critics of the science area contended that programs were outmoded and ill-suited to prepare scientists for the space age.

Out of this furor arose a number of elementary curriculum projects funded by large amounts of federal money. Money was allotted not only for the creation and development of these projects, but also for dissemination to schools across the country. Unlike previous curriculum revision efforts, these were national in scope and employed the services of scientists from all areas.

These curriculum projects had several major advantages over the existing science curriculum materials, which were primarily in the form of textbook series. First, they strongly emphasized a process approach to science and were inquiry oriented. This was a major change from most text series, which had a heavy emphasis on reading and memorization. Further, the national curriculum projects had highly structured materials with explicit directions for the teacher and the necessary laboratory materials for students. Usually these projects were manufactured and sold as complete kits to teachers, eliminating the need for extensive planning and avoiding problems of obtaining materials. Disadvantages included cost, a relative lack of emphasis on content, and inhibition of teacher creativity by overstructured lessons.

Keep these advantages and disadvantages in mind as we look at three curriculum projects. These three are representative of the group.

SAPA: Science—A Process Approach

Science—A Process Approach (SAPA), one of the more radical and innovative of the projects, exemplifies a number of recent changes in thinking about how science ought to be taught to little children. The entire program consists of a number of hierarchically sequenced process skills. A partial sequence for the process of inference follows.

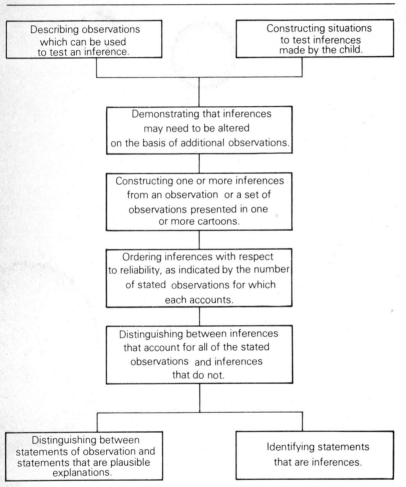

A SAPA Process Hierarchy (1967)

In this sequence, simpler, more fundamental processes need to be mastered before more advanced and complex ones are dealt with. The curriculum is laid out in terms of complex skills and activities. In the lower four grades (K–3) the basic process skills are emphasized (see list below), while in 4–6, the integrated processes are emphasized.

Basic Processes, (K-3)	*Integrated Processes, (4-6)*
Observing	Formulating hypotheses
Classifying	Making operational definitions
Measuring	Controlling and manipulationg
	variables
Communicating	Experimenting
Inferring	Interpreting data
Predicting	Formulating models
Recognizing space/time relations	
Recognizing number relations	

The instructional materials in this package include objectives, a teacher rationale, a list of materials needed, a proposal for initiating the lesson, and suggested instructional procedures. In keeping with the idea that science is doing, no written materials are provided to students. There are seven teacher guides, one for each level starting with kindergarten.

ESS: Elementary Science Study

This project is similar to SAPA in that it places major emphasis on development of students' process skills and their understanding of the scientific enterprise. However, ESS differ from SAPA in rigidity of structure. It is much more flexible and loosely sequenced. There are more than 40 units in the ESS curriculum, and although approximate grade levels are suggested for each of the units, there is no definite sequence. Teachers can use the units as they see fit. This characteristic has made the project attractive to teachers who want some control over the science curriculum. It has also made the project easily adaptable for use with a school's existing textbook program.

The units themselves usually take several weeks to complete, with lessons that stress individual, unstructured inquiry. One unit, "The Behavior of Meal Worms," encourages students to identify their own problems and investigate them through individual inquiry. For example, students are encouraged to observe meal worms and try to discover what senses they use in surviving. One way to do this is to shine a flashlight on the animals and observe their response. As one of the creators of the project described it, there is a heavy emphasis on "messing about in science." Other representative units are listed below.

Changes	Batteries and bulbs
Mystery powder	Bones
Pendulums	Growing seeds
Primary balancing	Gases and airs

Like SAPA, ESS attempts to provide individual students with their own materials to work with to encourage personal initiative and problem solving. A teacher's guide accompanies the units, but it is much less structured than the one for SAPA, reflecting the strong emphasis placed on responsive teaching and the encouragement of student inquiry.

SCIS: Science Curriculum Improvement Study

Of the three curriculum projects discussed in this chapter, SCIS is the most content oriented. Content orientation is not toward the memorization of facts, however, but is geared to an understanding of major concepts in science such as interactions, relativity, and ecosystems.

To teach these concepts, a tightly sequenced curriculum has been constructed, in which lessons in later grades depend upon understandings learned in earlier lessons. Three levels of abstraction of concepts are found in the program. First-level abstractions are the concepts of matter, living matter, conservation of matter, and variation. Second-level abstractions are interaction, causality, and relativity. Third-level abstractions include energy, equilibrium, behavior, and reproduction.

A three-step teaching sequence of exploration, invention, and discovery is used to teach these concepts. In the exploration phase, structured lab experiences allow students to manipulate objects and make observations. Out of these experiences comes the need for concepts and generalizations to describe the patterns and regularities observed in this phase. The teacher introduces these abstractions—concepts and generalizations—during the invention stage. Students are asked to test and apply these ideas during the discovery phase, which is designed to expand and reinforce ideas learned earlier.

Because the units are sequenced and the individual lessons structured, SCIS materials provide a lot of direction for the teachers. This structure, while providing guidance for the teacher, also makes SCIS less adaptable as a secondary resource and has been viewed by some teachers as too restrictive of their own initiative.

Comparison

These three curriculum projects illustrate the three major goals of science we discussed in this chapter. The SAPA curriculum shows how processes can form a major focus of the curriculum. SCIS illustrates the use of major concepts in organizing a science curriculum. ESS shows how student inquiry through autonomous investigations can be used to help students understand how science and scientists operate.

We mentioned that a major drawback to implementation of these curricula is cost. In times of tightened budgets school districts appear less and less willing to support science curricula that cost several hundred dollars a year to operate. In fact, a number of school districts that initially adopted these programs have since opted for cheaper, more teacher-centered science curricula. If you think you would like to use some of these ideas to teach science check in the school where you're working. See if any old science curriculum materials are being stored there. Our experience has been that these materials, in new or slightly used condition, are often sitting in school storage areas, waiting for a resourceful teacher to come along and use them.

Appendix B

Science Resource Books for Teachers

Abell, G. *Exploration of the Universe.* New York: Holt, Rinehart and Winston, 1975.

Asimov, I. *Asimov's Guide to Science.* New York: Basic Books, 1972.

Asimov, I. *Inside the Atom.* New York: Abelard-Schuman, 1958.

Asimov, I. *The Double Planet.* New York: Abelard-Schuman, 1967.

Asimov, I. *Twentieth Century Discovery.* New York: Doubleday, 1969.

Asimov, I. *To the Ends of the Universe.* New York: Walker, 1967.

Beck, L. *Human Growth.* New York: Harcourt Brace Jovanovich, 1969.

Bishop, M. and Lewis, P. *Focus on Earth Science.* Columbus, Ohio: Charles E. Merrill, 1972.

Brown, F., Kemper, G., and Lewis, J. *Earth Science.* Morristown, N.J.: Silver Burdett, 1973.

Carson, R. *The Sense of Wonder.* New York: Harper & Row, 1956.

Carson, R. *Silent Spring.* Boston: Houghton Mifflin, 1962.

Carter, J. et al. *Physical Science: A Problem Solving Approach.* Boston: Ginn, 1971.

Choppin, G., Jaffe, B., Summerlin, L., and Jackson, L. *Chemistry.* Morristown, N.J.: Silver Burdett, 1973.

Cole, F. *Introduction to Meteorology.* New York: John Wiley & Sons, 1970.

Colton, A., Darlington, L., and Lynch, L. *Chemistry Study Program.* Boston, Mass.: Houghton Mifflin, 1973.

Cornwall, I. *Prehistoric Animals and Their Hunters.* New York: Praeger, 1968.

Donn, W. *The Earth: Our Physical Environment.* New York: John Wiley & Sons, Inc., 1972.

Dunbar, C., and K. Waage. *Historical Geology.* New York: John Wiley & Sons, Inc., 1969.

Eisman, L., and C. Tanzer. *Biology and Human Progress.* Englewood Cliffs, N.J.: Prentice-Hall, 1977.

Elliott, A. *Basic Biology.* New York: Appleton-Century Croft, 1970.

Genzer, I., and P. Youngner. *Physics.* Morristown, N.J.: Silver Burdett, 1973.

Greenblatt, A. *Teen-Age Medicine: Questions Young People Ask About Their Health.* New York: Cowles Communication, 1970.

Harrington, J. *To See A World.* St. Louis: C. V. Mosby, 1973.

Headstrom, R. *Nature in Miniature.* New York: Knopf, 1968.

Hogg, H. *The Stars Belong To Everyone: How to Enjoy Astronomy.* Garden City, N.Y.: Doubleday, 1976.

Huffer, C. et al. *An Introduction to Astronomy.* New York: Holt, Rinehart and Winston, 1973.

Hulsizer, R. and D. Lazarus. *The World of Physics.* Reading, Mass.: Addison-Wesley, 1972.

Jastrov, R. and M. Thompson. *Astronomy: Fundamentals and Frontiers.* New York: John Wiley and Sons, 1972.

Jeffreys, H. *The Earth, Its Origin, History, and Physical Constitution.* New York: Cambridge University Press, 1970.

Keeton, W. *Biological Science.* New York: W. W. Norton and Co., 1972.

Laycock, G. *The Bird Watcher's Bible.* Garden City, N.Y.: Doubleday, 1976.

Marean, J., O. Johnson, and B. Menhusen. *Life Science, A Laboratory Approach.* Reading, Mass.: Addison-Wesley, 1972.

McAlester, A. *The History of Life.* Englewood Cliffs, N.J.: Prentice-Hall, 1968.

McCombs, L. and N. Rosa. *Ecology: An Introduction.* Reading, Mass.: Addison-Wesley, 1973.

Menzel, D. *Astronomy.* New York: Random House, 1970.

Merkin, M. *Physical Science with Modern Application.* Philadelphia: Saunders, 1976.

Miller, A. and J. Thompson. *Elements of Meteorology.* Columbus, Ohio: Charles E. Merrill Publishing Company, 1970.

Murphy, J. *Physics and Problems.* Columbus, Ohio: Charles E. Merrill, 1972.

Namowitz, S. and D. Stone. *Earth Science.* Princeton, N.J.: Van Nostrand, 1978.

Navarra, J. *Clocks, Calendars, and Carrousels: A Book About Time.* New York: Doubleday Company, 1967.

Navarra, J. *Nature Strikes Back.* New York: Natural History Press, 1971.

Navarra, J., J. Weisberg, and F. Mele. *Earth Science.* New York: John Wiley and Sons, Inc., 1971.

Navarra, J. *The World You Inherit: A Story of Pollution.* New York: The Natural History Press, 1970.

O'Brien, R. *Machines.* New York: Time-Life Books, 1964.

Oran, R. *Biology: Living Systems.* Columbus, Ohio: Charles E. Merrill Publishing Company, 1973.

Palmer, E. and H. Fowler. *Fieldbook of Natural History.* New York: McGraw-Hill, 1974.

Ramsey, W. et al. *Earth Science.* New York: Holt, Rinehart, and Winston, 1978.

Raymond, O. *Biology: Living Systems.* Columbus, Ohio: Charles E. Merrill Publishing Company, 1973.

Rumney, G. *The Geosystem, Dynamic Integration of Land, Sea and Air.* Dubuque, Iowa: W. C. Brown, 1970.

Thomson, T. *Chemistry: Introduction To Matter.* Reading, Mass.: Addison-Wesley, 1973.

Thurber, W. and R. Kilburn. *Exploring Earth Science.* Boston: Allyn & Bacon, 1970.

Turekian, K. *Oceanography.* Englewood Cliffs, N.J.: Prentice-Hall, 1968.

Weyl, P. *Oceanography.* New York: John Wiley and Sons, Inc., 1970.

Young, H. *Journey To Tranquility.* Garden City, N.J.: Doubleday, 1970.

Elementary Science Methods Texts

Abruscato, J. and J. Hassard. *Loving and Beyond.* Santa Monica, California: Goodyear, 1976.

Blough, G. and J. Schwartz. *Elementary School Science and How to Teach It, 6th ed.* New York: Holt, Rinehart, and Winston, 1979.

Butts, D. and G. Hall. *Children and Science: The Process of Teaching and Learning.* Englewood Cliffs, N.J.: Prentice-Hall, 1975.

Carin, A. and R. Sund. *Teaching Science Through Discovery.* Columbus, Ohio: Charles E. Merrill Books, 1970.

Carin, A. and R. Sund. *Teaching Modern Science, 2nd ed.* Columbus, Ohio: Charles E. Merrill, 1975.

DeVito, A. and G. Krockover. *Creative Science: Ideas and Activities for Teaching and Children.* Boston: Little-Brown, 1976.

Esler, W. *Teaching Elementary Science, 2nd ed.* Belmont, California: Wadsworth, 1977.

Gega, P. *Science In Elementary Education, 3rd ed.* New York: John Wiley, 1977.

George, K., Dietz, M., Abraham, E., and M. Nelson. *Elementary School Science.* Lexington, Mass.: D. C. Heath, 1974.

Good, R. *Science-Children: Readings in Elementary Science Education.* Dubuque, Iowa: W. C. Brown, 1972.

Hone, E., A. Joseph, and E. Victor. *A Sourcebook for Elementary Science,* 2nd ed. New York: Harcourt Brace Jovanovich, 1971.

Hungerford, H. and A. Tomera. *Science in the Elementary School.* Champaign, Ill.: Stipes, 1977.

Hurd, P. and J. Gallagher, New Directions in Elementary Science Teaching. Belmont, California: Wadsworth, 1969.

Ivany, J. *Science Teaching in the Elementary School: A Professional Approach.* Palo Alto, California: Science Research Associates, 1975.

Jacobson, W. *The New Elementary School Science.* New York: Van Nostrand, 1970.

Jenkins, E. and R. Whitfield. *Readings in Science Education.* New York: McGraw-Hill, 1974.

Kuslan, L. and A. Stone. *Teaching Children Science: An Inquiry Approach.* Belmont, California: Wadsworth, 1972.

Lansdown, B., P. Blackwood, and P. Brandwein, *Teaching Elementary Science Through Investigation and Colloquium.* New York: Harcourt, 1971.

Lewis, J. and I. Potter. *The Teaching of Science in the Elementary School.* Englewood Cliffs, N.J.: Prentice-Hall, 1970.

Navarra, J. and J. Zaffarone. *Science Today for the Elementary School Teacher.* Evanston, Ill.: Harper & Row, 1959.

Piltz, A. and R. Sund. *Creative Teaching of Science in the Elementary School.* Boston: Allyn and Bacon, 1974.

Renner, J., D. Stafford, and W. Ragan. *Teaching Science in the Elementary School.* New York: Harper & Row, 1973.

Rowe, M. *Teaching Science as Continuous Inquiry.* New York: McGraw-Hill, 1973.

Selburg, E. *Discovering Science in the Elementary School.* Reading, Mass.: Addison-Wesley, 1970.

Sund, R. and R. Bybee. *Becoming a Better Elementary Science Teacher—A Reader.* Columbus, Ohio: Charles E. Merrill, 1973.

Thier, H. *Teaching Elementary School Science.* Lexington, Mass.: D. C. Heath, 1970.

Trojcak, D. *Science With Children.* New York: McGraw-Hill, 1979.

Victor, E. *Science for the Elementary School.* New York: Macmillan, 1975.

Victor, E. and M. Lerner. *Readings in Science Education for the Elementary School.* New York: Macmillan, 1975.

Williams, D. and W. Herman. *Current Research in Elementary School Science.* New York: Macmillan, 1971.

Educational and Psychological Texts

Ahmann, J., and M. Glock. *Measuring and Evaluating Educational Achievement, 2nd edition.* Boston: Allyn and Bacon, 1975.

Ausubel, D. *Educational Psychology: A Cognitive View.* New York: Holt, Rinehart and Winston, 1968.

Ausubel, D., and F. Robinson. *School Learning: An Introduction to Educational Psychology.* New York: Holt, Rinehart and Winston, 1969.

Bloom, B. *Taxonomy of Educational Objectives, Handbook I: Cognitive Domain.* New York: McKay, 1956.

Blosser, P. *Handbook of Effective Questioning Techniques.* Worthington, Ohio: Education Associates, 1973.

Bourne, L., B. Ekstrand, and R. Dominowski. *The Psychology of Thinking.* Englewood Cliffs, N.J.: Prentice-Hall. 1971.

Bruner, J., J. Goodnow, and G. Austin, *A Study of Thinking.* New York: John Wiley, 1956.

Bruner, J. *"On going beyond the information given,"* in Contemporary Approaches to Cognition. Cambridge, Harvard University Press, 1957.

Bruner, J. *On Knowing: Essays for the Left Hand.* New York: Atheneum, 1965.

Bruner, J. *The Process of Education.* Cambridge, Mass.: Harvard University Press, 1960.

Bruner, J. *Toward a Theory of Instruction.* Cambridge, Mass.: Harvard University Press, 1966.

DeCecco, J. *The Psychology of Learning and Instruction: Educational Psychology.* Englewood Cliffs, N.J.: Prentice-Hall, 1968.

Ebel, R. *Essentials of Educational Measurement.* Englewood Cliffs, N.J.: Prentice-Hall, 1972.

Eggen, P., D. Kauchak and R. Harder. *Strategies for Teachers.* Englewood Cliffs, N.J.: Prentice-Hall, 1979.

Farnham-Diggory, S. *Cognitive Processes in Education: A Psychological Preparation for Teaching and Curriculum Development.* New York: Harper and Row, 1972.

Furth, H. *Piaget for Teachers.* Englewood Cliffs, N.J.: Prentice-Hall, 1970.

Furth, H., and H. Wachs. *Thinking Goes To School.* New York: Oxford University Press, 1974.

Gagné, R. *The Conditions of Learning.* New York: Holt, 1970.

Ginsburg, H., and S. Opper. *Piaget's Theory of Intellectual Development: An Introduction.* Englewood Cliffs, N.J.: Prentice-Hall, 1969.

Hunkins, F. *Questioning Strategies and Techniques.* Boston, Mass.: Allyn and Bacon, 1972.

Hunkins, F. *Involving Students in Questioning.* Boston, Mass.: Allyn and Bacon. 1976.

Isaacs, N. *A Brief Introduction to Piaget.* New York: Agathon Press. 1972.

Inhelder, B., and J. Piaget. *The Growth of Logical Thinking.* New York: Basic Books, 1958.

Kagan, J. *Understanding Children.* New York: Harcourt Brace Jovanovich, 1971.

Keislar, E., and L. Shulman, eds. *Learning by Discovery: A Critical Appraisal.* Chicago: Rand McNally, 1966.

Klausmeier, H., E. Ghatala, and D. Frayer. *Conceptual Learning and Development: A Cognitive View.* New York: Academic Press, 1974.

Krathwohl, D. et al. *Taxonomy of Educational Objectives, Handbook II: Affective Domain.* New York: McKay, 1964.

Lefrancois, G. *Psychology for Teaching.* Belmont, California: Wadsworth, 1975.

Lindsay, P. and D. Norman. *Human Information Processing: An Introduction to Psychology.* New York: Academic Press, 1973.

Mager, R. *Developing Attitude Toward Learning.* Palo Alto, Calif.: Pearon, 1968.

Mager, R. *Preparing Instructional Objectives.* Belmont, Calif.: Fearon, 1962.

McAshan, H. *The Goals Approach to Performance Objectives.* Philadelphia: Saunders, 1974.

Martorella, P. *Concept Learning.* San Francisco: Intext, 1972.

Maier, H. *Three Theories of Child Development.* New York: Harper & Row, 1965.

Phillips, J. Jr. *The Origins of Intellect: Piaget's Theory.* San Francisco, Calif.: Freeman, 1969.

Pikas, A. *Abstraction and Concept Formation.* Cambridge: Harvard University Press, 1966.

Sanders, N. *Classroom Questions: What Kinds?* New York: Harper and Row, 1966.

Sax, G. *Principles of Educational Measurement and Evaluation.* Belmont, Calif.: Wadsworth, 1974.

Schwebwl, M. and J. Ralph. *Piaget in the Classroom.* New York: Basic Books, 1973.

Sime, M. *A Child's Eye View.* New York: Harper and Row, 1973.

Smith, F. *Comprehension and Learning.* New York: Holt, Rinehart and Winston, 1975.

Stendler, C. *The Developmental Approach of Piaget and Its Implications for Science in the Elementary School.* New York: Macmillan, 1966.

Wadsworth, B. *Piaget for the Classroom Teacher.* New York: Longamns, 1978.

Understanding Science

Baker, R. *A Stress Analysis of a Strapless Evening Gown.* Englewood Cliffs, N.J.: Prentice-Hall, 1963.

Barzun, J. *Science: The Glorious Entertainment.* New York: Harper & Row, 1964.

Beveridge, W. *The Art of Scientific Investigations.* New York: W. W. Norton, 1957.

Bronowski, J. *Science and Human Values.* New York: Harper & Row, 1965.

Bronowski, J. *The Ascent of Man.* Boston: Little, Brown, 1974.

Beiser, A., ed. *The World of Physics.* New York: McGraw-Hill, 1960.

Cajori, F. *A History of Physics,* rev. ed. New York: Dover Publications, 1962.

Carson, R. *The Sense of Wonder.* New York: Harper & Row, 1965.

Conant, J., ed. *Harvard Case Histories in Experimental Science* (2 volumes). Cambridge, Mass.: Harvard University Press, 1957.

Conant, J. *Science and Common Sense.* New Haven: Yale University Press, 1951.

Davies, J. *The Scientific Approach* 2nd ed. New York: Academic Press, 1973.

Dillard, A. *Pilgrim at Tinker Creek.* New York: Bantam Books, 1974.

Fischer, R. *Science, Man and Society.* Philadelphia: Sauders, 1971.

Hempel, C. *Philosophy of Natural Science.* Englewood Cliffs, N.J.: Prentice-Hall, 1966.

Hildebrand, J. *Science in the Making.* New York: Columbia University Press, 1957.

Kuhn, T. *The Structure of Scientific Revolutions.* Chicago: University of Chicago Press, 1962.

Leopold, A. *A Sand County Almanac.* New York: Ballantine Books, 1971.

Margenau, H. and D. Bergamini. *The Scientist.* New York: Time Inc., 1964.

Martin, M. *Concepts of Science Education.* Glenview, Ill,: Scott Foresman and Co., 1972.

McCain, G. and E. Segal. *The Game of Science,* 3rd ed. Monterey, Cal.: Brooks/Cale, 1977.

Newman, J. *What is Science?* New York: Washington Square Press, 1962.

Piel, E. and J. Truxal. *Technology: Handle with Care.* New York: McGraw-Hill, 1975.

Ravetz, J. *Scientific Knowledge and Its Social Problems.* Oxford, England: Oxford University Press, 1971.

Roe, A. *The Making of a Scientist.* New York: Dodd, Mead, 1953.

Selye, Hans. *From Dream to Discovery: On Being a Scientist.* New York: McGraw-Hill, 1964.

Schwab, J. "Structure of the Disciplines: Meanings and Significances," in *The Structure of Knowledge and the Curriculum.* G. Ford and L. Pugno, eds. Chicago: Rand McNally, 1964.

Snow, C. *The Two Cultures, and the Scientific Revolution.* New York: Cambridge University Press, 1959.

Taffel, A. *Physics, Its Methods and Meanings.* Boston, Mass.: Allyn & Bacon, Inc., 1973.

Wartofsky, M. *Conceptual Foundations of Scientific Thought.* New York: Macmillan, 1968.

Watson, J. *The Double Helix.* New York: Atheneum, 1968.

Science Books and Periodicals For Students

Adams, F. *Catch A Sunbeam: A Book of Solar Study and Experiments.* New York: Harcourt Brace Jovanovich, 1978.

Aho, J. and J. Petras. *Learning About Sex.* New York: Holt, Rinehart, and Winston, 1978.

Anderson, L. *The Smallest Life Around Us.* New York: Crown, 1978.

Asimov, I. *Please Explain.* Boston: Houghton Mifflin, 1973.

Asimov, I. *How Did We Find Out About the Earthquakes?* New York: Walker, 1978.

Brandwein, P. *Invitation to Investigate.* New York: Harcourt, 1970.

Busch, P. *Exploring as You Walk in the Meadow.* Philadelphia: Lipincott, 1972.

Cole, J. *A Fish Hatches.* West Caldwell, N.J.: Morrow, William, & Co. 1978.

Cooper, G. *Inside Animals.* Wallham, Ma.: Atlantic/Little, Brown; 1978

Curious Naturalist, The (South Lincoln, Mass.: Massachusetts Audubon Society). For children; nine issues a year.

Fodor, R. *What Does a Geologist Do?* New York: Dodd, Mead & Co., 1978.

Ford, B. *Animals That Use Tools.* New York: Messner, 1978.

Goldberg, L. *Learning to Choose.* New York: Charles Scribner's Sons, 1976.

Gottlieb, L. *Factory Made: How Things are Manufactured.* New York: Houghton Mifflin, 1978.

Graham, A. and F. Graham. *Bug Hunters.* New York: Delacorte, 1978.

Grosvenor, D. *Zoo Babies.* Washington D.C.: National Geographic Society, 1978.

Hartman, J. *Looking at Lizards.* New York: Holiday, 1978.

Hever, K. *Rainbows, Halos, and Other Wonders.* New York: Dodd, Mead & Co., 1978.

Holter, P. *Photography Without a Camera.* Princeton, N.J.: Van Nostrand and Rinehold, 1972.

Hopf, A. *Animal and Plant Life Spans.* New York: Holiday, 1978.

Hutchins, R. *A Look at Ants.* New York: Dodd/Mead, 1978.

Junior Astronomer. Benjamin Adelman, 4211 Colie Dr., Silver Springs, Md. (C & T) 20906

Junior Natural History. American Museum of Natural History, New York, N.Y. 10024 (Monthly) (C & T)

Kerrod, R. *Rocks and Minerals.* New York: Warwick, Watts, 1978.

Lavine, S. *Wonders of Terrariums.* New York: Dodd, Mead & Co., 1978.

Leen, N. *Snakes.* New York: Holt, Rinehart, and Winston, 1978.

McCoy, J. *In Defense of Animals.* Somers, Ct.: Seabury Press, 1978.

Metos, T. and G. Bitter. *Exploring with Solar Energy.* New York: Messner, 1978.

Milgrom, H. *Paper Science.* New York: Walker, 1978.

Milgrom, H. *ABC Science Experiments.* New York: Crowell-Collier, 1972.

Monthly Evening Sky Map. Box 213, Clayton, Mo. 63105 (Monthly) (C & T)

Moorman, T. *How To Make Your Science Projects Scientific.* New York: Atheneum, 1974.

My Weekly Reader. American Education Publications, Education Center, Columbus, Ohio (Weekly during the school year) 43216

National Geographic. National Geographic Society, 1146 Sixteenth St. N.W., Washington, D.C. (Monthly) (C & T)

Natural History. American Museum of Natural History, 79th St. and Central Park West, New York, N.Y. 10024 (Monthly) (C & T)

Nature Magazine. American Nature Association, 1214 15th Street, N.W., Washington, D.C. (Monthly Oct. to May and bimonthly June to Sept.) (C & T)

Nixon, H. and J. Nixon. *Volcanoes: Nature's Fireworks.* New York: Dodd, Mead & Co., 1978.

Our Dumb Animals. Massachusetts Society for the Prevention of Cruelty to Animals, Boston, Mass. 02115 (Monthly) (C & T)

Outdoors Illustrated. National Audubon Society, 1000 Fifth Ave., New York, N.Y. (Monthly) (C & T)

Patent, D. *The World of Worms.* New York: Holiday, 1978

Patent, D. *Animal and Plant Mimicry.* New York: Holiday, 1978.

Patent, D. *Beetles and How They Live.* New York: Holiday, 1978.

Rahn, J. *Seven Ways to Collect Plants.* New York: Atheneum, 1978.

Ranger Rick's Nature Magazine (Washington, D.C.: National Wildlife Federation). Published eight times a year.

Schneider, H. *How Scientists Find Out: About Matter, Time, Space and Energy.* New York: McGraw-Hill, 1976.

Schneider, H. and N. Schneider. *Science Fun With A Flashlight.* New York: McGraw-Hill, 1975.

Schwartz, J. *It's Fun to Know Why: Experiments with Things Around Us.* New York: McGraw-Hill, 1973.

Schwartz, J. *Magnify and Find Out Why.* New York: McGraw-Hill, 1972.

Schwartz, J. *Earthwatch: Space-Time Investigations with a Globe.* New York: McGraw-Hill, 1977.

Scott, J. *City of Birds and Beasts.* New York: G. P. Putnam's Sons, 1978.

Simon. S. *Exploring Fields and Lots.* Champaign, Ill.: Garrard, 1978.

Space Science. Benjamin Adelman, 4211 Colie Dr., Silver Springs, Md. 20906 (Monthly during school year) (Formerly Junior Astronomer) (C & T)

Tuey, J. and D. Wickers. *How To Be a Scientist at Home.* New York: Van Nostrand and Rinehold, 1971.

Wickers, D. and J. Tuey. *How To Make Things Grow.* New York: Van Nostrand and Rinehold, 1972.

Wilson, M. and R. Scagell. *Jet Journal.* New York: Viking, 1978.

Appendix C

Sources of Free Educational Materials

Air Age Education
100 E. 42nd Street
New York, N.Y. 10017

Aluminum Co. of America
818 Gulf Bldg.
Pittsburgh, Pa. 15219

American Can Co.
100 Park Ave.
New York, N.Y. 10013

American Cancer Society
521 West 57th Street
New York, N.Y. 10019

American Dental Association
222 East Superior Street
Chicago, Il. 60611

American Diabetes Association
1 East 45th Street
New York, N.Y. 10017

American Forest Prod. Ind., Inc.
1816 N. Street, N.W.
Washington, D.C. 20006

American Forestry Association
919 17th Street N.W.
Washington, D.C. 20006

American Geological Inst.
2101 Constitution Ave.
Washington, D.C. 20037

American Heart Association
44 E. 23rd Street
New York, N.Y. 10010

American Iron & Steel Inst.
Education Dept. 150 E. 42nd Street
New York, N.Y. 10017

American Medical Association
535 Dearborn Street
Chicago, Ill. 60610

American Museum of Natural History
Education Dept.
Central Park W. at 79th Street
New York, N.Y. 10024

American National Red Cross
National Headquarters
Washington, D.C. 20013

American Petroleum Institute
50 West 50th Street
New York, N.Y. 10020

Eli Lilly
307 East McCarty
Indianapolis, IN. 46225

The Epilepsy Foundation
1729 F. Street, N.W.
Washington, D.C. 20004

General Electric
1 River Road
Schenectady, N.Y. 12306

Evaporated Milk Association
228 North LaSalle Street
Chicago, Ill. 60601

Kraft Food Educational Dept.
P.O. Box 6567
Chicago, Ill. 60680

Manufacturing Chemists Association
1825 Connecticut Ave. N.W.
Washington, D.C. 20009

National Aeronautics & Space Administration
Washington, D.C. 20502

National Association of Audubon Societies
1775 Broadway
New York, N.Y. 10019

National Association of Manufacturers
2 E. 48th Street
New York, N.Y. 10017

National Aviation Education Council
1025 Connecticut Ave. N.W.
Washington, D.C. 20006

National Canners Association
1133 20 Street N.W.
Washington, D.C. 20036

National Coal Association
1130 17th Street N.W.
Washington, D.C. 20036

National Cotton Council
P.O. Box 12285
Memphis, TN. 38112

National Council on Alcoholism
New York Academy of Medicine
2 East 103rd Street
New York, N.Y. 10029

National Dairy Council
111 N. Canal Street
Chicago, Ill. 60606

National Geographic Society
16 & M Streets
Washington, D.C. 20036

National Wildlife Federation
232 Carroll St. N.W.
Washington, D.C. 20012

National Science Teachers Assn.
("Publications" pamphlet)
1742 Connecticut Ave., N.W.
Washington, D.C. 20009

National Society for Medical Research
1330 Massachusetts Ave. N.W.
Washington, D.C. 20005

Proctor & Gamble
Education Department
Cincinnati, Ohio 45202

Union Carbide Research Center
Educational Aids Department
P.O. Box 363
Tuxedo, N.Y. 10987 and
Consumer Products Division
Advertising Department
270 Park Avenue
New York, N.Y. 10017

U.S. Atomic Energy Comm.
Division of Technical Information
P.O. Box 62
Oak Ridge, TN. 37830

Division of Public Information
Audio-Visual Branch
Washington, D.C. 20025

U.S. Department of Interior
Fish and Wildlife Service
Washington, D.C. 20242

Appendix D

Elementary Science Textbook Series

Addison-Wesley Publishing Company
School Division
Sand Hill Road
Menlo Park, California 94025

Bobbs-Merrill Company
4300 West 62 Street
Indianapolis, Indiana 46268

Ginn and Company
Statler Building
Back Bay, P.O. 191
Boston, Massachusetts 02117

Harcourt Brace Jovanovich
757 Third Avenue
New York, New York 10017

Harper & Row, Publishers, Inc.
Keystone Industrial Park
Scranton, Pennsylvania 18512

D.C. Heath and Company
2700 North Richardt Avenue
Indianapolis, Indiana 46219

Holt, Rinehart and Winston, Inc.
383 Madison Avenue
New York, New York 10017

Houghton Mifflin Company
110 Tremont Street
Boston, Massachusetts 02107

J.B. Lippincott Company
East Washington Square
Philadelphia, Pennsylvania 19105

The Macmillan Company
866 Third Avenue
New York, New York 10022

McGraw-Hill Book Company
Webster Division
Manchester Road
Manchester, Missouri 63011

Charles E. Merrill Books, Inc.
1300 Alum Creek Drive
Columbus, Ohio 43216

Rand McNally and Company
School Department, Box 7600
Chicago, Illinois 60680

Scott, Foresman and Company
1900 East Lake Avenue
Glenview, Illinois 60025

Silver Burdett Company
250 James Street
Morristown, New Jersey 07960

Index